mlr

Marxist Left Review

Number 27 – Autumn 2024

Editor
Omar Hassan

Editorial committee
Mick Armstrong
Sandra Bloodworth
Omar Hassan
Louise O'Shea

Reviews editor
Alexis Vassiley

© Social Research Institute

Published by Socialist Alternative
Melbourne, May 2024

PO Box 4354
Melbourne University, VIC 3052

www.marxistleftreview.org

marxistleftreview@gmail.com

Contributions to *Marxist Left Review* are peer-reviewed

ISSN 1838-2932
rrp. $20

Subediting and proofreading
Tess Lee Ack
Diane Fieldes

Layout and production
Susan Miller and Oscar Sterner

Cover
Susan Miller

Printed by IngramSpark

Marxist Left Review is a theoretical journal published twice-yearly by Socialist Alternative, a revolutionary organisation based in Australia.

We aim to engage with theoretical and political debates on the Australian and international left, making a rigorous yet accessible case for Marxist politics. We also seek to provide analysis of the social, political and economic dynamics shaping Australian capitalism.

Unless indicated otherwise all articles published reflect the views of the individual author(s).

We rely on our readers' support to continue publication.
You can help by subscribing at *marxistleftreview.org*

mlr
Marxist Left Review

Number 27 – Autumn 2024

FEATURES

REVIEWS

OMAR HASSAN

Editorial: Amidst a genocide, solidarity with Palestine grows

Omar Hassan is the editor of *Marxist Left Review*. He has been active in anti-fascist and Palestine solidarity work, and has written extensively on the Middle East.

F OR OVER SIX months the Western world has witnessed an unprecedented mobilisation against Israel's genocidal assault on Gaza. From New York to Paris and Berlin, London to Melbourne, hundreds of thousands have stood up against the destruction of the Gaza Strip. This is a mass movement in every sense of the word. It has combined enormous central demonstrations in major capital cities with myriad local actions. In some places the size of the central demonstrations have been comparable with those against the Iraq War, despite enjoying little to none of the institutional support from mainstream liberal organisations that the latter received.

But unlike Iraq, the mobilisations have been regular and sustained, with millions of people refusing to go back to business as usual while the Western-backed slaughter of Palestinians continues. In many places demonstrators have faced severe repression. In France and Germany, protests were banned for weeks, before activists managed to defeat government attempts at censorship. In Germany in particular, the situation is out of control. A progressive conference supported by Yanis Varoufakis, former Greek Finance Minister, was raided and shut down by police on accusations of anti-Semitism. Police have now taken the extraordinary move of banning rally speeches in languages other than English and German, and have been arresting rally organisers, including left-wing Jews. All of this points to the violent hypocrisy at the heart of Western "democratic" values our leaders are so fond of extolling.

Unable to defend Israel's atrocities directly, the establishment attack on the pro-Palestine movement has relied on accusations of anti-Semitism to stifle the movement. Governments and countries that have vilified Muslims, refugees and other minorities for decades have suddenly discovered that racism exists and can be a problem. Yet instead of confronting bigotry in its deeply established and institution-alised forms, especially on the far right, it is the anti-war movement that is somehow accused of discrimination and harassment. We are through the looking glass, so much so that figures of the far right with recorded histories of anti-Semitic views have been allowed to argue that migrants are entirely responsible for European anti-Semitism. This, in the lands of Vichy, pogroms and the Holocaust. Meanwhile the US Congress passed a motion moved by far-right Republicans condemning the chant "from the river to the sea" as anti-Semitic, after winning the support of the vast majority of Democrats.

In Australia, Zionists released a fake and edited video of protesters in Sydney supposedly chanting "gas the Jews", which was used to argue for a blanket ban on future demonstrations. The police eventually admitted the footage was doctored, but not before the anti-Semitism narrative had been firmly established. Rally organisers in Sydney were correct to both distance themselves from any bigotry, while insisting on the democratic and anti-racist credentials of the movement, and successfully carried on the protests.

In Australia, the weekly protests in a number of cities have been vital for maintaining momentum, keeping the issue in the public eye and as an entry point for those looking to join the movement. But for a committed minority, the desire to do more has propelled them into a series of impressive local actions targeting weapons companies, Zionist politicians, local councils, and more. In Melbourne the scope of organ-ising is so broad that more than six months after the protests began, there are still days where there can be four separate solidarity actions taking place. The breadth and scale of this organising is inspirational and enormously positive.

A particular highlight has been the campaigning led by students and youth. Late last year socialist high school students initiated walkouts of hundreds in cities across Australia, with a peak of 1,000 in Melbourne. At the time, this was the biggest school student action in the world. They were subsequently joined by university students, who have organised strikes, sit-ins and public forums on campuses everywhere. Students have played a vital role overseas too. In the US Students for Justice in Palestine and Jewish Voices for Peace have led impressive campaigns and stood up to serious repression both on and off campus. As we go to print, a student occupation of Columbia University in New York has become an international sensation, and has inspired similar actions elsewhere.

As a result of all this organising, support for Palestine has expanded beyond the traditional bases of the left and migrant communities. Demonstrations in the US have often been instigated by left-wing Jews and the broader community. Links with various anti-racist organisations and campaigns have been made everywhere. Here in Melbourne, where this journal is published, well under half of the attendees at the demonstrations are from Arab or Muslim backgrounds. This represents a huge shift from previous rounds of mobilisation, and creates a deeper and broader basis for ongoing organising into the future.

All of this is reflected in opinion polls conducted in the West, which have been steadily – albeit slowly and unevenly – shifting in favour of the Palestinian people. A Gallup poll conducted in the US in March found that 55 percent of Americans opposed Israel's military actions in Gaza, while just 36 percent were still in favour. This is an important result, given the overwhelmingly pro-Israeli slant of news media there, yet the overall picture is that far more people identify as broadly sympathetic with Israel than Palestine. Polls are better in the UK, where the number of firm supporters of Palestine (28 percent) is double that of firm supporters of Israel (14 percent). The caveat, however, is that most people are uninformed and uncommitted.

In Australia the situation is similar. On the concrete issues of the war, an Essential Poll in March found that 37 percent supported Israel withdrawing from Gaza, while just 18 percent thought Israel was justified in continuing its attacks.

Presumably after Israel's highly publicised assassination of the seven World Central Kitchen aid workers, public opinion will have shifted even further. Yet there is a strong strand of isolationism and indifference, which would prefer Australia to "not get involved", even when our government and military-industrial complex is actively assisting Israel's war crimes. Thus a Resolve Strategic poll conducted in April found that 57 percent of Australians thought our government should "take no action" on the war on Gaza, up from 45 percent on the same question in November.

Importantly, the movement here has also adopted an unusually firm stance against the ALP, which has once again disgraced itself by backing Israel so firmly. Its initial stance repeated all the talking points of Zionist *hasbara*, supporting Israel's (non-existent) "right to defend itself". The government also decided to give $75,000 aid packages to each and every Australian citizen who happened to be in Israel on October 7, but nothing to Australian citizens in Gaza or the West Bank who have suffered from Israel's subsequent brutality. Since then it has attempted to speak out of both sides of its mouth to avoid alienating Muslim voters, but few have been taken in by this rhetorical tweak. Aside from the isolated arguments of a few union officials and left sects, the Palestine movement has been clear that Labor is complicit in the genocide until it cuts all military and economic ties to the apartheid regime. That they refuse to do so is a product of Labor's long-term commitment to the US alliance and the system of imperialism that the Americans oversee.

In any case, Israel's atrocities and the movement's response have clearly created a new and wider audience for anti-war and anti-impe-rialist politics, particularly in the West. But we cannot be complacent. The lies and propaganda of the media and political class retain much of their power, even if social media and the radical press gives a minority access to alternative perspectives. The solidarity movement cannot be satisfied with current mobilisation numbers and retreat into a bubble, but must continue reaching out to try to connect with new audiences by linking up with different issues and other movements.

Strangely enough, this is something of a debate. In the typically declamatory style of online discussions, there has been an observable tendency to denounce those who have only recently become aware of Israel's criminal policies. But rather than moralistically dismissing such people, the campaign needs to keep reaching out and expanding our capacity to influence, educate and mobilise. This means welcoming those who are new to the cause, and trying to consolidate and deepen their commitment.

There are also political debates, especially around forces in the Middle East that are cynically using the Palestinian cause to build their popularity. For instance, some in the movement have fallen into the trap of championing Iran, the Houthis or Hezbollah as allies of the Palestinian people. This is a profound mistake: the enemies of our enemies are not necessarily our friends. Just last year the Iranian government was repressing women, national minorities and workers who rose up under the slogan "women, life, freedom". How can the Palestine solidarity movement uphold our stance as principled defenders of democratic rights and liberation if we celebrate such a regime? While Hezbollah and the Houthis are not responsible for the same scale of oppression, they are both conservative movements that have played counter-revolutionary and anti-democratic roles in their own countries and, in Hezbollah's case, abroad.

As well, the issue of identity politics has raised its head once again, manifesting in a new tendency to isolate the Palestinian cause from the broader anti-imperialist struggle. Given the highly reactionary situation in the Middle East, with countries like Jordan, Saudi Arabia, the UAE and even Qatar and Turkey being deeply implicated with both America and Israel, this is a profoundly unhelpful position. Freedom in Palestine is inherently bound up with the revolutionary fight against imperialism and capitalism across the region and the world. The Palestinians cannot win such a battle on their own.

In this contradictory situation, socialists have a special role within the solidarity movement. We have to continue to throw ourselves into the struggle, trying to deepen and broaden its scope wherever possible. The student actions and the unprecedented strike by community sector workers in Melbourne[1] indicate that organised revolutionaries can

---

1.   See Bassini 2024.

make a serious contribution, and are just two examples of our leadership. In many cities our branches provide much of the infrastructure for the weekly demonstrations. But of course, others have taken excellent initiatives that we have supported, such as the regular pickets of Heat Treatment Australia and AW Bell in Melbourne, the union-backed pickets of Zim ships in Perth and elsewhere, and much more besides.

But there is also a need to deepen the political and strategic understanding of people in the movement. This means grasping the nature of Zionism, imperialism and the struggle for Palestinian liberation. Rage at the ongoing genocide is an important starting point, but to confront Israel, the US empire and its allies – including the Australian state – we need the historical and theoretical grounding, strategic thinking and long-term organising that only the socialist movement can offer. Radical media sources such as *Red Flag* and this journal are vital in this project, allowing incoming activists to gain a more thorough understanding of the issues than what is possible from social media.

Yet the context into which socialists must intervene is intensely contradictory. On one hand, millions have made new connections between their recent experiences with Black Lives Matter and other campaigns against racism, and the Palestinian cause. With the so-called war on terror fading into the background, this new generation is far less influenced by the traditional justifications for Israeli atrocities. The extraordinary energy of activists thrown up by this movement has been demonstrated. Yet inevitably, there is a fairly profound ignorance about the historic experiences and strategic debates in the decades-long movement for Palestinian liberation, in particular, the role of the left and workers' movement within it. This is made worse by the fact that class struggle remains at a low ebb, and so appeals to working-class agency as a possible step in such a movement are mostly fairly abstract.

Nor is it particularly obvious that workers and the poor of the Middle East and North Africa can be the basis for Palestinian liberation. The terrible defeat of the Arab Spring – in different ways constrained, coopted and destroyed by the dominant nationalist and Islamist politics of the region – has isolated Palestine and given Israel a relatively free hand. There has been very little space for mass mobilisation, which is why recent protests in Jordan are of enormous significance.

But overcoming these challenges and building a new revolutionary left is vital. In some ways, Israel's war on Palestine is only a portent of imperial crimes to come. We only narrowly avoided a devastating regional conflict between Israel and Iran. Netanyahu is an increasingly beleaguered prime minister, with opposition growing on his left and right flanks. A poll by the Israeli Democracy Institute in January found that just 15 percent of Israelis wanted Netanyahu to remain in office once the assault on Gaza ends. For a self-interested genocidal maniac such as Bibi, this is potentially a rationale for many more months of slaughter. And while it seems like Biden successfully convinced Netanyahu to vent his anger on Rafah instead of Tehran, there is still a chance of the conflict escalating into a wider regional war.

The horror of war is not confined to the Middle East. Russia's invasion and occupation of Ukraine continues to grind on, leaving enormous death and destruction in its wake. The US and its allies, including Australia, are desperate to curtail China's rise as a global power. They are deploying an increasingly aggressive set of economic and military politics to prepare for the possibility of a world war. Reflecting these imperial tensions, a report by the Stockholm International Peace Institute found that arms spending globally has increased by almost 7 percent this year, the fastest growth in fifteen years. So at a time when governments are "tightening their belts" to avoid feeding inflation, they're investing trillions into bombs, tanks, submarines and fighter jets. Our challenge is to overthrow these murderous parasites before they get a chance to use them.

References

Bassini, Louisa 2024, "Community workers walk out for Palestine", *Red Flag*, 27 February. https://redflag.org.au/article/community-workers-walk-out-palestine

JOEL GEIER

Socialist alternatives: The Portuguese Revolution

Joel Geier has been a revolutionary Marxist activist for over six decades, and has written extensively on economics, history and Marxist theory. He was a co-founder of the International Socialists (US), and was an eye-witness to the Portuguese Revolution.

F IFTY YEARS AGO, the Portuguese Revolution represented the climax of the radical 1960s and 1970s. In Portugal the working class confronted the questions of taking state power, ending exploitation and oppression by emancipating itself and initiating a socialist transformation of society. This amazing proletarian revolutionary process has not been equalled in the struggles since. Yet unfortunately it remains virtually unknown or ignored, with little recognition even within the radical left, which under reactionary climate has drifted away from the questions of self-emancipation, working-class revolution, insurrection and the conquest of power. These questions, fundamental to liberation, were posed in Portugal under modern conditions, and provide important judgements for revolutionary theory and practice. This brief introductory sketch of a revolutionary class struggle of nineteen months is limited to only a few of the major events.

My assessment of the revolution comes from personal experiences and interactions with workers and soldiers, meetings with workers' and residents' commissions, occupied farms, factories under workers' control, and prominent revolutionaries from many political tendencies during the revolutionary and counter-revolutionary periods, as well as numerous reports by comrades who took part in the events in Portugal.

The International Socialists were allied and worked with the Party of the Revolutionary Proletariat (PRP), the leading proponents of the Revolutionary Councils of Workers, Soldiers and Sailors (CRTSM in Portuguese), and of a state based on autonomous organs of workers' democracy. They were an inspiration, and for all their strengths and weaknesses, remain a creative model for revolutionary functioning in the midst of revolution.

I arrived in Portugal in July 1975, eager to see the revolution first-hand, yet unaware I would witness the "Hot Summer", the onset of the struggle for state power. On the bus from the airport into Lisbon I was amazed as every wall was covered with revolutionary posters, and even more so as we passed factory after factory with red flags flying over them and signs proclaiming: "This factory is under the control of the workers' commission". My mind echoed George Orwell's words from *Homage to Catalonia*, as he entered Barcelona in 1936: "It was the first time I had ever been in a town where the working class was in the saddle... There was much of this that I did not understand...but I recognized it immediately as a state of affairs worth fighting for". It is in this spirit that I convey my account of the revolution.

Portugal in Africa
The Portuguese Revolution began on 25 April 1974, when 400 junior officers, organised as the Armed Forces Movement (MFA), carried out a military coup. The rebels met virtually no resistance as they toppled a 48-year-old fascist dictatorship, and had no idea that they were unleashing a proletarian revolutionary process that would push far beyond the limited goals they had set out to accomplish. It would be another confirmation of Trotsky's theory of permanent revolution – the idea that a bourgeois democratic political revolution can transform uninterruptedly into a socialist revolution, with class struggle driving workers to realise their goals by attempting to take power. It was a complex process, at times confused, but it was in the direction of socialist revolution that the working class moved.

The Portuguese Revolution began in Africa. The revolution developed as the culmination of years-long opposition to Portugal's African colonial wars, both domestically and in the colonies themselves.

Portugal was regarded as a serious world power – despite being a small, poor country of 9 million – because of its huge African empire in Angola, Mozambique and Guinea Bissau. Together these colonial possessions totalled 22 times the size of Portugal, with extraordinary natural resources (oil, diamonds, coal, coffee and more) and were key to the holding of southern Africa for the West and its allies, Rhodesia (now Zimbabwe) and South Africa.

Portugal was the first European nation to colonise Africa in the fifteenth century, and it was "the last to leave". It launched the transatlantic African slave trade as a source for primitive capital accumulation, and to create a forced labour supply for the sugar plantations in Brazil.

Portugal's empire slowly evolved to more modern imperialist practices, forcing the colonies to export raw materials to Portugal at below world market rates and to be a captive market for higher-priced Portuguese exports of finished goods. But this arrangement was limited: while more advanced capitalist nations in the post-World War II period moved to neocolonialism, backward Portuguese capitalism, dependent on the colonies for capital accumulation, continued to maintain direct colonial control. Portugal's fascist regime feared that if it moved to a more limited form of economic domination over its colonies, Portuguese capital could find itself supplanted by its more developed rivals.

But the regime could not hold back historical tides. When most of Africa gained political independence, the Portuguese colonies rebelled. In Angola a national liberation movement arose in 1961, followed within two years by movements in Mozambique and Guinea Bissau.[1]

The Portuguese Army

The new provisional government, the Junta of National Salvation, which came to power in Portugal in 1974, was based on an unstable alliance between the MFA's insurgent junior officers and the armed forces' General Staff led by General Spínola, which represented the interests of capital. The Portuguese bourgeoisie, facing anti-colonial struggles abroad and opposition to the colonial wars at home, finally

---

1.   Ponte 1974; Figueiredo 1975, pp.186–216.

opted to attempt a neocolonial solution: local autonomy for the colonies within a Portuguese federation. In contrast, the MFA was for the right of self-determination for the colonies, whose national liberation movements would not settle for anything less than independence. These divergent interests manifested as a power struggle within the military, and became a dynamic for a deepening revolutionary progression, similar to that of the February 1917 Russian Revolution. In both Russia and Portugal, a democratic government replaced a dictatorship because of popular opposition to an ongoing imperialist war. The still-dominant ruling class in each country tried to continue the war for modified imperialist aims, while the workers, who have no imperialist interests, shifted to ever more radical alternatives to finally end the wars. Workers refused to accept democratic imperialism as a substitute for fascist imperialism; they were not just for ending the colonial wars but for the end of colonialism. This intertwining of class struggle with anti-imperialism became one of the most impressive attributes of the Portuguese revolutionary working class, whose strong, ardent anti-imperialism remains an inspiration for international socialism.[2]

The weight, over more than a decade, of Portugal's simultaneous fight against three wars of national liberation, transformed every aspect of Portuguese society, and ended in revolution. Portugal was armed by its NATO allies, with its officers trained in the US in Vietnam War-era doctrines – of strategic hamlets, napalm, direct bombing, body counts, civilian massacres, of "dirty wars". These imperialist policies were as disastrous for Portugal as they were for the US in Vietnam. By the late 1960s, it was clear that Portugal's position was hopeless; its endless wars were lost. Anti-war opposition had also convinced conscious workers that Portugal itself was both a part of and controlled by international imperialism, and functioned as a semi-colony of the advanced capitalist countries.[3]

Throughout the long wars and economic crisis, working-class consciousness developed. As a result of the colonial wars the Army underwent a social explosion, expanding from 10,000 men to 220,000. The soldiers drafted were workers and peasants. They experienced

---

2.   Varela 2019, p.64; Hammond 1998, pp.75–6; Insight 1975, pp.96–7.
3.   Insight 1975, pp.33–53.

terrible treatment in an institution riddled with rotten class prejudice; were paid an unbelievably low wage starting at $6 dollars a month; and were fed in separate, inferior messes. The mandatory two-year draft service was extended to four years, with up to 24 months of overseas combat in the colonies. To avoid military service around 200,000 draft dodgers and 25,000 deserters fled the country; by 1973, 20 percent of yearly draftees did not show up at induction. Together these figures comprised a significant number of young men in their twenties.[4]

The officer corps grew to 7,000, of whom only 2,000 were professional officers, recruited from lower middle-class backgrounds. The other 5,000 officers were *milicianos*, recently-drafted university students. There were only 14,000 university students in Portugal, children of the upper middle class, in a country where only 4 percent of working class students could afford to go to high school. University students were automatically made officers when drafted. Many of them had taken part in the radical left student activity of the 1960s, influenced by the student radicalism of the American anti-Vietnam War movement and the Paris May 1968 uprising. Many spread their radical views to their professional officer colleagues, the base of the MFA.[5]

Workers radicalise

Half of the government budget went to the wars, in a country with the lowest wages in Europe, virtually no social welfare, and appalling levels of illiteracy, disease, life expectancy, maternal and infant mortality. Almost a million and a half workers, peasants and ex-servicemen, seeking to escape poverty wages, emigrated during the wars, mainly to Western Europe. Eight hundred thousand of them were concentrated in the Paris region, the "second largest Portuguese city", many of them radicalised as participants in the general strikes and factory occupations of May 1968. They marched in demonstrations with banners proclaiming: "Death to Salazar, Franco and fascism". Many rushed home after 25 April 1974 to take part in the revolution.

Meanwhile, the global economic crisis, runaway inflation, and the international working-class upsurge that began in the late 1960s was

---

4. Figueiredo 1975, p.103–4; Varela 2019, pp.56–62; Mailer 1977, pp.185–7.
5. Hammond 1998, pp.63–70; Insight 1975, pp.16–18.

already also shifting Portugal's workers to the left. By the early 1970s, Portugal had yearly inflation rates of 20, 30 and 40 percent. Although strikes were banned by the fascist unions, inflation is the mother of all strikes; illegal strikes broke out at the end of 1960s, and continued to grow. In 1973, there were a hundred and fifty illegal strikes.

Most strikes were crushed by the PIDE, the secret political police that had been set up and trained originally by the Gestapo. Later, when Portugal was incorporated into NATO, the PIDE received training in the United States by the CIA. PIDE agents were placed in the large factories, usually paid for by the owners. When strikes broke out, workers were fingered by the PIDE, and by foremen, management and some working-class spies. At TAP, for example, the national airline with 8,000 employees, underground cells – of the Communist Party, the Movement of the Socialist Left (MES) and the PRP – existed alongside 200 PIDE informers. In the last years of the dictatorship, strike leaders were routinely arrested, tortured and jailed in prisons and concentration camps.[6] But the movement kept growing and radicalising.

The revolution begins
Most of the drafted soldiers and many of the junior officers became politically influenced by the national liberation movements they were sent to fight. They came to realise that they had been sent to fight people like themselves, politically oppressed and impoverished. They were horrified at being forced to fight for the control of a social system, and for the ownership of vast colonial natural resources, by the six great monopolies that dominated the Portuguese economy and were allied with the fascist regime. Over time, they started to take seriously the anti-colonial injunction issued by the African liberation movements to form a fourth national liberation movement in Portugal itself. And it was the ultimate success of the wars for national liberation that finally destroyed the corrupt fascist regime in Portugal and opened the space for the workers' revolution that followed.

Many draftees and junior officers came to believe that the wars were hopeless, that victory was impossible and Portugal was already

---

6.   Figueiredo 1975, pp.105–45; Mailer 1977, p.108.

defeated. As opposition to the war grew, the government in June 1973 called a "Combatants Conference" to mobilise the army to regain support for the wars. A group of junior officers circulated a petition stating that the Conference decisions did not apply to them since they had been excluded from taking part. Hundreds of officers signed the petition, a high level of support that convinced the initiators to organise a meeting of officers who opposed the war, which became the MFA. Within a few months, this group of junior officers grew to 400. They were politically diverse, ranging from unpolitical, to conservative, to the left. By their second meeting, they came to the decision that the only way to end the wars was to overthrow their own government. The rest of the officers were uncommitted or more conservative, passive on 25 April, but supporters of the MFA so long as it was ending the colonial wars. They also decided to passively follow the MFA because of the unexpected strength of the civilian mass movement.

The MFA was politically diverse, but from the start its leadership bodies were dominated by the broad left, including its eight-person coordinating committee, and its three-person executive committee. The program of the MFA was written by Ernesto Melo Antunes, a Marxist and self-described Gramscian, and it called for "decolonization, democracy, and development," with a heavy emphasis on anti-monopoly and pro-working-class measures.[7]

The MFA's 1974 military coup lifted the lid on a volatile situation and the working class exploded. On the very first day, masses awakened to the possibilities of open, legal struggle. Tens of thousands of workers took to the streets, cheering on the army as it entered Lisbon. The clandestine resistance movements, the Communist Party and the revolutionary left, came up out of the underground within hours, and started organising people on the streets. Thousands marched singing the *Internationale*. Resistance fighters led masses of people to the prisons, demanding the release of all political prisoners, many of whom had been strikers. The government capitulated within a day, freeing all political prisoners.

The next day, the order to free political prisoners was extended to

---

7.   Ferreira and Marshall 1986, pp.15–16; Insight 1975 pp.31–52.

thousands of African prisoners in the colonies. Meanwhile, revolutionary students led thousands of people to the Lisbon airport to demand that no troops be sent out to the African colonial wars. The new government refused to accept that demand, but the next day granted amnesty to all draft dodgers and deserters. On the streets, in the factories and in government offices throughout Lisbon, workers sought to hunt and lynch members of the secret police. The government stepped in to protect the PIDE agents from their long-suffering victims, but abolished the secret police, and arrested hundreds of them that day. In response to the stormy upheaval from below, the government was making the first of what was to be many concessions to militant working-class action, and everyone felt that. In turn, the power of the mass movement demoralised the agents of repression, the regular police and the national guard, who, fearful for their lives, refused to go out onto the streets The forces of law and order disappeared for a period of time.[8]

The new government then declared May Day a national holiday. From 25 April to 1 May, most workplaces and all the schools were closed. For 47 years May Day rallies had been illegal and had led to clashes with the police. Now, 600,000 people demonstrated in Lisbon, a city of just one million people. The rally was addressed by the Junta, the MFA, Mário Soares of the Socialist Party, and Álvaro Cunhal of the Communist Party. Political consciousness, developed by the years of war and economic crisis, soared overnight as May Day awakened many workers to the depth of support for a socialist transformation. Few, however, understood what a socialist transformation entailed or how one could occur.[9]

Political engagement and sophistication had been impossible for most people, but now, with the lid lifted, the masses were awakening with every variety of radical ideas on offer. Political discussion broke out everywhere, in the bars, cafés and workplaces, on the buses and on the streets. Consciousness was transformed by enormous leaps, and ferment was everywhere. Daily life became dominated by strikes, demonstrations, occupations and meetings, endless meetings, setting

---

8.   Mailer 1977, pp.37–59; Varela 2019, pp.16–28.
9.   Hammond 1998, pp.74–7; Mailer 1977 pp.59–61; Varela 2019 pp.29–30.

masses into motion. Working-class consciousness was further stimulated by the liberation of the media, the newspapers, radio and TV, as fascist owners of media enterprises were driven out, and the press and TV were opened up to all the left-wing groups that had emerged, further stimulating political dialogue, as participants in the struggle read and debated the competing proposals of various left forces.

On 2 May, the schools and the factories reopened. Revolutionary groups took over the universities, abolished exams and fired all deans, heads of universities, and fascist collaborators among professors and administrators. High school students held general assemblies and demanded that all teachers with ties with fascism be fired and that attendance records be abolished so students could take part in political demonstrations.[10]

The Workers' Commissions

But the greatest transformation of class consciousness took place in the factories. Assemblies were held as all who worked for wages – manual, skilled, technical, office, and often lower management – met together. All questions of working life and politics were now open for discussion. Workers started discussing all conditions of their employment: wages, wage differentials, length of the working day and working week, mandatory overtime, harassment, sexism, poor working conditions, as well as broader debates over capitalism, exploitation and imperialism. The assemblies would then draw up lists of the workers' demands, unleashing struggles for immediate improvements of conditions. Factory assemblies during the revolutionary period usually met on a weekly basis in the hours after work, with sub-groups assigned to working on specific topics met more frequently. In a few working-class strongholds, like the Lisbon Naval Yards (Lisnave), assemblies met bi-weekly during paid work time.

The assemblies elected factory committees, in Portugal called workers' commissions, Comissão de Trabalhadores (CTs). Factory assemblies and CTs were the first independent workers' organisations formed. The existing fascist unions were not independent, they were

---

10. Insight 1975, pp.103–4, Varela 2019, p.160.

state-controlled labour fronts. The assemblies and the CTs started the self-organisation of the working class, and were the basic organs of workers' democracy.[11]

Workers' commissions were the organisations which the working class recognised as their own. They became the core of workers' power, the locus of the class struggle, the organs of workers' control, the mobilisers for mass demonstrations, the nucleus for popular power, the most distinct feature of the Portuguese revolution. Representatives to the workers' commissions were elected in the workplaces by the factory assemblies, or by different sections of the factory. In the large factories CT members were full-time representatives, akin to shop stewards. Their term was usually for a year but they were subject to immediate recall, and made no more than a worker's salary. It is no accident that this followed the guidelines of Lenin's *State and Revolution*, which was number two or three on Portugal's best-seller list for the next eighteen months, running only somewhat ahead of Lenin's *Imperialism* (at number six or seven).

Within three or four months the number of workers' commissions grew to between 2–4,000. The most politically advanced were in the 50 large factories with over 1,000 workers. The largest, most modern factories contained the most militant and class-conscious workers, the vanguard of the revolution, many of them veterans of the colonial wars. These skilled workers, particularly at workplaces like Lisnave, Setnave, TAP, Siderurgia and Efacec, were part of the international economy. Many militant strikes were carried out by poorly paid, unskilled, assembly, agriculture and building workers. But the skilled workers at the largest factories were the best-paid and most self-confident. They were the most needed by the international corporations, the most secure in their position in the economy, and the least afraid of losing their jobs. Often such conscious workers had a history of involvement in political struggles under fascism, within cells of the underground organisations, or as participants in the illegal strikes prior to 1974.[12]

The Communist Party, the only well-organised political force in Portugal, initially decided to boycott the workers' commissions, but

---

11.   Varela 2019, pp.32–9; Robinson 1987, pp.90–1; Mailer 1977, pp.131–44.
12.   Hammond 1998, pp.77–81.

felt forced to join them nine months later, in February 1975. The CP was antagonistic to the workers' commissions, which they feared as rivals to the trade unions that they now controlled. Almost all Portuguese trade unions had been fascist-controlled, with a dozen or more craft unions in a single workplace. These unions were not allowed to strike or hold democratic elections. Immediately after the overthrow of the dictatorship, the Communist Party occupied the fascist trade union offices, tossed out the officials, and took the unions over from the top down, with no elections and no input from workers. The CP thereby controlled almost all the trade unions in the country, which they used as leverage for influence and power in the new government. The CP used similar tactics to take over local government authorities, occupying government offices, replacing the fascist officials with their own members, and preventing local elections.[13]

Both the Spínolist wing of the Junta and the MFA agreed that the CP had to be in the cabinet in order to control the working class and the mass movement. This proved to be an inaccurate evaluation of working-class forces. The absence of the CP, thanks to their Stalinist sectarian blindness, opened the workers' commissions and – with them the mass movement – to much more radical leadership direction, and action. When the CP was forced to flip-flop and enter the CTs in February, 1975, the CTs became an ongoing battleground between the CP and the revolutionary left, with the CP forced to take more left-wing positions that put them at odds with their coalition partners.

The CP's original boycott of the CTs left a healthy legacy of suspicion and hostility towards the party, and allowed for the development of rank-and-file-based democratic internal life that included discussion, decisions and resulting actions, unlike the situation within the trade unions and other CP-dominated groups. The workers' commissions were the organised force that prevented the CP from controlling the working class, and opened up space for the revolutionary left.[14]

---

13. Robinson 1990, pp.73–9.
14. Varela 2019, pp.67–71 and 124–7.

The strike wave

The Portuguese working class entered the revolution as an active participant in the making of history, becoming a class-for-itself, and altering the politics and class goals of the MFA coup. The first stage of the revolution was a mass strike wave, the most basic proletarian method of struggle. In revolutionary periods, strikes deepen the political consciousness of both participants and observers. In Portugal, led by the workers' commissions, 400 hundred strikes rocked the country in the first two months of the revolution, May and June of 1974. Many of those strikes united economic and political demands, a quality Rosa Luxemburg explained as the essence of the mass strike.[15]

Most strike demands were for wages, the reinstatement of workers fired during the illegal strikes, and *saneamento*. *Saneamento* meant purging the workplaces of all fascist collaborators: owners, foremen, managers, executives, even working-class stool pigeons. Fascist supervisors were often locked out or chased out of factories, and in a few cases expelled, during the first factory occupations. In some plants where purging forced out all the foremen, workers began to decide who the foremen were, or simply run things themselves, with good results. *Saneamento*, when carried out by workers themselves, and not the state, created the first ideas of workers' control that would become powerful in the next stage of the revolution. Through the assemblies and *saneamento*, the CTs were becoming a dual power in the workplaces, challenging bosses' control over production.[16]

The strike wave's economic emphasis was on wages and salaries. In the first four months of 1974, inflation in Portugal was running at 63 percent. Many strikes demanded a doubling of wages for striking workers and often, a doubling of the minimum wage. Some strikes were for creating greater working-class equality by reducing wage differentials. At Lisnave, there were 11 different pay grades, and the strike aimed to raise all workers to the highest pay grade. The Communist Party and its unions opposed all 400 strikes and actually attempted to break some of them. The assumptions of the Junta, the MFA and the CP – that the CP and its unions could act as a disciplinary agent of the

15. See Luxemburg 1906, chapter VI.
16. Varela 2019, pp.32–51; Hammond 1998, pp.78–83.

government and control the working class – were a complete failure. The CP claimed that higher wages were irresponsible, unrealistic and threatened the stability of the new government, which could lead to the return of fascism. The CP, prior to joining the government, had called for a minimum monthly wage of 6000 escudos ($240), and then supported the Junta proposal for 3300 escudos ($132), which workers called "the wage of misery", further antagonising militant workers, who felt betrayed by the CP.[17]

The Communist Party

During the revolution, the Portuguese far left was the strongest in the world. Every radical tendency existed and was tested by the actuality of revolutionary practice; most failed miserably. With the bourgeois parties tainted by their fascist collaboration, politics flowed through the MFA, left parties and popular power organisations.

The Communist Party was the only large, well-organised political party at the start of the revolution. The CP had been the underground party of resistance to fascism; many of its members had been tortured and jailed for years. The CP's bravery and consistent fight against fascism gave it enormous prestige and respect in the working class, which it regularly betrayed. The CP was an unreformed Stalinist Party that never deviated from Moscow's line, and was capable of overnight shifts between incredible sectarianism and fantastic opportunism. Its sole consistency was to oppose every revolt from below, including strikes, factory occupations, housing take-overs and workers' control. The CP viewed the power and passion of the mass movement as a threat to its manoeuvres from above. Put simply, as the largest party of the working class, the CP also functioned as the main barrier to socialist revolution.

The CP emerged from the underground with 5,000 members. With a vigorous open recruitment campaign at Lisnave and other factories, it grew within months to 100,000 members. Many radical groups, the PRP included, missed early opportunities, and were handicapped by continuing the underground organising culture limited to strict cadre

---

17.   Varela 2019, pp.69–71; Cliff 1975, pp.16–17.

recruitment. CP membership dwarfed the combined membership of all the left groups, and allowed it to build a massive bureaucratic apparatus of thousands of paid full-timers, union and local government officials and organisers. This made it a formidable opponent in the factories, holding back working-class militancy and advancement.[18]

When the CP opposed the workers' committees and the strike wave, many party members and sympathisers left and joined the Maoists, second-rate Stalinists whose ideology and perspectives were closest to the ideas they had received through CP education. Some others joined revolutionary left groups, but many became *apartido*, or non-party. This was a strong current that appeared in the working class, distrusting the CP and all other political parties, reinforced by the sectarian operations of certain left groups which put their organisation's interests over those of the working class. Many of the best revolutionary militant workers were *apartido*, the strength of which most revolutionary groups had to accommodate to at demonstrations and joint actions, but which held back necessary party-building.

The CP's political strategy throughout the revolution was to attach itself to MFA officers and to give unwavering support to the MFA and its decisions. CP strength in the MFA increased with the almost accidental appointment of Vasco Gonçalves, who was considered no threat by President Spínola, as prime minister. Gonçalves had been, and possibly was still, a member of the CP; even if not, he acted as a disciplined supporter.

Communist Party theory maintained that Portuguese capitalism was not developed enough for socialism, and therefore the party was against a workers' revolution. Instead it advocated for collaboration with the middle classes and even sections of capital against the monopolies and fascism. The CP supported a two-stage revolution plan: for the foreseeable future, a democratic revolution for national independence and development, followed in the distant future by a socialist revolution. This was orthodoxy in Communist Parties after the Stalinisation of the Comintern.

---

18.   Cliff 1975, pp.12–17; Varela 2018.

The Socialist Party

The other main party in the various provisional governments that emerged during the revolution was the Socialist Party. The Portuguese SP was formed in Bonn in 1973, under the auspices of the German Social Democratic Party, with 200 middle-class members, including professionals, lawyers, journalists, professors and intellectuals. It gained massive electoral support from workers, but in the factories it was smaller than the revolutionary left. To gain this support, it initially took positions verbally to the left of the CP, supporting the mass strike wave and calling for workers' control and overthrowing capitalism. As the workers radicalised and increasingly imposed power from below, the SP snapped back to its petty-bourgeois origins, opposed workers' power, and became financed by the CIA as the single most important force in the bourgeois counter-revolution.[19]

The Maoists

Portugal's revolutionary left was the largest in the world. Many dozens of far-left groups suddenly emerged or formed. They represented, and put to the test, every conceivable shade of radical ideas, riddled with confusions and problems. They also contributed to the fragmentation of the left, and in the sorting-out process of the next year there were a dozen survivors. Most left groups had no independent role, but politically tailed after or tried to influence the CP or SP. Four radical groups – the PRP, the MES and the Maoist Movement to Reorganise the Party of the Proletariat (MRPP) and Popular Democratic Union (UDP) – were at times real forces in the military and the working class, particularly in the CTs, with influence in the revolutionary process. Maoism, however, was a political disaster for the left.

The MRPP was initially the largest revolutionary organisation and played a very militant, albeit sectarian, role in the early strike wave. Unreconstructed Stalinists, they disgraced themselves with their dogmatic adherence to China's line that the CP was social-fascist, its ties to Moscow representing a greater danger than the capitalists. This led the MRPP to an early alliance with the SP against the CP, and

___

19. Birchall 1979.

later the MRPP became a useful instrument for the right. The MRPP joined the reactionary physical assaults on CP offices and members, and supported the counter-revolutionary coup of 25 November 1975. As the MRPP discredited itself, the UDP, formed through the merger of over a dozen small Maoist groups, became the main Maoist organisation. The UDP shared the CP's two-stage theory, opposed socialist revolution as unrealistic, originally considered workers' control to be utopian and anarchist, and argued that revolution was premature until a new, real Communist Party was built. Their main programmatic demand for struggle was for national independence. The UDP grew primarily by positioning itself as the most militant group in actions, even when that led to ultra-left positions. UDP membership was double or triple that of the PRP, which made them a major competitor for influence and support from the most radical workers and soldiers. The UDP was forced at times to cooperate in joint work with the PRP and other revolutionaries, but they were always prepared to engage in treacherous manoeuvres for sectarian raids of popular organisations, for their real objective of building the Reconstructed Marxist-Leninist Communist Party.[20]

The PRP – party building in the revolution

A proletarian revolution requires two necessary entities to be successful: workers' councils (soviets), as the governmental bodies for a workers' state; and a revolutionary workers' party that provides political leadership during each stage of the revolution to move it forward, with the goal of winning the working class to the conquest of state power. The Portuguese Revolution began with neither of these two essentials and after 19 months it only had rudiments of them.

The most difficult task revolutionaries can face is to build a revolutionary workers' party from scratch in the midst of revolution itself. The absence of a mass revolutionary party has been the decisive cause of the defeat of many revolutions, including Portugal's. It is a question that will often reappear in the future, given the state of the contemporary revolutionary left. Defeat, however, is not inevitable; the Hungarian

---

20. Cliff 1975, p.20; Robinson 1987, p.97.

Revolution of 1919 occurred with a Communist Party being formed weeks before the revolution, and the defeated 1905 Russian Revolution was the dress rehearsal for revolutionary victory in 1917. The lack of a revolutionary party at the beginning of revolution is not an excuse to fatalistically accept or await defeat. The job of revolutionaries is to work as best they can with existing conditions, as they attempt to build a revolutionary workers' party during revolution, however difficult that may prove to be.

The only force in Portugal that genuinely worked to build a revolutionary workers' party was the Revolutionary Party of the Proletariat (PRP), an organisation that stood uncompromisingly for revolutionary communist ideals: for a proletarian socialist revolution, for a state based on worker's councils, for workers' democracy, for workers' control of production and the state, for opposition to all imperialism, and for an armed insurrection for the seizure of state power. It was the only group that fought for these ideals in the popular power organisations and in the barracks, in an honest, non-sectarian manner.

The PRP began with a small underground cadre of 80, but with enormous recognition and prestige for its military operations under fascism. Its two most famous accomplishments were blowing up a NATO base outside Lisbon, and penetrating the officer corps, stealing the war plans for Guinea Bissau and turning them over to the national liberation movement. It had also controlled the underground Radio Free Portugal, which operated from Algiers and had broadcast news every night into Portugal that sustained the resistance. With legality, the PRP quickly drew in hundreds of its existing sympathisers. During the revolution it grew to 3,000 members, with 150 factory cells in the Lisbon industrial belt.

The PRP originated as a faction in the CP in 1969, opposing both the Russian invasion of Czechoslovakia and Stalinism. It rejected the two-stage theory of revolution and proposed that a proletarian socialist revolution was on the agenda in Portugal. It had opposed CP passivity and advocated for armed struggle against the fascist regime. Its main strength was that it was linked to militants in the most important factories in Marinha Grande and the Lisbon-Setúbal industrial belt, whose assessment of working-class consciousness informed the PRP's perspectives and ability to make rapid shifts in the turbulence of the revolution.

As an interventionist organisation the PRP was unequalled in the international revolutionary movement of the 1970s, but its weakest point was theory. PRP ideology was an eclectic mixture of Lenin, third worldism, Guevara, Luxemburg and Trotsky. They refused to be labelled as followers of any of them. From Trotsky, they took three important theories: permanent revolution, the united front against fascism, and the revolution betrayed. They considered the Stalinist states to be state-capitalist class societies, but had illusions about the progressive character of "third world socialism". But on the most important question of theory and practice, that of the working class, they were excellent, with total commitment to the working class, its interests, its independence, and to learning from its struggles. They believed in and fought for workers' power, for the self-organisation and self-activity of the working class, for the necessity of both a revolutionary party and autonomous organisations of the working class. Implementing these views, whatever other theoretical weakness the PRP had, placed them head and shoulders above much of the international left.

A powerful advantage of the PRP was their cohesive functioning on the basis of shared political analysis, through a unique method unlike any other revolutionary group internationally. In the rapidly changing conditions of the revolution, they regularly produced extremely sophisticated analyses of all social, economic and political events, of the evolving role of the political parties, of shifting consciousness among the working class and soldiers, and drawing conclusions for what was to be done. PRP membership cohesion and discipline was based on these perspectives and the organisation went over each new analysis individually with every cadre and member, which provided them the basis for functioning in the mass movement. These analyses were also shared with sympathisers in the CTs, the residents' commissions (CMs) and among soldiers and officers of the Continental Operations Command (COPCON), who were dependent on them to function through the chaotic shifts in the revolution.

Despite its small size, the PRP was the most influential group in shaping the ideology and political initiatives of the revolutionary left.

Central to major turning points in the revolution were key initiatives that the PRP proposed to advance the revolution at critical moments: the Inter-Empresas, CRTSMs, the COPCON document, United Revolutionary Front (FUR), Soldiers United for Victory (SUV), and the Setúbal Committee of Struggle, all of which will be discussed later.[21]

Tensions in the Junta

The government that came to power after 25 April, the Junta, was a coalition of the MFA army officers, the bourgeoisie, the Socialist Party and the Communist Party. The main bourgeois goals were twofold. First, a transition to bourgeois democracy to allow for Portugal's entry and integration into the European Economic Community (the predecessor of the European Union). This would allow for exports from Portugal's low-wage economy to the Common Market without tariffs or restrictions and to attract foreign investment for modernisation and development. The second main bourgeois goal was ending the colonial wars on a platform of partial local self-government within a Portuguese federation, with Portuguese control of defence and foreign policy. This would protect Portuguese companies' dominant position in the colonial economies. These goals were stymied however, by the strength of the mass movement. Despite SP and CP support, they could not contain the working-class revolt, nor the revolt against the colonial wars, spearheaded by the troops and the MFA.

A month after the MFA coup, the troops in Guinea Bissau mutinied and demanded that the government grant independence to the national liberation movement. In August police fired upon mass demonstrations in Lisbon, demanding independence for Mozambique, killing one and wounding others; but the state was incapable of suppressing growing working-class opposition to colonialism. The bourgeoisie was determined to prevent the loss of Angola, its most important colony, with the richest natural resources and greatest potential wealth. There were other imperialist considerations; on 19 June, Spínola met with President Richard Nixon who promised American support, with the

---

21. Program of the PRP in Peoples Translation Service 1975, pp.26–31; Cliff 1975, pp.18–19; Geier 1975; Geier and Finkel 1976.

proviso that the right to independence of Angola and Mozambique would not be recognised, to which Spínola completely agreed.[22]

COPCON

As the strike wave mounted, it became clear that the government was incapable of simply suppressing the movement because the apparatus of state repression was in disarray. The secret police had been abolished. Both the regular police and riot police often refused to go on the street or near the strikes for fear of the working class. The government solution was to create a new organ of state repression, the Continental Operations Command (COPCON), to serve as the military police of the Lisbon region. That proved to be yet another cruel illusion for the bourgeoisie – COPCON would soon evolve as the main army support for the popular power movement and the revolutionary left.

COPCON originally had a dual function. It was designed to change the balance between the Junta and the MFA. COPCON was to be the MFA's power base in the army, out of Spínola's control, charged with overseeing government implementation of the MFA program. COPCON's other function was to hold down workers' strikes and housing occupations by mediation, and coming to agreement with the workers involved, so that the popular forces whose support the MFA wanted were not totally antagonised. COPCON operated by those guidelines for a few months, and broke some important strikes in the name of law and order.[23]

But over time the body changed and was radicalised by proletarian struggle – and its own working-class soldiers. The COPCON troops who tried mediation, arbitration and compromise increasingly ended up identifying with the workers, their demands and actions. A significant turning point was the demonstration at the Lisbon Naval Yard (Lisnave), Portugal's largest and most important factory. The demonstration demanded the *saneamento* of the remaining fascist collaborators in the Lisnave administration, as well as expressing opposition to the new government strike law, supported by the CP and SP, which banned

---

22. Insight 1975, pp.135–8.
23. Ferreira and Marshall 1986, pp.106–7 and pp.147–50; Insight 1975, pp.140–5 and 169–75.

factory occupations, political and sympathy strikes, and sought to severely limit strike action across the board, while legalising employer lock-outs. The Lisnave demonstration was banned by the government and opposed by the CP cells operating in the factory, but supported by the factory assembly and workers' commission. As Lisnave workers began to start the march to Lisbon carrying banners reading "Death to Capitalism", COPCON troops who had been sent with loaded rifles to prevent the march began fraternising with the workers. They responded by chanting at them: "Sons of the working class. Brother Workers. Future Workers. Always, always on the side of the people" and "The People, Armed and United, Will Never Be Defeated".

Faced with such a scene, working-class soldiers broke down, some crying, and put down their guns. For the first time in the revolution, troops had refused to be used against the workers. Officers understood they could not force the troops to stop the march, and so withdrew them. This turning point began a period in which the government could not rely on COPCON as its repressive apparatus against workers.

The commander of COPCON was Otelo de Carvalho (Otelo to everyone in Portugal), the hero of the victory over fascism. His background was that of a fairly apolitical, naïve officer, devoted to the military, and perceived as a political lightweight. Yet he was a brilliant military strategist. Otelo was the organiser and architect of the 25 April coup, who had successfully executed every detail of the complex plan. When COPCON moved to the left, Otelo became the most popular figure in Portugal. He and many troops under COPCON's command became radicalised, sympathetic to the revolutionary left, and often served as the armed strength of the popular power movement. Otelo remained politically unsophisticated and often erratic: loyal to the military and its officer corps, which included initial opposition to the rank-and-file Soldiers United for Victory. But he was also led, as he said, by the "spontaneity and creativity of the masses which gives them the ability to solve their own problems", to become a revolutionary defender of soviet power and of arming the working class.[24] This culminated in COPCON offering outright support to working-class occupations.[25]

The coup of 8 September 1974

The culminating impact of all these events – the mass strike wave, the factory commissions, the revolt of the troops in Guinea Bissau, the growing shift of power to the MFA, the unreliability of COPCON, and the coalition of the Junta and the MFA being ripped apart by the radicalism of the class struggle – convinced the bourgeoisie that they had lost control over the democratic revolution. Their solution was to plan a coup to restore their authority, halting the process of decolonisation and democratisation from below. Spínola, supported by right-wing parties that were little more than reorganised fascist groups, called on "the silent majority" to march on Lisbon on 28 September 1974, patterned after Mussolini's march on Rome. The plotters were confident their coup would succeed, as they took over key army bases and re-established control over the major sources of information, the newspapers, television and radio stations. They preemptively arrested Otelo and other left-wing officers to avert military resistance.

The working class sprang into action to prevent the coup from succeeding. The Communist Party and the trade unions finally took action, calling on railroad workers and bus drivers to halt all transport into Lisbon. Workers, along with the PRP and other armed revolutionaries, built barricades around Lisbon, and COPCON troops joined them to prevent right-wingers from entering the city. The right-wing coup was defeated by this combination of spontaneous actions by the working class and the revolutionary left, with the strike calls of the CP and the unions. The march was called off. The Spínola government collapsed, replaced by the rule of the MFA without the General Staff, and the balance of forces shifted sharply to the left.[26]

---

24. Ferreira and Marshal 1986, pp.114–21; Insight 1975, pp.73–8 and 139–40; Faye 1976, pp.46–9.
25. Mailer 1977, pp.115–6 and 373–4; Varela 2019, pp.75–6.
26. Insight 1975, pp.166–80; Mailer 1977, pp.120–6; Robinson 1987, pp.93–6.

Factory occupations

28 September was a turning point for the revolution, opening the second, more radical phase, with a rise in class struggle and growing opposition to the capitalist system. The right-wing coup plotters were leading figures from the old order, a fact that convinced the left that fascism had not yet been fully eradicated. While the fascist superstructure had been eliminated, the economic, social and political forces that were the base for fascism remained intact and could reassert their power. All the gains of the revolution could be lost, and the fear of arrest and prison radicalised both MFA officers and working-class cadres. The working class, having broken out of the prison of fascism, now broke with the prison of capitalist politics as well. All the neofascist parties, which compromised the bulk of the capitalist parties, were now banned. Well-dressed people, luxury cars, exclusive shops, and expensive restaurants disappeared from the streets and public view.

The radical second stage of revolution, with its greater class polarisation, introduced new revolutionary proletarian methods, including the occupation of the factories, and the beginning of workers' control of production. As the working-class revolution progressed, so did the counter-revolution, with each class engaged in dynamics of self-protection. As workers became more confident, combative and insistent, the owners grew frightened that they could lose everything. Having failed in their coup attempt, the capitalists tried more economic methods of protecting their property and wealth. These included economic sabotage, laying off workers, cutting work to part-time, closing or threatening to close the factories, and removing equipment from the factory. The bosses began a capital strike, ending investments for new machinery and refusing the money needed to replace or repair worn-out, damaged or obsolete machinery. The multinationals cancelled orders and shifted production to plants in other countries. The six great Portuguese monopolies used the banks they owned to transfer money out of the country – which was revealed by the bank workers' union when they opened the books.

Such polarising measures are intrinsic to the logic of capitalism during proletarian revolutions in general, not only to Portugal's. In working-class revolutions, as capital engages in economic sabotage to protect their wealth, class struggle is forced to shift and workers must create new methods of self-defence. Workers moved from strikes over wages and conditions to the struggle for the right to work and defence of their jobs. They started occupying the factories to prevent them from being closed. They demanded that the books be opened and called for worker-control of company finances, so that the money to keep the plant functioning didn't simply disappear. As this occurred, factory assemblies and workers' commissions drew the conclusion that to maintain their employment, they had to control the workplace. To control the managers, they started democratically electing their own foremen. When workers realised that they had to control production, or else the factory would go bankrupt and they would lose their jobs, they begin the process of establishing workers' control inside the factories. This began to take place in Portugal in the autumn of 1974.[27]

Housing occupations

Complementary to factory occupations were the occupations of housing which had begun in April but accelerated after the failed coup. Tenants and shanty town dwellers formed neighbourhood residents' commissions, *comissão de moraderes* (CM), which were patterned after the workers' commissions of the factories, with assemblies and elections of representatives who were all recallable. Together the CMs and CTs formed the core of the popular power movement, and militants were often active in both.

A hundred thousand members of Lisbon's working class resided in shanty towns on the outskirts of the city, living in tin huts lacking running water and indoor toilets. Such conditions produced horrendous health problems. To cite just one example, one of every twenty infants died before their first birthday. The shanty town dwellers, along with tenants of other terrible housing, moved into empty apartments and challenged the right of landlords to maintain a large quantity of unoccupied housing for purposes of speculation. They defended the housing occupations with the slogan: "As long as there are people

---

27. Varela 2019, p.84–90; Geier 1975.

without houses, there should not be houses without people". During the revolution some 80,000 people in Lisbon moved into occupied housing.

The MFA, SP and CP were against the housing occupations. They defended the property rights of the landlords, arguing that they were for maintaining a coalition with the petty bourgeoisie, not losing its support. COPCON troops were the exception, as they supported the "illegal" occupations, and later enforced the occupations as legal. Armed COPCON troops selected places for workers to occupy, physically defending them against the owners. This further divided COPCON from the MFA and the coalition parties, increased the split within the armed forces and further enhanced the image of COPCON and Otelo. The CMs also fought against the landlords to freeze rents, as well as for determining fair rents of what workers could afford based on their salaries and family sizes.

Since the CP and SP were against occupations, the neighbourhood committees became heavily influenced – even more than the CTs – by revolutionary militants from the PRP, UDP, the League of Revolutionary Unity and Action (LUAR) and MES. The CMs became mobilising forces for the revolutionary demonstrations of the Hot Summer of 1975. Since the occupations were illegal under capitalist law, they appealed to the newly-forming Popular Justice Courts. The CMs raised the slogan "A revolutionary situation demands a revolutionary legality". They did not recognise the capitalist laws, including the fascist constitution of March 1933 that was still in effect. What they were doing, they stated, was acting in accordance with legality for the working class, establishing revolutionary justice.

After a second failed coup in March, these occupations would spread to vacant houses, mansions and luxury hotels. The neighbourhood commissions took charge of these buildings and turned them into medical clinics, child-care centres, senior centres, libraries, workers' clubs, canteens and laundries, as well as providing for other social needs. Workers who ran these social centres felt an enormous sense of liberation, pride and accomplishment.[28]

---

28. Hammond 1998, pp.126–34; Varela 2019, pp.128–30; Ferreira and Marshall, 1986, p.152; Downs 1989.

Inter-Empresas and land occupations

All of these revolutionary actions divided the MFA government and political parties while increasing the size and influence of the radical left. In February 1975, a mass demonstration against unemployment, for the right to work, would become pivotal to the shifting political alliances. The demonstration was called by the Inter-Empresas, a coordinating committee of 37 workers' commissions, and represented one of the first attempts to link the CTs across individual factories for unified working-class support of strikes and occupations. PRP members were key initiators of this attempt to unify the CTs. The Inter-Empresas called for a mass demonstration against unemployment on 7 February. At the same time, NATO was aggressively holding exercises off Lisbon's harbour as a warning that it could intervene against the revolution. Fearing NATO, the CP and SP opposed the right-to-work demonstration as overly provocative, and the government decided to ban it. The workers' commissions were not intimidated, and in response the demonstration added the second demand of "NATO Out, National Independence". The Inter-Empresas met with and won the support of COPCON, which then had the MFA Assembly overturn the ban on the demonstration. Thirty thousand workers turned out triumphantly, backed by the same revolutionary groups that would later that summer form the United Revolutionary Front (FUR). For the first time, the MFA had broken with the CP and SP to support radicals from the popular power movement. All the political forces understood this as a political opening to the left, and recognised that the existing government coalition could not last.[29]

Joining with the working-class movement in the factories and neighbourhoods, the farm workers of the south began occupying the huge agricultural estates. These farms, many of them spread over thousands of acres, were owned by the old nobility and were often kept uncultivated as hunting grounds. The agrarian proletariat, reliant on seasonal work, was the most exploited and poorly paid sector of the working class. And as a result, many farmworkers were radical communists. In 1962, under fascism, 200,000 farmworkers, led by the

---

29.   Robinson 1990, pp.153–63; Robinson 2011, pp.267–71; Varela 2019, pp.119–22.

Communist Party, had carried out a general strike and won the eight-hour day. During the revolution, the farmworker occupations occurred under the banner of "land to those who work it". The workers did not break up the estates to divide the land; instead they reorganised the farms as co-ops and collective farms. The farmworkers were given government credit for tractors and machines to increase the food supply and overcome Portugal's heavy dependence on food imports. In some places, links were made between the farms and neighbourhood commissions, bringing food to urban workers at lower prices. Many farmworkers from the south regularly came into Lisbon on trucks and tractors to take part in the revolutionary demonstrations.[30]

March 1975: Another botched coup

The encroachment of popular power on the social relations and legal system of capitalism, the mass occupations of factories and housing and the revolt of troops who refused to go to Angola all convinced leading capitalists to gamble on a second military conspiracy. This coup was planned by General Spínola along with senior army officers, leading industrialists and owners of the six great monopolies and the banks, all of whom were convinced that repression could bring popular compliance. It was an even bigger failure than the first failed coup, technically incompetent and politically misjudged to an extraordinary degree.

The coup began by seeking vengeance on the Light Artillery Regiment (RALIS), one of the most revolutionary of the COPCON forces, who would later become famous when they dropped the required military oath to the country, instead swearing allegiance to the working-class revolution. The RALIS barracks were shelled and bombed, killing one and wounding a dozen enlisted men. Right-wing paratroopers were sent into battle to gain the surrender of RALIS. Instead, when they were surrounded by thousands of enraged workers, they went over to the left.

In response, impromptu mobilisations of workers spread every-where. A general strike of virtually all factories opposed the coup. Workers rushed to known left-wing barracks and demanded guns.

---

30. Mailer 1997, pp.155–67; Hammond 1998, pp.178–85; Varela 2019, pp.183–93.

Armed workers then began to patrol the streets. Masses of workers surrounded barracks thought to be sympathetic to the right, and soldiers arrested right-wing officers. The coup plotters did not receive the military backing they had expected from Spínolist military supporters, who later that day were expelled from the MFA. COPCON moved to organise the military defence of Lisbon and was decisive in defeating the coup. Workers' barricades went up throughout Lisbon, and were reinforced by armed revolutionaries from the PRP and LUAR, as well as COPCON troops. For days workers ran the city. The coup collapsed almost before it started, and many capitalists involved with it fled the country, abandoning their factories, while others, including owners of the six monopolies, were arrested. The MFA Assembly and its Council of the Revolution now had full control of state power.[31]

But this could not be the revolution's final resting point. The class struggle went right through the MFA, splitting it into factions that represented different social forces and their political proposals.

Nationalisations

On the day of the coup, militant bank workers and their unions occupied the banks, arrested the managers and prevented all attempts to withdraw money or transfer it abroad. They opened the books and exposed how the banks, owned by the six great monopolies, had been subsidising the right wing, organising economic sabotage and stealing from the people and the government. In one case they revealed that the owners of the Espirito Santo bank had stolen two billion dollars from government subsidy funds for job protection and transferred the funds out of the country. The bank workers declared that they would occupy the banks until the they were nationalised under workers' control. The next day, the government nationalised all of the nation's domestic banks and insurance companies, which together owned one quarter of national industry. This was a dramatic reversal of its economic plan released just one month earlier, and reflected the enormous impact of the popular revolt against the coup.

The nationalisations were carried out without compensation to the

---

31. Insight 1975, pp.219–31; Cliff 1975, pp.23–5; Mailer 1977, pp.196–201, Varela 2019, pp.140–1; Ferreira and Marshall 1986, pp.190–2.

owners, which for capital was a declaration of total war. At other times and in other countries, social democratic governments have carried out nationalisations, but always with compensation, which preserves the wealth and social power of the capitalist class. But this massive confiscation of private capitalist wealth placed the MFA and the revolutionary masses into direct conflict with the capitalist system.[32] In response, domestic and international capitalism united to crush the revolution economically and politically. Their aim was to create chaos and hunger. An economic blockade by the European Community (EC) and international capitalism began to try to starve Portugal into submission. Orders to Portugal were cancelled, or not renewed. Tariffs were placed on Portuguese goods. The EC reduced imports from Portugal and blocked it from accessing credit. Foreign direct investments and all international aid and subsidies to Portugal were ended; they would not be restored until after the final, successful right-wing coup. At the same time, the CIA now stepped up its preparations for a third counter-revolutionary coup.[33]

Workers' control

The 11 March coup marked another stage in the revolutionary process; an intensification of class warfare, of factory land and housing occupations – and the beginning of dual power. Factories whose owners had fled, or been expropriated, came under workers' control. In other factories, strikes broke out demanding nationalisation under workers' control as a pre-emptive measure. These strikes demanded financial backing from the government in order to maintain production and employment.

In May there were strikes for workers' control at the major factories of TAP, CUF (the largest monopoly), CTT (postal and telephone), as well as at *República*, one of the newspapers that supported the Socialist Party, and Rádio Renascença, owned by the Catholic Church. Troops were sent in to break the strikes, but in every case, the troops went over to the strikers, shifting the MFA Assembly leftwards.

As political workplaces, *República* and Rádio Renascença became

---

32. Hammond 1998, pp.141–54; Varela 2019, pp.150–64; Insight 1975, pp.216–8.
33. Cliff 1975, pp.35–7; *Workers' Power*, No.126.

the flashpoints for the fight over workers' control. The SP, when it left the government in July, used *República* as an excuse, claiming that it was the work of the CP attempting to end press freedom as a step toward establishing a Stalinist state. Despite this, most workers understood that the SP was out to crush workers' control as an idea.[34]

Hundreds of factories were under workers' control, with the workers' commissions supervising the administration. Still, it was an uneven process. In more backward factories, the old administrative or technical staff often ran the factory. In the large, advanced factories, the workers and the CTs organised production, set the hours of work, wages and salaries, replaced piece-rates with fixed salaries, ended dangerous and unsafe working conditions, determined line speed, health and safety measures, and supervised technical personnel. In some workplaces, they raised wages for the lowest paid, froze higher wages, and moved to implement equal pay for women workers. It was an inspiration for every visiting socialist to experience workers' control – the hallmark of every great proletarian revolution – alive in 400 factories in Portugal. Now working for themselves, the workers humanised working conditions, and simultaneously raised productivity by drawing upon the organising genius that exists in the working class. Workers understood the productive process better than foremen and administrators; they knew how to increase production if the ends would benefit them, not the bosses.[35]

The workers' commissions' primary objective was to keep the factory running in order to pay the wages of the workforce. Firms under worker control were faced with difficult decisions about how to finance the plant and market its products, pay bills and prevent bankruptcy. They needed to gain orders, replace materials and machinery and find markets for their products. Factories under workers' control, where there was self-management, were still regulated by the capitalist market, and would remain so as long as capitalism persisted. Workers' control is necessary for socialism, but not sufficient. Without workers

34. Radical America 1975; Mailer 1977, pp.227–36; Varela 2019, pp.194–8; *Workers' Power*, No.135; Geier, meeting with *República* Workers' Commission, July 1975.
35. Robinson 2011, pp.263–80; Hammond 1998, pp.159–71; Varela 2019, pp.143–50; *Workers' Power*, No.126.

taking state power and instituting a planned economy, self-managed factories become co-ops in a capitalist economy.

Many CTs quickly realised this, and did not want to be in the position of exploiting themselves, cutting labour costs in order to sell on the capitalist market. They therefore recognised the need for national planning under workers' control. But such an approach – that is, the development of a socialist economy that can meet its potential as a force for humane, creative work – can only come about by workers taking state power. In the Portuguese Revolution, this was not simply a desirable socialist goal, but a necessity that could not be postponed. It was workers' control that forced open the debate on state power and placed it on the immediate agenda.[36]

Dual power

Dual power is usually presented in terms of two political powers, and the struggle between them. But at a sufficient scale and Portuguese level of militancy, workers' control can introduce an economic dual power to the capitalist market, in which one side or the other must triumph and bring the struggle to conclusion fairly rapidly. Workers' control and the capitalist market are the representatives of the two incompatible social systems of capitalism and socialism. The capitalist market will force occupied workplaces to compete on the market, subjecting workers to the laws of capitalist competition. In contrast, under workers' control, production is not carried out for profit and accumulation, the fundamental dynamic of capitalist production. These two systems were in a deadly competition in which one or the other must destroy its adversary. The intense Hot Summer was the dramatic expression of this life-or-death situation.

In Portugal, while dual power had developed in the factories, farms and neighbourhoods, there were still no working-class political bodies that could pose an alternative to the political power of the state. Without this, the working class had no way of making political decisions – let alone governing – on local or national questions. Factory commissions were not sufficient to respond to Portuguese the economic sabotage

---

36. Geier 1975. Geier, discussions with Setnave Workers' Commission, July 1975 and August 1976.

engineered by capital, end the colonial wars, deal with the crises in health, education, pensions, social welfare and more. There was no alternative to the existing state and its policies.

Because of this, during the revolution, dual power in Portugal was often humorously derided as dual powerlessness. The government was incapable of enforcing its decisions. This situation reached a climax in November during the building workers' strike, when the government announced that it was itself "on strike" because it lacked the power to enforce any of its decisions. But there was no working-class alternative government lying in wait to fill this vacuum.

This impasse was a part of the chronic political crisis during the long Hot Summer, as the third stage of the revolution emerged: an advanced revolutionary situation where the central question was deciding which class would hold state power.[37]

Revolutionary councils

The first proposal for workers to take power had arisen shortly after the failed coup of 11 March, when the PRP proposed the formation of a state based on revolutionary councils of workers, soldiers and sailors (CRTSMs). This proposal was launched through the workers' commissions of Marinha Grande, where the PRP held a majority of the city's CTs. Marinha Grande, a small city of 40,000 that was centre of the glass-blowing industry, had a legendary reputation. Its workers had risen against fascism in 1934 and had set up a soviet republic, although it was subsequently crushed. Now its workers were issuing the call for a new soviet republic across all of Portugal. The CRTSMs became the first in a series of proposals on state power that were to follow and that would split the MFA. Discussions in workers' commissions and army units in some of the most important factories and radical barracks provided support for the CRTSMs. In mid-April, a founding conference of the CRTSMs was held, with representatives from over 200 workers commissions and 40 military units. It was an encouraging start, one that could not be ignored, and led to debates in many workplaces and military units, and within the MFA Assembly.

---

37. Varela 2019, pp.267–9; Hammond 1998, pp.236–7.

The first CRTSM public event was a Lisbon demonstration on 17 June, that helped propel the subject of state power to a central position in public debate for the next five months. This demonstration was co-sponsored by the workers' commissions of Lisnave and Setnave and the PRP and called for workers' power and the defence of workers' control at *República* and Rádio Renascença, both of which were under attack by the SP and Catholic Church respectively. The demonstration of 40,000 workers was led by ten thousand shipyard workers from Lisnave and Setnave. They carried banners calling for all power to the working class, for a state based on workers' councils, and for the dictatorship of the proletariat. They also raised a slogan that became a favourite chant at many Hot Summer demonstrations: "Fora com a canalha, o poder a quem trabalha" – Out with the scum, power to those who work (the ruling class often referred to the "lower classes" as "canalha").[38]

The MFA splits

The MFA Assembly met the next day and came out against the dictatorship of the proletariat. Meanwhile COPCON officers, most notably Otelo de Carvalho, endorsed the CRTSMs. In an indication of the influence of the radical left, Otelo stated that councils and neighbourhood committees were the essence of the Portuguese revolution, and were like soviets that existed in Russia in 1917 before the bureaucracy set up a new class society.

In the weeks that followed, the MFA split into three factions, politically broadly represented by the SP, CP and revolutionary left. Each faction made a proposal to solve the crisis of dual power, through reconstructing political, state and economic power. The three groups mobilised their supporters to battle it out in what was called the Hot Summer, which continued until the coup of 25 November.

The Socialist Party and its collaborators inside the MFA, led by Ernesto Melo Antunes, drafted a proposal called the Document of the Nine, which was signed by 400 officers. It was for parliamentary democracy, and opposed the radicalism of the popular power

---

38. Peoples Translation Service 1975, pp.20–6; Robinson 1990, pp.175–218; Varela 2019, pp.167–77; Geier 1975.

movement as an obstacle to "real" democracy. It was for resolving the economic crisis of dual power by joining the European Economic Community and accepting the dictates of the capitalist market. It charged the Communist Party with trying to destroy the free press and democracy and attempting to set up a state modelled on Russia and Eastern Europe. The Nine's main enemy, however, was the revolutionary left and workers' councils. It attacked the radicalism of what it dismissed as a wild revolutionary vanguard confined to Lisbon and the south; considered workers' control to be anarchist; and argued that military discipline had to be restored in the barracks, where the troops, in its view, were out of control.[39]

The Communist Party, and its allied Gonçalvist officers, proposed a state based on Committees in Defence of the Revolution (CDR). Their blueprint was for political power to rest with the MFA and its government, with decisions made from above, but coordinated with tightly controlled popular mobilisations from below. Their model was based on the Cuban state. The Castro government tried behind the scenes to convince radical leftists estranged from the CP to support the CDR proposal. This had some influence on the MES. PRP members, by contrast, shed their illusions in Castroism as they began to understand what it meant in practice, and what its meaning was if applied to the Portuguese working class and to themselves. The CDR plan to resolve the economic crisis was the Battle for Production, for workers' control to be co-managed with supervisors and local government authorities in order to increase production through voluntarism, gutting real workers' control. These bureaucratic proposals that tried to straddle and avoid firm decisions on dual power had limited appeal beyond the CP.[40]

COPCON presented the third alternative, that of the revolutionary left, for a state based upon the popular power organisations – the workers' and neighbourhood commissions, farmworkers' co-ops and barrack units. The COPCON document denounced both the CP's attempt to control the state apparatus and the social democratic Document of the Nine as hostile to popular power and a way of keeping the means of production in the hands of the bourgeoise.

---

39. Faye 1976, pp.165–71; Hammond 1998, pp.214–5; Insight 1975, pp.262–3.
40. Varela 2019, pp.171–2.

The COPCON document was written by COPCON officers (primarily from the PRP, with input from officers from the UDP and MES as well) and by Isabel do Carmo (General Secretary of the PRP). The PRP explained that the COPCON document was a compromise since it maintained the MFA and the MFA-Peoples Alliance. This was not the same, they said, as soviet power, but would hopefully be a transition towards it. The idea was that if implemented, this set-up would Gonçalves be given the content by the working class that would quickly lead to a soviet state. The economic emphasis of the COPCON document was for the extension of workers' control to the entire economy, while developing economic self-sufficiency and trade with the third world in order to break from the "imperialist" market.[41]

The Hot Summer

By the Hot Summer, which continued into November, the MFA was moving to the right as the three factions struggled for power. The summer featured mass mobilisations, demonstrations, strikes, occupations, dramatic battles over *República* and Rádio Renascença, and clashes between military units. Demonstrations in Lisbon were the largest since the first May Day, with tens and hundreds of thousands participating. In the working-class quarters, in all the cafés, bars, neighbourhood clubs, subways, buses, even at soccer games, people were talking and arguing about the meaning of each of the three political programs, the strength of the contending forces, and what could be done to take power.

The revolutionary left was being forced to act together as a more united force. This was given urgency by the question of state power and their shared support for the COPCON document, as well as the threat of the right within the MFA and the reactionary riots in the north of Portugal. The PRP proposed and organised a united front, the United Revolutionary Front (FUR), with the other revolutionary left groups: LUAR, MES, LCI, and the Popular Socialist Front (FSP), with the occasional support of the UDP. The FUR became the organising centre for the mass demonstrations and activity in support of the COPCON

---

41.   Faye 1976, pp.172–9; Ferreira and Marshall 1986, pp.115–21; Varela 2019, p.202.

document and in defence of workers' control at *República* and Rádio Renascença. As the united alternative to the CP and SP, the FUR gave the revolutionary left the ability to win many workers, neighbourhood commissions, farmworkers, co-ops and radical soldiers to its proposals and demonstrations. As a whole, the groups in the FUR functioned as greater than the sum of their parts; a unified revolutionary left that was recognised as a serious contender for power.

The FUR and the UDP, with the support of 250 workers' and neighbourhood commissions, called the first demonstration in support of the COPCON document, which attracted, 120,000 workers, soldiers and sailors.

But the two great weakness of the revolution remained: the absence of soviets and of a mass revolutionary workers' party. The PRP, despite its remarkable and creative achievements, was still a small party of a few thousand, and therefore not a credible alternative to the major parties. The FUR was an attempt to bridge this gap, but was a coalition, not a revolutionary party. The FUR's cohesion would be challenged by sharp political differences, sometimes over minor points. These inevitably required negotiations to resolve, limiting the FUR's ability to make rapid sharp shifts, or to function as a disciplined body. The coalition was necessary to defend the revolution from the growing right, and to advance the revolution as the alternative to social democracy and the CP. But it was not the force that could arm and politically prepare the working class for a revolutionary uprising, an armed insurrection and a possible civil war.[42]

The prospect of a civil war was being foreshadowed as the north of the country was rocked by armed right-wing mobs that attacked 100 offices of the CP and left groups, burning them down, and beating and shooting those on the scene, leaving some dead in their wake. These attacks were supported by the right, the SP, the Catholic Church and the Maoist MRPP and PCP-ml. The PRP was the only group to shoot back when armed mobs attacked its headquarters in the north.[43]

---

42. Mailer 1977, p.390; Varela 2019, pp.207–10; *Workers' Power*, No.128.
43. Mailer 1977, pp.264–9; Insight 1975, pp.256–9; Hammond 1998, pp.209–13.

Soldiers United for Victory

As the MFA officers shifted to the right, their bonds with working-class troops grew increasingly strained and broken. This led to a growing soldiers' revolt, characterised by insubordination, the collapse of military discipline, the creation of an underground soldiers' press, outright mutiny, and finally the formation of a united revolutionary organisation in the barracks, Soldiers United for Victory (SUV).

SUV began in the Oporto area in the north, which had been the first place right-wing officers had taken over the MFA in the summer of 1975. The northern region MFA defended the right-wing mobs and replaced General Eurico Corvacho, the Gonçalvist commander of the north, with a right-winger who then purged left-wing soldiers and officers. An underground meeting of hundreds of soldiers took place in August to defend Corvacho and the expelled soldiers. That meeting was quickly followed by the founding of SUV, the largest rank-and-file soldiers' organisation since the Russian Revolution. SUV was organised by soldiers from the PRP, UDP, MES, the Internationalist Communist League (LCI) and LUAR, the same groups that supported the COPCON document. For the first time, soldiers from these groups created a joint organisation in the army, moved by the bursting of illusions in the MFA as it shifted to the right.

At SUV's first public appearance, a press conference on 7 September, they announced their program and purpose: to organise inside the army, to defend left-wing soldiers, to democratise the army and to end MFA rule. SUV identified themselves as workers in uniform, and raised working-class demands for better conditions, better pay, a single mess with officers' food, and free transport for soldiers (trips home often took the whole month's pay). Their manifesto charged that a reactionary offensive was underway in and out of the barracks, and that the MFA was now in the service of the counter-revolution. SUV raised as its slogans: "Reactionaries Out of the Barracks" and "Soldiers are Always on the Side of the People".

SUV's vision for a democratic army involved mass assemblies and the elections of recallable soldiers' committees. They sought to link these soldiers' committees with workers' and neighbourhood commissions, with the goal of strengthening the Popular Assemblies.

They were against all imperialisms. They viewed themselves as the armed wing of the working class, in struggle with all workers for the destruction of the MFA and the bourgeois army, for the creation of a revolutionary army of the working class. SUV was the reflection and intensification of dual power, now also inside the military.[44]

The working class immediately rallied around SUV, as the hoped-for defence against the right-wing offensive. Workers' support for SUV rapidly led to mass demonstrations. On 10 September, three days after the appearance of SUV, 40,000 workers, alongside 2,000 soldiers, demonstrated in Oporto. The next day, in Lisbon, 33 military units took part in the SUV demonstration. The SUV demos were the biggest ever held in Portugal's provincial cities. One of the most sensational demonstrations of the Hot Summer was the united FUR and SUV demonstration of 120,000 people in Lisbon on 25 September, in defence of jailed SUV members, with thousands of soldiers making up the largest military presence ever at a demo. Masses of workers and soldiers then seized the city buses, driving them to the military jail outside Lisbon where they forced the authorities to free the political prisoners.[45]

Soviets and guns

Also on 7 September, the same day as SUV's public appearance, left-wing units of the military police revolted and refused to be sent to Angola. Then on September 10, Captain Álvaro Fernandes, an Angolan PRP officer and one of the authors of the COPCON document, went underground after turning over 1,500 G-3 automatic weapons to the PRP and workers' commissions. Otelo publicly defended this action, saying: "The guns are in good hands". (At the same time, however, Otelo was also denouncing SUV, since it called for the destruction of the MFA and the bourgeois army, which reflected Otelo's confused loyalties over dual power.)

At this point, the workers' commission at Lisnave was already armed, and the PRP was forming armed worker militias in other factories. These events were creating an insurrectionary mood inside the

---

44. Peoples Translation Service 1975, pp.37–8; *Inprecor* 1975; Varela 2019, pp.225–9; Robinson 1987, pp.109–10; *Workers' Power*, No.129.
45. Levitan 1975.

working class. The PRP then made its famous announcement that the working class should arm itself to prepare for an insurrection, which, they argued, was the only road to prevent civil war.[46]

In September, the first soviets appeared, but there were only two of them. One was located in the city of Marinha Grande, the stronghold of the PRP mentioned earlier. The second soviet was a broader, more representative council of dual power that appeared in Setúbal at the end of September. It called itself the Committee of Struggle of Setúbal, and was formed under the initiative and influence of the PRP cells in the city's factories. It had representatives from Setnave and most of the city's workers commissions, from the neighbourhood commissions and from all the army units in Setúbal. The Setúbal newspaper placed itself in support of the Committee of Struggle, publicising its events, decisions and actions. The Committee was so popular that it drew in the periphery of the Communist Party, which forced the CP itself to support it. It was a workers' council, a dual power in the city of Setúbal, which served as a governing power, enforcing rent control, supporting occupations and mass demonstrations, supervising the city government, and more. It called itself a committee of struggle, rather than a council, because its objective was to struggle for a working-class seizure of power.[47]

Another promising development was the strengthening of a few Popular Assemblies in some parts of Lisbon. The Assemblies came out of an earlier MFA proposal to coordinate neighbourhood committees, workers' commissions and soldiers' units with local authorities, as functioning local governments. The Popular Assemblies were against the right and for defence of the revolution, but were highly uneven politically and often lacked political clarity. They had been set up by, and were loyal to, the MFA, and were paralysed as the MFA became an instrument of the right. Some of the better Popular Assemblies were potential nuclei of workers' councils, had the revolution continued.

When the centre-right bloc gained a majority within the MFA, the government fell. The new, sixth provisional government represented a

---

46. Mailer 1977, pp.311–2; Hammond 1998, pp.233–4; *Workers' Power*, Nos.133 and 136.
47. Varela 2019, pp.231–3; Robinson 1990, pp.269–90; Robinson 2011, pp.274–8; Downs 1989, pp.58–62; *Workers' Power*, No.132.

drastic shift to the right. It was dominated by the SP and the Group of Nine, with Vasco Gonçalves dismissed and CP influence curtailed. In an attempt to regain power, the CP then moved dramatically to the left, aiming to increase and use its popular support as a bargaining chip in negotiations with the SP and MFA. The CP now took some positions similar to those of the revolutionary left, blocking the continued growth of the revolutionary left, and shifting some working-class support back to the CP.

Since both the CP and the revolutionary left were battling the same SP-MFA-Right bloc, cooperation occurred among their supporters, who came out for each other's demonstrations, without official co-sponsorship. Sharp political differences persisted which limited joint activity. But the CP was a mass force that was now making radical statements, supporting radical actions, and verbally flirting with the popular power movement. For some worker supporters of the FUR, the CP was seen as a lesser evil than the social democrats. The CP had led the building workers' strike, the most radical strike of the period, that barricaded the presidential palace and held the cabinet and the parliament as hostages. The CP's flirtation with radicalism convinced many workers that the CP was the necessary force to defend the revolution, defeat the right and open the road to state power. This belief was an understandable illusion, but an illusion nonetheless. As the CP manipulated the workers' and popular power movement in order to negotiate the terms of its return to the government with the SP and the MFA, it remained the major barrier to the working class taking power.

The coup of 25 November 1975

All of these developments came to a climax with a third, successful, coup on 25 November. Officers associated with the CP, under the impression that the CP supported their action, started the motions for a peculiarly amateurish attempted coup, which in turn was the signal for the successful joint social democratic and-right-wing coup that would end the revolutionary situation.

At the start of these competing coups, the CP pulled the plug, abandoning its military supporters and imposing discipline on its trade unions to block all attempts to strike or mobilise against the right.

At a meeting the night before, the CP's leader, Cunhal, had come to an agreement with Melo Antunes, the organiser of the next day's coup. The details of that meeting have never been made public. But on 26 November, Melo Antunes went on television to defend the CP from charges of plotting a coup, and to prevent any measures against the CP. Melo Antunes argued that including the CP in the government was necessary to defend democratic stability. The deal perhaps had been for the CP to tolerate a social democratic coup as a lesser evil than a right-wing coup. For Melo Antunes, the real danger was not the CP, but what he referred to as the Lisbon Commune, after the Paris Commune of 1871. It was the revolutionary left, and the PRP in particular, that would be slandered with coup-plotting and repressed.[48]

The coup of 25 November was not the right-wing coup that had been expected. Until then, the revolutionary left, as well as most other political forces, had thought a new coup would mean the return of fascism, or some facsimile of fascism. The chant at left demonstrations had been "Portugal will not become the Chile of Europe", in reference to the CIA-backed coup that had overthrown the left-wing government of Salvador Allende and installed the Pinochet dictatorship just two years earlier. But the 25 November coup in Portugal was to be carried out by the social democratic centre of the MFA, albeit with right-wing support.

The key players in the coup, besides Melo Antunes, were Frank Carlucci, Mário Soares and António Ramalho Eanes. Carlucci, a sophisticated imperialist, was the US Ambassador and a CIA agent, who would later be promoted to second-in-command of the CIA. Carlucci had been secretly organising for a social democratic coup for over a year, convinced that after two failed right-wing attempts, a similar third one had no better prospects for popular support and success. He was convinced that a Chilean solution in Portugal would only bring on civil war, with the final outcome uncertain. Instead he hoped that a social democratic solution and entry into the Common Market would stabilise Portugal as a capitalist country in the Western bloc.

Carlucci's main agent and co-thinker was Mário Soares of the SP. Carlucci arranged for substantial CIA funding of the Socialist Party

---

48. Faye 1976, Otelo testimony, pp.41–6; Varela 2019, pp.243–8; Hammond 1998, pp.242–8; *Workers' Power*, No.138.

as the logical organiser of popular forces for a coup. The CIA's large monthly financing of SP activity was laundered through the German Social Democratic Party and British Labour Party. Thus international social democracy maintained its historical record of backing counter-revolutionary violence .

Melo Antunes and the MFA reformers would not finalise coup preparations until after Angolan Independence on 11 November, for fear that if the right-wing won the coup, they would continue the colonial wars. Melo Antunes was the MFA's house intellectual: a self-described Marxist and Gramscian, author of the MFA's major programmatic documents, and the leader of the MFA majority and Group of Nine. He was a left social democrat, who supported the educated elite implementing reforms for the masses, as long as the masses did not take matters into their own hands.

Ramalho Eanes, the other main figure in the coup, organised the military operations. Eanes had one foot in each camp – the Group of Nine, all of whose meetings he attended, and the centre-right. He became the main beneficiary of the coup, becoming president of the Republic the following year. His operational troops were the right-wing Amadora commandos led by the far-right Jaime Neves, whose role Eanes had kept secret from the Group of Nine.[49]

Social democratic counter-revolution

Social democratic repression differs from right-wing repression. In Portugal, social democratic piecemeal "reform" tactics were used over a period of years to restore full capitalist functioning, with a tempo designed to avoid violent working-class resistance. The immediate action was to crush what it viewed as its most dangerous enemies, the revolutionary left in the military. On the day of the coup, COPCON was abolished and Otelo arrested. Radical units were then purged, reorganised or dissolved. Restoring army discipline was the first step to restoring state repression over society.

The next step was to restore disciplined functioning in the state apparatus. Revolutionary groups were persecuted, the PRP more than

---

49. Ferreira and Marshall 1986, pp.193–8; Melo Antunes interview pp.163–7, Otelo de Carvalho interview p.117–21, Vasco Lourenço interview pp.134–7.

any other, with 100 members jailed, and arrests continuing for years. The two main leaders of the PRP, Isabel do Carmo and Carlos Antunes, later received long jail terms; meanwhile, Spínola and right-wing coup plotters were welcomed home from exile.

Still, it took a few years for the state to gain the confidence to crack down on the factory committees and on workers' control, often through financial pressure. Workers' control had come into existence to defend employment; now, to maintain jobs it was forced to accept management control. It took more years still to undo the nationalisations and restore them to private ownership, and longer still to give financial compensation to the former owners. The government proceeded step by step, in a more sophisticated counter-revolutionary process than the traditional right-wing counter-revolutionary dictatorship and savage repression.

The Portuguese revolution ended on 25 November 1975, but many revolutionaries did not immediately accept defeat. Revolutionaries are trained to always be the last to leave the field of battle, and in some past instances, what could seem to be defeats turned out to be only temporary setbacks. The immediate revolutionary situation was over, but the revolution might have revived, in conjunction with international events in Italy, Greece, and most importantly, in Spain. Franco had died on 20 November 1975. Until then, there had never been a democratic transition away from fascism. As a result, the left expected a revolution in Spain, which could then revive the Portuguese revolution. That did not occur, thanks to the atrocious politics of the Spanish Communist Party, which was desperate to engineer a peaceful transition.

The defeat of the Portuguese Revolution turned out to be the final act of the 1960s–'70s radicalism. The neoliberal offensive had begun germinating in the 1975 recession. There would be no more reforms for the working class, but rather a decades-long attack by capital, with right-wing advances and working-class retreats.

Had the Socialist and Communist Parties been for the working class taking power, the Portuguese Revolution would not have been defeated. Social democracy and Stalinism were responsible for this missed opportunity for workers to take power in the heart of Europe.

Still, the Portuguese Revolution provides many important lessons for the revolutionary left that have been lost owing to the defeat of the revolution, and by decades of neoliberal reaction internationally. Those lessons are not all that different from those of other great working-class revolutions. The most basic is that the coming revolution will be a proletarian revolution or there will not be a revolution. Building organs of workers' democracy and dual power is necessary, but not sufficient for victory. The revolutionary process is also a process for the counter-revolution, and both sides have time constraints. If the revolutionary workers do not take state power, the counter-revolution will end the revolutionary situation and workers' democracy will be destroyed. Never underestimate reformism. In a revolutionary period, vehicles for reformism backed by powerful sponsors can be reinvented overnight as the agents of reaction. The indispensable instrument for the working class to emancipate itself is its own revolutionary party. The greatest chance for successful revolution is to not postpone party building, whose every advance now is a bridge to future liberation.

References

Birchall, Ian 1979, "Social Democracy and the Portuguese 'revolution'", *International Socialism*, 2:6, Autumn, pp.71–84. https://www.marxists.org/history/etol/writers/birchall/1979/xx/portrev.html

Cliff, Tony 1975, "Portugal at the Crossroads", *International Socialism*, 1:81/82, September 1975. https://www.marxists.org/archive/cliff/works/1975/portugal/index.htm

Downs, Charles 1989, *Revolution at the Grassroots*, State University of New York Press.

Faye, Jean Pierre 1976, *Portugal: The Revolution in the Labyrinth*, Spokesman Books.

Ferreira, Hugo Gil and Michael Marshall 1986, *Portugal's Revolution: Ten Years On*, Cambridge University Press.

Figueiredo, Antonio de, 1975, *Portugal, Fifty Years of Dictatorship*, Holmes & Meier.

Geier, Joel 1975, "Out With the Scum, Power to Those Who Work", *Workers' Power*, No.128, 14–17 September. https://www.marxists.org/history/etol/newspape/workerspower/wp128.pdf

Geier, Joel and David Finkel 1976, "The Portuguese Revolution and the PRP", Documents of the International Socialists (U.S.), 1969–1986. https://www.marxists.org/history/etol/document/is-us/IS-documents/76-77/76-(8).pdf

Hammond, John 1998, *Building Popular Power: Worker's and Neighbourhood Movements in the Portuguese Revolution*, Monthly Review Press.

Inprecor 1975, "The Soldiers Show the Way", No.35, 9 October. https://www.marxists.org/history/etol/newspape/inprecor/inprecor-no-35-october-9-1975.pdf

Insight Team of the *Sunday Times* 1975, *Insight on Portugal: The year of the captains*, Andre Deutsch.

Levitan, Mark 1975, "Portugal Won't Be the Chile of Europe", *Workers' Power*, No.130, 2–15 October, pp.8–9. https://www.marxists.org/history/etol/newspape/workerspower/wp130.pdf

Luxemburg, Rosa 1906, *The Mass Strike, the Political Party and the Trade Unions*. https://www.marxists.org/archive/luxemburg/download/mass-str.pdf

Mailer, Phil 1977, *Portugal, The Impossible Revolution?*, Free Life Editions.

Peoples Translation Service, Berkely 1975, *Portugal: Key Documents of the Revolutionary Process*.

Ponte, Bruno da 1974, *The last to leave, Portuguese colonialism in Africa*, International Defence and Aid Fund.

Radical America 1975, "Documents of the Workers' Struggle", Vol.9, No.6, November–December. https://files.libcom.org/files/Rad%20America%20V9%20I6.pdf

Robinson, Peter 1987, "Portugal 1974–75: Popular Power", in Colin Barker (ed.), *Revolutionary Rehearsals*, Bookmarks.

Robinson, Peter 1990, *Workers' Councils in Portugal 1974–75*, Open Research Online. https://oro.open.ac.uk/19940/1/pdf115.pdf

Robinson, Peter 2011, "Workers' Councils in Portugal 1974–75", in Immanuel Ness and Dario Azzellini (eds), *Ours to Master and To Own. Workers' Control from the Commune to the Present*, Haymarket Books.

Varela, Raquel 2018, "The PCP in Portugal's Revolution 1974–75", *International Socialism*, 2:157, Winter. https://isj.org.uk/the-pcp-in-the-portuguese-revolution-1974-5-crisis-state-and-revolution/

Varela, Raquel 2019, *A People's History of The Portuguese Revolution*, Pluto Press.

Workers' Power 1975, "News Direct from Revolutionary Portugal", Nos.129–138.
https://www.marxists.org/history/etol/newspape/workerspower/index.htm

OMAR HASSAN

Hamas: From resistance to containment

Omar Hassan is the editor of *Marxist Left Review*. He has been active in anti-fascist and Palestine solidarity work, and has written extensively on the Middle East.

T HE NEW *NAKBA* taking place in Gaza has made it clearer than ever that the struggle for Palestine is a struggle against the entire system of capitalism and imperialism in the Middle East. Israel is a nuclear-armed ethno-state backed to the hilt by the US empire and all its allies. International organisations such as the UN have been powerless to intervene, reduced to putting out press releases pleading for aid to be restored. For months the Western media were uncritical cheerleaders of the Israeli genocide, regularly calling on supporters of the war while silencing Palestinians and their allies. Though the narrative is more mixed now, there is still an overwhelmingly pro-Zionist bias. As well, the Arab and Muslim regimes have been utterly passive in the face of this catastrophe, offering their tacit approval as Israel unleashes its destructive power against a defenceless population.

All of this can be explained with reference to the international system of profit and power. The Middle East is a strategically vital region for both oil and trade, and Israel is the most powerful state within it. Given the US is Israel's primary ally, there is no chance that NATO members or other US allies such as Australia will do anything to seriously challenge or constrain Israel's ambitions. And of course, institutions like the media are tools of the establishment, more likely to mindlessly reproduce imperialist propaganda than offer a critique.

Within the Middle East, many of the region's most important countries – think Saudi Arabia, Egypt, UAE – have long been integrated into the Western orbit, and have been steadily normalising their relationships with Israel. Those that haven't are not interested in risking their own positions for the sake of solidarity with the Palestinians.

Within this situation, the first task of socialists across the world is to offer our solidarity to the Palestinians and their liberation struggle, and to respond to the endless lies and propaganda put out to justify Israel's racist existence. To do this socialists in Australia and across the world have thrown ourselves into organising protests, sit-ins, pickets, blockades, camps, strikes and forums to grow and deepen the movement. But in the midst of this vital activism, there's an urgent need to convince activists of the fundamental connection between capitalism and Palestinian oppression.

Within the broader movement, the question of Hamas looms large. For Israel and its allies, Hamas is a terrorist organisation, the latest manifestation of the savagery and violence inherent in the Arab peoples. Its very existence serves as a self-evident justification for Israel's most brutal actions. This argument reached its climax in the immediate aftermath of Hamas's military operation on October 7, which shook a complacent and rightward moving Israeli society to its core. Led by a vulnerable yet tenacious Netanyahu, Israel has sought to save face by launching an unprecedented assault on the people of Gaza, ludicrously justified as self-defence. The enormous casualties and cruelties unleashed on the people of Palestine need not be described here, as they are well known and ever increasing. All of this has been outrageously justified as a campaign of self-defence against Hamas.

The issue of Hamas also arises in the international solidarity movement, often for opposite reasons. Many supporters of Palestine have little idea about the history, politics or practice of Hamas (or its allies in Hezbollah or the Houthis). They are seen simply as the only group willing to resist Israeli aggression, which leads many to fall into fairly uncritical support for its actions and leaders.

In developing an independent assessment of Hamas, we have to avoid simplistic reactions to Zionist propaganda or glorification of an abstract "resistance". On one hand, we absolutely defend the

Palestinians' right to fight for self-determination, including with force. Yet defending these essential national rights does not require us to champion whatever organisation rises to the fore at a particular time, and certainly not to defend any and every tactic employed. That would be third world nationalism, not Marxism. Anti-imperialism is not as simple as putting a plus where the imperialists put a minus.

This article will therefore attempt to put forward a Marxist assessment of Hamas as a political organisation. It will begin by exploring the decline of secular nationalism across the region and in Palestine, compounded by the Palestine Liberation Organization's (PLO) acceptance of the treasonous Oslo accords. By then exploring their conservative approach to governing Gaza, their cosy relationship with reactionary capitalist forces in the region, and their inconsistent struggle against Israel and imperialism, it will become apparent that Hamas is incapable of achieving any kind of Palestinian liberation.

Much discussion about Hamas focuses on their conservative religious views or their attitude to armed struggle. But while these factors are important, they are secondary. The most essential thing to establish is their position within the political economy of Palestinian society, which invariably shapes their attitude to a range of vital political, economic and strategic issues. My argument is that the organisation represents a conservative form of bourgeois nationalism, one that marks a qualitative degeneration from previous eras of mass resistance in Palestine. As a bourgeois force, it is totally incapable of mobilising the type of revolutionary mass movement required to defeat the imperialist powers that oppress the Palestinians alongside the workers and poor across the Middle East.

The rise of Hamas

In developing a serious analysis of Hamas, we should start with its rise as a political tendency in Palestinian society. Hamas has built for itself a profile as a resistance movement within Palestine and in the broader Arab and Muslim world on the back of its rejection of the disastrous Oslo Accords. Its commitment to resistance resonated with those who refused to placidly accept the status quo of Israeli dominance, and its heartland being the beleaguered Gaza Strip meant that it has been on the front line of substantial social, economic, military and cultural attack by the Israelis. All these factors, in addition to their long-standing and relatively efficient welfare networks, transformed Hamas from its origins as a marginal rival to the hegemonic PLO into the most popular political organisation in Palestine.

Hamas was launched in December 1987, just as the first Palestinian Intifada was kicking off. But its roots go back to the early part of the twentieth century, with the formation of the Muslim Brotherhood. Initiated in Egypt by Hassan al-Banna in the late 1920s, the Brotherhood developed into a transnational network of clerics and activists organised around a modern yet socially conservative brand of political Islam. The Brotherhood sought to build up their supporter base by providing welfare services to the poor, funded by donations from the middle- and upper-class figures who led the organisation. This reliance on landowners, mosques and urban businessmen shaped its fierce hostility to Arab nationalism and the left. It was used as a weapon against socialists and nationalists throughout the anti-colonial era, and received substantial funding and support from the British puppet, King Farouk of Egypt. At various points during the Cold War the Brotherhood played an important role in fighting the left, both ideologically and physically. As reward the organisation would often receive funding and political support from various reactionary governments and sources.

In Palestine, the Brotherhood had only a small base in Gaza from before the *Nakba* of 1948. Though Islamism was always stronger in Gaza than the West Bank, it was largely sidelined by the secular nationalists for decades. Islamic organising only really began to gain mass influence in the 1970s. Having said that, the Islamists had been encouraged first by Egypt, then after 1954 by Israel. This had allowed generations of Islamic organisers to patiently embed their religious, cultural and welfare organisations and their ideology in the wider population even as the nationalists and the left were harshly repressed.[1]

The standing of political Islam was given an immense boost by the Iranian revolution of 1979. Though it started as a popular and democratic rebellion against the Western-backed Shah, Khomeini was

---

1.   Caridi 2023, pp.61–3; Filiu 2012.

able to hijack the revolution to install a repressive theocracy, assisted by the leading Stalinist organisations. Despite its authoritarian and reactionary nature, the new Islamic republic skilfully played on the themes of anti-imperialism and social justice and won an international following.

The seeming success of this new regime in challenging the West contrasted greatly with the disastrous policies of the secular nationalists who headed increasingly authoritarian and neoliberal nationalist governments across the region. These regimes were no longer interested in even pretending to stand with the people of Palestine, highlighted by Egypt's decision to make peace with Israel in 1978. The PLO had been unable to achieve any form of statehood; its terrible defeats in Jordan in 1970 and Lebanon in 1982 sent people looking elsewhere for inspiration.

The left in the Middle East, totally dominated by Stalinism, was also unable to pose an alternative. Communist parties and new left formations across the region largely tailed behind the reactionary post-colonial dictatorships, and in many cases even formed part of their pseudo-democratic governing coalitions. The Palestine Communist Party was never much of an attraction, having supported the partition of Palestinian territory in 1948 and for decades defended the right of Israel to exist, the most conservative position of any of the main Palestinian parties. The Popular and Democratic Fronts, which formed in a later era with an initially more radical platform, quickly moderated under the influence of their Stalinist "stages" theories and their opportunist alliances with reactionary figures such as Hafez al-Assad and Saddam Hussein.

Having grown substantially as a result of their own efforts and the failure of the nationalist and left forces, the Palestinian Muslim Brotherhood was coming under increasing pressure for refusing to engage in resistance to Israel. A minority split to form the more militant Islamic Jihad in 1981. As sentiment for rebellion grew in the build-up to the First Intifada, a fierce debate broke out regarding the future of the group. The traditional view of the organisation was that charity work and the gradual "Islamisation" of society was a precondition for any liberation struggle. The majority, however, had now come to the conclusion that it was impossible to delay their engagement in active resistance any longer. This wing of the party did not explicitly reject the importance of Islamic welfare work, but rather argued that religious proselytising could and should co-exist with armed resistance. In this way the organisation known as Hamas was born.

Already viewed with scepticism by the other factions, Hamas's inaugural intervention into Palestinian politics did little to reassure its detractors. On one hand, it actively took part in the First Intifada along with everyone else. Yet even then there was a tendency towards militarising the struggle, and their activities were generally conducted separately from the other organisations grouped under the rubric of the PLO. Tareq Baconi, author of *Hamas Contained*, summarises their sectarian and politically reactionary approach:

> Rather than joining the local leadership that was coordinating with the PLO to sustain the uprising, Hamas openly competed against it… The leaflets it published were different in language and feel from those officially issued by the intifada's leadership. They introduced a religious element into an uprising that was not thought of by most Palestinians in particularly religious terms. Slogans from Hamas proliferated, its graffiti attacking Jews and Christians as well as secular nationalists.[2]

But like any mass rising, the Intifada could not sustain itself forever. Years of mobilisation and brutal repression saw thousands of leaders and activists imprisoned, and the base somewhat exhausted. The leader of the PLO, Yasser Arafat, picked this moment to start negotiations with Israel that have gone down in history as the Oslo Accords. From the outset these so-called "peace talks" were a trap to defuse the mass rebellion and convince the PLO to abandon central planks of its liberation program. But Arafat and the other bourgeois leaders of Fatah and the PLO were not simply victims of some Israeli trick: they were willing and active participants in the betrayal of the liberation struggle, selling all their principles for a cushy position within the international

---

2. Baconi 2018, p.25.

order of states. Sections of the left, alongside nationalist intellectuals like Edward Said, argued that Oslo would not grant Palestinians meaningful self-determination. But these criticisms were ignored, with Arafat and his team prepared to settle for a statelet consisting of Gaza and fragments of the West Bank. As a downpayment for this dubious result, the PLO accepted Israel's right to exist as a Jewish ethno-state, along with its right to control 80 percent of historic Palestine, and renounced the armed struggle.

The political structure of Palestinian life we know today essentially took shape in this period. In return for giving up every single principle of Palestinian liberation, the PLO was allowed to set up a pseudo-state structure in the form of the Palestinian Authority. Critics remarked that the PA was neither Palestinian nor an authority, with Israel granted indefinite control over security, borders, trade, water, electricity and a host of other functions typically carried out by a state. Oslo ultimately collapsed because Israel had no intention of giving the Palestinians a single concession. But the failure of the negotiators to achieve a deal at Camp David in 2000 angered the Palestinian street, who rightly felt they had given up much and received nothing in return.

Hamas had steadily gained support and authority among Palestinians by opposing this disastrous process every step of the way. They denounced Arafat's acceptance of the two-state solution, the growing security collaboration between Palestinian and Israeli forces and the tacit abandonment of Palestinian demands, including the right of refugees to return to their homes. Instead, it argued for a renewed resistance. It gained prestige from the Second Intifada, which definitely ended the Oslo process. This Second Intifada was a far more militarised affair than its earlier namesake, and far more under the control of the political factions. The rebellion saw guerrilla fighters from Fatah, Hamas, Islamic Jihad and the Popular Front engage in escalating armed attacks against Israeli targets. The mass of the population supported the uprising, but were far less involved than the last time around.

The end of Oslo, the Second Intifada and the election of a new Israeli government led by mass murderer Ariel Sharon pushed Hamas in new and contradictory directions. Hamas now sensed an opportunity to build on its support in Gaza and, for the first time, entrench itself as a leading faction in Palestinian politics. It decided to run in a series of local and municipal elections in 2005 and 2006, and achieved strong results. It then decided, after much internal debate, to contest for positions in the Palestinian Authority (PA). This was a big step for the party, which had rejected the PA as the bastard child of the Oslo process. The PA has no real power or control over the Palestinian territories. It is instead better understood as a quisling government, a Palestinian Vichy, which receives international funding and support in exchange for administering – and repressing – the Palestinians on behalf of Israel.

Hamas saw running in these elections as a means of confirming their new role as a major party within the Palestinian establishment. Party spokesman Ghazi Hamad set out the new approach:

> Hamas presented an alternative, we said *negotiations alone are not enough* [my emphasis] to achieve our rights. What is needed is a Palestinian-led strategy, with a genuine consensus over aims and a proper balance between political and military struggle. But we also said the priority was reform and change in the way we are governed. How can we promise Jerusalem and the right of return when we can't deliver our people a loaf of bread?[3]

This superficially attractive formulation entailed a lowering of horizons from liberation to successful governance under occupation, a shift that has entailed policing the armed factions, repressing rivals and political compromise. Initially, their goal was not to win outright, but to form a coalition with Fatah and the other existing parties. But Hamas-backed lists did surprisingly well, giving the party unexpected control of most urban councils and a substantial majority in the Palestinian Legislative Council. This shocking result transformed Palestinian politics.

Elected on a platform of "change and reform", Hamas promised a break with the previous ten years of negotiations and humiliation. Although it continued to defend the right to resist Israel's expanding occupation, the concept of resistance had now been radically redefined. Far from calling for a new round of protest or armed struggle, Hamas

---

3.   Usher 2006, p.21.

leaders offered modest promises: they would improve the corrupt and inefficient provision of essential services and walk away from negotiations that seemed one-sided. While on paper it upheld the long-term goal of unifying Palestine from the river to the sea, on repeated occasions Hamas offered Israel long-term truces based on the previously unthinkable: a Palestinian state within the 1967 borders.[4] This programmatic convergence with Fatah and the PLO was designed to facilitate a coalition government. Even after winning a majority, Hamas offered Fatah a number of ministries – this despite the fact that the latter had an established history of collaboration with Israel and was led by US President George Bush's hand-picked stooge, Mahmoud Abbas.

But these historic concessions were not enough to placate Hamas's enemies. Israel and its Western allies refused to accept the democratic process, lightly dismissing the outcome of a free and fair election because they did not like the result. Israel, the US and the EU immediately cut financial, diplomatic and military ties to the PA and placed sanctions on the new government. Emboldened by these acts of aggression – and, presumably, behind the scenes lobbying – Mahmoud Abbas initiated a partially successful coup against the newly elected legislature. Hamas easily rebuffed Fatah to maintain control over Gaza, but Fatah was able to use their existing power to establish a dictatorship in the West Bank that lasts to this day. The result was a Palestinian polity now divided in two.

Israel responded to Hamas's victory by turning the Gaza Strip into a disaster zone, even before the latest offensive. They set out to punish the population for daring to elect Hamas. Prior to the latest assault, more than 2 million people lived in the tiny territory, more than 50 percent of whom were unemployed. According to the UN Relief and Works Agency, around 80 percent of the population relied on international aid for their survival, and 95 percent lacked access to clean water due to systematic Israeli policies. The situation was established and maintained by a callous siege that denies the people of Gaza sufficient materials to live their lives. Israeli political and military leaders regularly talk of the need to "mow the lawn":

---

4.   Caridi 2023, pp.171–78, Hroub 2010, pp.56–7.

> Israel must wean itself from the naïve belief that improving the standard of living of the Palestinians in Gaza will reduce terror. Actually, the opposite is probably true. … Israel [has] wisely adopted a patient military strategy of attrition or "mowing the grass," which was conceived, first and foremost, to harm the enemy's capabilities.[5]

This thinly coded language refers to the regular massacres of civilians in the Strip, and should put to rest once and for all the false narrative that Israel is merely responding to Palestinian provocations. The current genocidal attack is thus best understood as a new stage in this historic process of suppression and mass murder.

Hamas: repackaged bourgeois nationalism

When Hamas emerged from the 2006 elections as the most popular party in Palestine, it reflected the desire for a less corrupt and more resistance-oriented political leadership. Yet its time in government has seen it fall into many of the same practices and dead ends as its predecessors in Fatah and the PLO. Indeed, its slide from resistance organisation to an authoritarian regime prepared to negotiate with Israel was far more rapid than that of the PLO.

In Marxist terms, Hamas is a classic bourgeois nationalist party. While many of their founders were impoverished refugees and low ranking clerics, the organisation has since evolved to being an institution with an annual budget measuring in the tens of millions of dollars. Much like the PLO, the party is both pro-capitalist and pro-market. Many of its leaders are filthy rich and possess huge investment portfolios, particularly in Turkey and the Gulf. This wealth was accumulated through real estate, Islamic finance and skimming off the top of international aid destined for Gaza. The party has cultivated relations with a range of capitalists across the Muslim world, using them to bypass sanctions, open diplomatic doors and as a source of donations. Hamas also has close connections with wealthy Palestinians in Gaza. Among other things, these figures help to fund and run the tunnel network that

---

5.   Inbar 2018.

Hamas runs as a sort of public-private partnership. This raises revenue for the group in the form of taxes and bribes. This layer has also profited from the agriculture and hospitality sectors, and generally enjoyed much better lives than the millions of regular Gazans. There was no debate within the party when Hamas proposed a wealthy Palestinian businessman to be the minister of economy, trade and industry in their first cabinet, and two of the three candidates seriously considered for the key post of prime minister were Palestinian capitalists.[6] This reflects the pro-capitalist attitudes of Hamas and the broader Muslim Brotherhood tendency within Islamism, which have always championed trade and private property as core pillars of society.

Many commentators and experts have documented the way in which Hamas has gradually moderated its politics over time. The factors behind this shift include their growing affiliations with sections of Palestinian and international capital, their situation in Gaza shifting the group from resistance to governance, and the objective challenges of dealing with Israel's ongoing siege on Gaza. In any case, Hamas has clearly shifted further towards reconciliation with Fatah's governing principles – if not always the organisation itself – and, in a contradictory and uneven way, the Israeli occupation. Their practice right up until the attack on October 7, which will be discussed separately, also confirms this approach.

1. The Liberation of Palestine

The traditional position of the Palestinian liberation movement was – rightly – to refuse to recognise the legitimacy of the Israeli state. Facing a colonial settler project originally initiated by British imperialism on an indigenous population, the Palestinians were and are fully within their rights to demand the destruction of the structures of occupation and their replacement by democratic institutions open to all those who live in the area formerly known as Palestine. This perspective is not simply a more just alternative to the status quo. Rather, the very existence of the apartheid structures and the perpetual expansion of Israel – which has racism and imperialism encoded into its very

---

6.   Caridi, pp.234–35.

DNA – precludes any lasting and just peace. The abandonment of this perspective in favour of the so-called two-state solution was a disastrous concession to imperialism and a symptom of the broader degeneration of the left and nationalist forces. Accepting the two-state solution and Israel's "right to exist" has never resulted in any gains for the Palestinian people. In fact after decades of negotiations and the creation of institutions designed to move in that direction, the situation for Palestinians in Gaza and the West Bank has never been worse.

As mentioned earlier, Hamas benefited greatly from being the largest faction to publicly and systematically oppose the Oslo Accords and the idea of a bantustan state. Article 13 of its first charter states that "so-called peaceful solutions and international conferences, are in contradiction to the principles of the Islamic Resistance Movement".[7] Yet as Hamas approached and eventually entered into positions of power, they quietly abandoned this position. The concept of a *hudna*, or long-term ceasefire, gradually entered their lexicon and has become an accepted element of their strategy. Based on a particular reading of Islamic texts, the concept developed as an attempt to straddle the conflicting requirements of diplomacy and resistance. It allows Hamas leaders to negotiate with Israel and the imperial powers while shielding the group from the accusation of selling out.[8]

Given all this, the persistent accusations that Hamas refuses to acknowledge Israel's supposed right to exist are cynical and disingenuous. In practice, Hamas has repeatedly accepted Israel's existence. Its 2017 charter maintains the organisation's formal opposition to the foundation of Israel, the Oslo Accords that recognise it, and the PA's subsequent collaboration with the Israel Defence Forces. But more importantly, the new document positions Hamas as a potential partner of government and negotiations within the framework of a reconstituted PLO, declaring the two-state solution to be a "formula of national consensus".[9]

But of course, what's written in a party's charter or platform is far less important than what the party says and does on a daily basis.

---

7.   Hamas 1988.
8.   Caridi 2023, pp.171–78, Hroub 2010, pp.56–7.
9.   Hamas 2017.

In practice, Hamas's attitude to Israel looks strikingly similar to that of Fatah in the early years of Oslo. Thus in 2001, just as the Second Intifada was getting started, a leading figure in Hamas put out a leaflet explaining that "Hamas and Islamic Jihad may agree to a temporary ceasefire, for a set time period such as ten years, during which the Palestinian people can create their own state within the 1967 borders, with Jerusalem as its capital, without giving up one inch of historic Palestine".[10] In 2003 Hamas agreed to a unilateral ceasefire with Israel, and by 2005 Hamas had conceded further, signing up to the Cairo Declaration which promised to "maintain an atmosphere of calm" – that is, to stop attacks on Israel – in exchange for peace and the release of prisoners.[11] In the aftermath of their election victory in 2006 Hamas agreed to "'respect' all past agreements signed by the PLO, on the basis that they supposedly 'safeguard the interests of our people.'"[12]

But like Fatah before them, Hamas have gained nothing from this backsliding. Israel has never accepted the Palestinian right to genuine self-determination, nor has it ever stopped building illegal settlements on stolen Palestinian land. Indeed, it refuses to even define its own borders. In January of this year, Netanyahu openly declared his opposition to ever granting the Palestinians any sort of statehood.

2. Anti-democratic rule
One of the tragedies of the Palestinian people is that they live with the weight of multiple layers of authoritarianism. They suffer under the genocidal Israeli occupation and the siege on Gaza imposed by Israel and Egypt, but also the authoritarian rule of the PA in the West Bank and Hamas in Gaza.

It's true to say that Hamas won a majority of seats in free elections back in 2006, and were immediately denied the chance to govern by Fatah and its imperialist supporters. In this sense, it's impossible to say whether they would have governed in a democratic manner given the chance. Yet the party has clearly grown comfortable with its position as unquestioned rulers of Gaza. Fatah and its subsidiary organisations

10. Baconi 2018, p.40.
11. Usher 2005.
12. Baconi 2018, p.119.

in Gaza have been repressed repeatedly over the years, and while Islamic Jihad and the Popular Front for the Liberation of Palestine can operate openly, they self-censor for fear of repression. Hamas have at times indicated they would tolerate new elections, but at other times indicated some wariness. Recently elected leader Yahya Sinwar made his reputation by personally executing a dozen Palestinians accused of being "collaborators" as part of his role heading up the organisation's feared Internal Security Force. While it's possible some of the accused *were* working with Israel, some were killed simply for being gay or for being part of an opposing faction.[13]

When it comes to class struggle, Hamas have proven totally reactionary. Their hostility to the organising efforts of workers and the poor was exposed early in 2019 when protests across Gaza threatened to spark a general strike under the slogan of "we want to live".[14] The movement was a response to persistently high unemployment in the Strip – not primarily Hamas's fault, of course, given Israel's siege – but also the government's decision to raise taxes on cigarettes and a series of essential food items. The protest demands included establishing a labour office to protect workers' rights, reduction of prices on staples, and the suspension of all taxes on essential goods. The protests were organised by a broad coalition of grassroots activists backed by every faction aside from Hamas and Islamic Jihad. When Mahmoud Abbas and the PA tried to use them as a means of undermining Hamas's rule in Gaza, the activists put out a statement clarifying their stance, which sheeted home the blame for the crisis first to Israel and Egypt, then to the PA for not paying the wages of their employees in Gaza, and only then to Hamas.[15]

None of this sophisticated messaging and political positioning stopped Hamas from physically crushing and politically slandering the movement. They responded by subjecting protesters to harsh beatings to drive them off the street. According to an excellent article by Salem Al-Rayes for the pro-resistance publication *Raseef22*, Hamas then arrested more than 1,000 people – including dozens of journalists and

---

13. Zilber 2023.
14. Abuheweila and Kershner 2019.
15. Humaid 2019.

Palestinian human rights observers – whose cases were then referred to military courts.[16] The pretext was that stones were thrown; the Israelis would have been proud. All this repression was justified by depicting the movement as an agent of Israel and the right-wing Palestinian Authority. Thus the Hamas minister for refugee affairs, Atef Udwan, was quoted in an Emirati newspaper as asking protesters to leave: "Hamas will not fall and we will not hand over power to anyone, so for those who don't like this, the Rafah crossing is open for them to emigrate."[17]

The protesters also pointed to the huge inequality among Palestinians in and around Gaza. Some held signs saying "we want to live the same life of luxury, money and cars as Hamas' leaders' sons", while one viral video featured a woman attacking the same injustice:

> Are we forbidden from saying we are in pain? Let people say what they want, why do you oppress them? All of Gaza is unemployed. Our children have lost 12 years of their lives. Why? Each child of a Hamas official, as soon as he is 20 years old, will own an apartment, a car, a jeep, a building and be married, while our sons have nothing in this life.[18]

This sentiment has grown as Hamas has become increasingly corrupted by an extended period of one-party rule. The most infamous symbol of this is the extraordinary wealth of Hamas leaders and family members outside of Gaza, who live the decadent lives of luxury you would expect from members of the Gulf royal family. So while many supporters of Hamas are happy to cite Fanon's defence of anti-colonial violence approvingly, his denunciation of the corruption and self-interest among the post-colonial elite is at least as pertinent. His final book, *The Wretched of the Earth*, is famous for its defence of revolutionary violence, yet it is also filled with rage at the new class of local leaders that replaced the old colonial elite. The chapters on the perils of national consciousness and spontaneity are chock-full of insights as

---

16. Al-Rayes 2019.
17. Adam 2019.
18. Liebermann 2019.

to the limits of bourgeois nationalism and the self-appointed leaders of the struggle:

> Certain natives continue to profiteer and exploit the war, making their gains at the expense of the people, who as usual are prepared to sacrifice everything, and water their native soil with their blood. The militant who faces the colonialist war machine with the bare minimum of arms realises that while he is breaking down colonial oppression he is building up automatically yet another system of exploitation. This discovery is unpleasant, bitter, and sickening: and yet everything seemed to be so simple before: the bad people were on one side, and the good on the other. The clear, unreal, idyllic light of the beginning is followed by a semi-darkness that bewilders the senses. The people find out that the iniquitous fact of exploitation can wear a black face, or an Arab one; and they raise the cry of "Treason!" But the cry is mistaken; and the mistake must be corrected. The treason is not national, it is social.[19]

In the case of Palestine, the situation is even worse than Fanon imagined, because the elites have been corrupted while colonialism remains in place. Yet his insistence on grounding the failures of bourgeois nationalists in their material privileges is absolutely spot on, and is forgotten by third world nationalists.

As with ruling classes across the world, Hamas has attempted to use culture wars around issues of oppression to consolidate their popularity and clamp down on opposition. In Gaza this has taken the form of soft-Islamisation drives, and it is women who have been the most public and sustained victims of these efforts.[20] Hamas has attempted to force women to wear the hijab in public institutions and to ban them from smoking in public, along with other generalised policing of their behaviour. Resistance on the ground has resulted in many of these policies being abandoned or delayed. In one incident, two prominent women publicly unveiled themselves, in opposition to the increasing

19. Fanon 1963, pp.144–5.
20. Kear 2018, pp.157–63.

religiosity of Gazan society. In their public statement the activists were careful to blame Israel's siege and occupation, as well as Hamas, for the growth of conservative politics in the strip.[21] LBGT people have also been harassed and killed by the regime, on the reactionary basis that LBGT individuals can be more easily turned into informers. For all these reasons and more, as early as 2010 Palestinian researcher Khaled Hroub was arguing that:

> The Islamization that has been forced upon the Gaza Strip – the suppression of social, cultural, and press freedoms that do not suit Hamas's view[s] – is an egregious deed that must be opposed. It is the reenactment, under a religious guise, of the experience of [other] totalitarian regimes and dictatorships.[22]

In practice then, Hamas have long abandoned the full liberation of Palestinian territory, and their rule over Gaza is characterised by pro-market and pro-rich policies, anti-democratic suppression of free speech and assembly, and conservative clericalism.

These experiences have led Gazans to be increasingly critical and distrusting of Hamas over the years. An extensive survey of Palestinian public opinion organised by the Palestinian Centre for Policy and Survey Research, conducted just before October 7 last year, found that just 32 percent of likely voters in Gaza would have voted for Hamas in hypothetical elections, with 32 percent preferring Fatah. This is down from 44.5 percent Hamas won in the 2006 legislative elections.[23]

Hamas and the armed struggle
Despite Hamas offering endless concessions and compromises, Israel has refused to grant any of their core demands. The paralysing siege has been maintained, as have Israel's strict controls over food, migration, the economy, and everything else.

---

21. Kear 2018, p.162.
22. Hroub 2010. His comments were republished on a right-wing site, for reasons that are fairly obvious, but he is no Israeli stooge. See Middle East Media Research Institute 2010.
23. Shikaki 2024.

In this context, faced with endless Israeli oppression and a growing domestic hostility to Hamas's reactionary policies, armed resistance takes on a new meaning. To some extent it remains a tactic deployed to improve Hamas's negotiating hand, and at times has resulted in the release of Palestinian prisoners, a partial loosening of the siege, or some other minor concession. But just as importantly, the use of armed force is a form of political communication to a *Palestinian* audience, and is a proven way of winning mass support. For instance the October 7 attack has massively boosted its support among Palestinians and the wider Arab world, particularly in the West Bank. The same polling agency that identified cratering support for Hamas prior to October 7 found its popularity nearly doubled in Gaza and more than doubled across Gaza and the West Bank.[24] This surge in public opinion would seem to be matched across much of the Arab world, where figures from Hamas's armed wing, such as Mohammed Deif and Yahya Sinwar, are lauded as heroes in the struggle against Israeli colonialism.

From a Marxist point of view, it has to be said directly that occupied peoples have the right to resist their oppression, including using armed force. Even bourgeois legal theory recognises this right, which is enshrined in the Geneva conventions of 1949. Resistance to unjust foreign and colonial occupation forms a core part of the folklore of countries as politically diverse as France, Iraq, India, and Vietnam. And there is no question that Palestine is being occupied, not just in lands stolen since 1967, as is usually understood, but across the land spanning from the Jordan River to the Mediterranean Sea. So armed resistance by Palestinians is a legitimate tactic.

Yet the Palestinian people have consistently been defined as terrorists for resisting the occupation of their country. From the very beginning of the Israeli occupation of their land, a racist narrative was established that distinguished between Arab savages and civilised European Jews. Israel and its Western allies opposed Palestinian resistance long before the existence of Hamas. This reflects an Israeli desire to crush any and all sources of opposition to the entrenchment and expansion of Israel's colonial expansion.

---

24. Shikaki 2024.

Confronted with endless Israeli violence and provocations, multiple generations of Palestinian activists have insisted that resistance in general, and armed resistance in particular, is both their right and an absolute necessity. Yet given the overwhelming advantages possessed by the Israeli military, attempts at specifically *armed* resistance have generally failed to weaken the Israeli occupation or deliver lasting results. For decades Fatah oscillated between phases of armed struggle and tortured peace talks, neither of which effectively hindered Israel's colonial expansion. Oslo was their final surrender, but it could have been foretold from the very beginning, given the utopianism of their alternative strategy.

The First Intifada was a brief respite from this pattern precisely because of its mass character. Tens of thousands of Palestinians found their voice by taking part in the years-long uprising, which involved street protests, strikes, union organising, student actions, rent-strikes, boycotts and more. The mass nature of this resistance made it harder for the Israelis to unleash overwhelming violence, and gained the movement access to international support. Unfortunately, rather than build on the possibilities created by this movement, Arafat and Fatah sought to leverage it into hopeless peace talks that later became known as the Oslo Accords.

Hamas started on this journey from military resistance to diplomatic dead ends decades later, but has traversed similar ground. Their early attacks targeted the Israeli military and illegal settlements. This position was abandoned following the massacre of Palestinian worshippers at the Ibrahimi mosque by a fascist Israeli settler during Ramadan in 1994. This outrageous attack pushed Hamas to adopt a similar tactic of targeting civilians. But every attack by Hamas and other resistance groups was followed by Israeli reprisals, each more brutal than the last, a chain of escalating violence which led to thousands of dead Palestinians.

This campaign of terror attacks – the correct technical word for blowing up cafés or buses in civilian areas – continued for years, and was a total disaster for the Palestinians. It did not weaken the Israeli occupation one iota. In fact, the attacks gave Israel the excuse to expand and deepen its control over the West Bank and Jerusalem, including the construction of the apartheid wall. At the same time, it gave the Israelis and their international propaganda machine – otherwise known as the mainstream media – an excuse to smear the Palestinian movement. Less importantly, but still of some relevance, the attacks helped accelerate the Israeli public's trajectory towards the far right, and empowered the most militaristic and aggressive factions. So the campaign of terror attacks – which also included members of other factions, including Fatah – was a total disaster.

This failure to achieve anything positive is fairly typical of terrorist tactics, which is why Marxists have generally opposed them, from the Irish Troubles right back to the days of Bakunin and the Russian Narodniks. Even when they are successful, the type of secretive and minoritarian organising involved in these methods undermines the possibilities of democratic, let alone socialist, outcomes for the struggle.

After much internal and external debate, Hamas gave up the suicide bombing tactic in 2005. Aside from the most recent events on October 7, the crux of Hamas's military struggle in the last 20 years has involved the fairly indiscriminate firing of rockets towards Israel. News of a round of rocket fire is inevitably reported with breathless horror by international journalists based in Israel. But the reality is that Hamas's relatively primitive rockets pose almost no threat to Israeli society. According to the Israeli Ministry of Foreign Affairs, just 21 people in Israel were killed by this method between 2000 and 2013, some of whom were temporary migrant workers.[25] By comparison, 183 Palestinians were murdered by Israel during peaceful protests at the Gaza border in 2018 alone.[26] So as a military tactic, rockets have proven woefully inadequate.

Supplementing the rocket attacks have been occasional incursions into Israeli territory, where Hamas and other armed groups seek to capture Israeli soldiers to trade for Palestinian political prisoners and the slight loosening of the siege on Gaza. This tactic has been of some utility, at times forcing Israel to release thousands of Palestinian prisoners. But it is by nature a fairly defensive measure, with no prospects of ending the occupation.

25. Israel Ministry of Foreign Affairs 2013.
26. Human Rights Council 2019.

In the aftermath of October 7, a debate has emerged on the left about how to respond to the attack, and by proxy, armed resistance more broadly. Many have adopted an approach of unconditional and uncritical support for Hamas and its military actions, celebrating October 7 as a moment of liberatory potential. But Marxists need to judge tactics concretely and politically. While armed self-defence and insurrection can be an important part of mass mobilisations, and certainly revolutions, the military aspect must always be subordinated to a broader political strategy.

There are two factors in assessing any tactic and strategy. The first is to judge whether it can assist in the struggle for Palestinian self-determination. Of course, no single act or campaign will achieve full liberation, so the assessment is whether it helps take the struggle even one small step forward, either by strengthening our side or weakening the enemy in some way. When judging the utility of any action, we should ask whether it contributes to the building of a movement that can achieve genuine liberation, and whether it is deployed as part of a coherent strategic vision to that end. That is as much true of a strike or protest, say for a wage rise or climate action, as it is of the armed struggle. The second is what type of social system and political dynamics are implicit in or unleashed by the method of struggle.

In Palestine, the armed struggle has always had an attraction due to the violence and brutality of the Israeli state. Through their resistance Palestinians have discovered and rediscovered their national pride and dignity. But the problem with any strategy that relies primarily on armed resistance is that Israel possesses by far the most powerful military in the region. Imperial powers have offered Israel billions in military and economic aid, meaning that its military capacities dwarf those of the Palestinians. And while the early PLO was rightly inspired by the heroic Vietnamese resistance to US occupation, the two situations are fundamentally different. The US empire could eventually be forced to retreat from Vietnam with its tail between its legs, but the Israeli ethno-state state has nowhere to go, it must fight to the death. So while the willingness to participate in or support armed resistance often expresses the courageous refusal of the oppressed to give up their struggle for freedom, in the Palestinian context there are real limits to its utility. That's especially the case now that the Israeli state is an entrenched presence in the Middle East, with abundant weapons, deep pockets and powerful friends.

Even as Hamas have adopted many of the same principles of Fatah, their commitment to armed resistance has remained their primary distinguishing characteristic. There is no argument put forward about how sporadic rocket fire or kidnappings can help achieve a free Palestine. Indeed, aside from October 7, which took Israel totally by surprise, Hamas's attacks are fairly symbolic gestures. There is simply no possibility of a substantial *offensive* military victory against the Israeli army, and Hamas does not present a serious program to overcome the structural imbalance of power. In this sense, the armed resistance the party launches from time to time is more usefully understood as a political stunt, a means by which Hamas leaders exploit the admirable bravery and commitment of their rank and file to gain attention and assist the party in winning small improvements through their negotiations with Israel.

Of course stunts can be effective, if paired with a broader strategy. Yet as well as being incapable of defeating Israel, the armed struggle is also directly counterposed to the type of mass revolutionary resistance that can achieve the type of radical democracy and economic equality needed for true liberation for the Palestinians. Military struggle, especially by guerrilla fighters, is inherently top-down and secretive. Planned attacks cannot be promoted in advance, and its protagonists are restricted to small groups of fighters rather than the mass of the population. The evidence for this counterposition is abundant. The radical potential of the Second Intifada was quickly subsumed by the armed attacks unleashed by the various political factions. A similar process took place in 2021, where an ongoing grassroots campaign of protests and strikes against the eviction of Palestinians from occupied East Jerusalem was essentially squashed after Hamas decided to fire rockets at Israel – and thereby initiate a cycle of violence. This action increased Hamas's popularity as a national resistance force, but curtailed the possibilities of ongoing mass mobilisation. Even in countries where the armed struggle has succeeded, national liberation by this means did not deliver democratic results. So in Vietnam,

Algeria and elsewhere, the elite bands of guerrilla fighters who led the national liberation struggles simply installed themselves as the new oppressive dictators. For socialists, who are not nationalists, but are interested in pushing every struggle towards revolutionary democracy and economic justice, such an outcome in Palestine would be totally unsatisfactory.

Perhaps the most damning proof that the armed struggle as carried out by Hamas poses no threat to Israel can be found in the actions of the Israelis themselves. Paula Caridi's invaluable book on Hamas documents in detail how Israel has repeatedly intervened to prevent the party from silencing its armed wing. On multiple occasions the Palestinian factions have been close to agreeing to ceasefires based on a program of dialogue with Israel on the grounds of the Oslo agreements, only to have the talks sabotaged by Israel. During its suicide bombing phase, Hamas offered to stop targeting civilians on three separate occasions, on the proviso that Israel agreed to do the same. Israel did not agree. Another time, the Palestinians were close to negotiating a truce among themselves, and to abandon suicide attacks altogether. When Israel found out, they dropped a one tonne bomb on the home of a Hamas leader, scuttling the prospect for years to come.[27]

This history makes it clear that Israel has never been interested in peace with the Palestinians, and certainly not with Hamas. But it also reflects their supreme confidence that armed Palestinian resistance poses no threat to Israel's survival. Reinforcing this point, Israeli journalists have recently exposed the extent to which Netanyahu had been happy to fund Hamas – including its military wing – via Qatar. His rationale was that maintaining the division between Hamas in Gaza and the PA in the West Bank precluded any implementation of a two-state solution. This strategy of supporting the Islamists to weaken Fatah goes back decades. But if Hamas or its strategy posed any fundamental threat to Israel, this would not have been a viable option.

To some extent, the events of the last six months have fundamentally transformed the situation. It is too soon to know exactly what Hamas was thinking in launching the attack on October 7, what the result of

---

27. Caridi bases all this on the recollections of former MI6 agent Alastair Crooke, at the time a key advisor to the EU on Middle Eastern policy; Caridi 2023, p.303.

Israel's murderous response will be, or indeed what will happen inside Israel itself. There are many, many moving parts. But already it's clear that the military "achievements" of October 7, dramatic as they were, have not advanced the Palestinian cause by a single step. Never before has any Arab force done so much damage to Israel, and yet the result has been an unimaginable setback for the Palestinian cause, comparable only to the *Nakba* of 1948.

Hamas and its supporters have attempted to argue that the current situation marks a victory for the Palestinian cause. Sometimes it is argued that Hamas can claim credit for the current surge in public support for the Palestinians around the world. But this is a real stretch – by that logic Osama bin Laden could have taken credit for the historic movement against the Iraq War. The mass rallies have not occurred as a result of October 7, but despite it. They reflect a humanistic and solidaristic response to Israel's genocidal massacre, and the integration of the Palestinian struggle within a broader anti-racist framework popular among sections of youth. Others have argued that Hamas simply needs to survive Israel's onslaught to have achieved victory. But the best case scenario for Hamas is a new "truce" that allows them to maintain their hegemony over what's left of a ravaged and diminished Gaza. It is hard to see how anyone could argue that such a scenario would represent an advance for the people of Palestine from the status quo before the war. The fundamental error here is conflating Hamas's interests – for whom surviving the war would clearly be an achievement won at the expense of enormous Palestinian misery – with those of the Palestinians.

In any case, there is much yet to play out before a definitive judgement can be made on recent events. But for now we can say that the attack has given the bloodthirsty Israeli establishment an excuse to inflict an historic defeat of the Palestinian people. The numbers of Palestinian casualties and refugees are unprecedented, as is the physical obliteration of the Gaza Strip and Gaza City, Palestine's second largest urban centre. While it is understandable that people seek to psychologically cushion themselves from the terrible truths about the unfolding genocide, socialists have a responsibility to look reality in the face. How many more such "successes" can the Palestinian people afford?

Revolutionary alternatives

The Palestinians' struggle has oscillated between armed resistance and peace talks for decades, in two major cycles. The first was led by Fatah, starting around the time of the battle of Karameh in 1968, and ending with the betrayal of the Oslo agreement. The second was driven by Hamas, starting in the late 1990s, spurred on by growing frustration with Oslo, and ended with the decades of uneasy coexistence between Hamas and Israel. October 7 shattered that status quo, and it is too early to know what comes next. But regardless, it's clear that the bourgeois nationalist leaderships of both Fatah and Hamas have failed to bring the Palestinians a single step closer to liberation. In the words of Palestinian intellectual and journalist Haidar Eid, Palestinians face the choice "between the religious right and the secular right, while a necessary alternative is absent from the field".[28]

The fundamental reason is that both are trapped within the framework of bourgeois nationalism, which seeks simply to claim a place for Palestine in the international capitalist order. The problem with this perspective is that the Israelis and their imperial backers do not want such a situation, and have not accepted any limits to their colonial expansion. The Arab and Muslim states, which have been looked to for support by generations of Palestinian organisations, similarly have no interest in confronting the complex web of economic and geopolitical relationships that prop up Israel. Indeed, they are part of the system. The Palestinians cannot defeat the armed might of this international alliance of capitalist reaction on their own.

This is why the left has always understood the issue of Palestine as intrinsically linked to that of regional and global imperialism. Partly this is because the creation of Israel was never simply about disempowering the Palestinian people, but was an attempt to implant a loyal, pro-Western entity in a region that has enormous strategic significance due to its large oil reserves. Since its creation Israel has helped maintain first British and then American hegemony in the region, in the process disciplining any Arab states that have threatened to challenge the status quo, even in minor ways. Israel has been an attack dog that has

---

28. Eid 2021.

sought to preserve the unequal economic and geopolitical structures of the Middle East and North Africa, often in conjunction with sections of the ruling class in the Arab world, most notably the Gulf States, to stem the revolutionary movements that have periodically swept the region. In this way the settler society set up by the Zionists has proven to be a highly effective outpost of Western imperialism.

There is also another reason it's important to understand the Palestinian struggle as a regional and even international one. This relates to the structure and nature of the society that has emerged as a result of the historical struggle between Zionist settlers and the indigenous Palestinian inhabitants. In this case, rather than incorporate the indigenous population into the workforce as in South Africa, the European colonists attempted to ethnically cleanse the land entirely. But unlike in Australia, Canada and the US, the Zionists have not been so successful as to wipe out the vast majority of the original inhabitants. Instead, the numbers of settlers and indigenous inhabitants are roughly equal, with millions more Palestinians dispersed as refugees.

The result is a hybrid structure, where a highly sophisticated capitalist society has been built on top of and in opposition to the former inhabitants of the land, but one that is still forced to engage in frontier wars. The result is a perpetually mobilised and racialised Jewish society which, despite its various social and economic stratifications, is easily united against its Palestinian or Arab enemies. The Jewish Israeli working class has never acted from an internationalist perspective, prevented from doing so by the ideological prison owned and organised by the Jewish colonial elites. There are few countries on earth where nationalism has been more effective in deferring and distorting the dynamics of class struggle than Israel, and there is no prospect of this changing in the short to medium term.

At the same time, there is no sense in which the Palestinian working class is capable of fundamentally challenging the racist structures of Israeli society on its own, as occurred in South Africa during the 1980s. For Palestinians, the exclusionary and genocidal policies of Israel mean there is not a sufficient working-class base from which to launch a revolutionary insurrection against the racist superstructure of the Israeli state. There are a few hundred thousand Palestinian workers who live in the West Bank and work in Israel. Then within Israel itself there is a sizeable number of Palestinian workers. But it is the case that Palestinians are not central to production except in a few secondary areas like construction and agriculture. For the most part, Palestinians are forced to live on the margins of Israeli society. They are subject to its whims while lacking any serious capacity to influence its decision-making.

A regional strategy is necessary to find such a force, which is why Arab revolutionaries have long argued that the road to Jerusalem runs through Cairo, Baghdad and Damascus. There, millions of workers exist and have the capacity to bring down the capitalist and imperialist networks of power that dominate the region. Fatah's refusal to play a role in catalysing this sort of struggle saw the Palestinian movement and the broader left crushed in both Jordan and Lebanon through the 1970s and early '80s. An international movement that links the democratic and economic demands of the people of the region with freedom for Palestine is the only hope for justice.

The Arab Spring was a moment of momentous opportunity for the Palestinian cause. While enormous sympathy for Palestine was evinced as part of the Arab Spring of 2011, the Palestinian leaders failed to offer it meaningful political support or make demands for practical solidarity. Fatah, tied to the Saudi elites, essentially backed the old order. Hamas allied itself closely with the neoliberal government of the Muslim Brotherhood in Egypt and its co-thinkers internationally, which used Palestine as a fig leaf to distract from its reactionary economic and social policies. But this too was done out of pragmatism, rather than democratic principle. While Hamas initially supported the protest movement against the criminal Assad regime, when it became clear that Assad would survive thanks to the intervention of Iran and Russia they turned their back on the rebels and sided with the regime.

In contrast to these sordid dealings, a genuinely revolutionary resistance would have understood that the fate of Palestine lay with the fate of these revolutions. But as well as exposing the limits of Fatah and Hamas, the revolutions of 2011 and 2019 proved that simply overturning the old regimes and replacing them with another form of capitalist rule would not be sufficient to achieve the changes desired.

Only a socialist revolutionary movement that sweeps the capitalists, militaries, the clerics and the sectarians from power across the region could then set its sights on Palestine. Such a movement would necessarily be led by the working class, the only genuinely anti-capitalist and anti-imperialist force in the Middle East.

Today this argument is obscured by the fact that this new generation of Palestine supporters are being politicised in a context where working-class and socialist politics are at an historic nadir. This is true not only in the Middle East, but across much of the rest of the world. In this ideological vacuum it is common for people to fall into classless third world nationalism, manifesting now as "anti-colonial" discourse. In this rubric, Palestine supporters can find themselves cheering on the military stunts conducted by the Houthis in Yemen, the neoliberal South African government's decision to take Israel to the International Court of Justice and the October 7 attack by Hamas. Each of these actions are believed to represent opposition to Western imperialism, but there is no broader strategic vision which would allow for a judgement about their efficacy or utility for the liberation movement.

This article has attempted to advance a more serious assessment of Hamas and its strategies. The Palestinian people have suffered far too much over the years, primarily at the hands of the Israelis, but also the Arab regimes, and due to the missteps and failures of their own leaders. The situation today in Gaza is intolerable. The strangulation of the Strip by Israeli and Egyptian forces has continued for over a decade, leaving many unable to access the most basic necessities of life. There have been no national elections since 2006, as Fatah and Hamas have preferred to entrench themselves in their respective bases than risk the political judgement of the people they claim to represent. Nor are there political parties that can challenge the domination of these two organisations, offering an alternative to their failed approaches. Meanwhile Israeli society continues its drift towards fascistic authoritarianism, backed by a bipartisan consensus in the US congress.

In this desperate situation, socialists have a duty to try to win this new generation of activists to a perspective that can actually achieve liberation. And while the conditions in Palestine make the development of popular resistance extraordinarily difficult, the heroism of the

Great March of Return of 2018–19 indicates that Palestinian aspirations for a just future remain unextinguished. More than twelve months of continuous mass protests served to unify Gaza in an unprecedented way, led by independent activists who imposed a vision of collective struggle that harks back to the glory days of the First Intifada. In the context of a regional counter-revolution, this inspirational campaign failed to receive the practical and political solidarity that it both needed and deserved. Yet the movement highlighted one means by which the Palestinians can organise themselves to resist the occupation, and in the process reimpose themselves on the political imagination of progressives across the world.

Ultimately, the Palestinians, like workers and the poor the world over, need to develop a new revolutionary movement that can challenge the stifling, decades-long domination of bourgeois nationalists in Fatah and Hamas.

References

Abuheweila, Iyad and Isabel Kershner 2019, "Hamas Crackdown on Gaza Protests Instills Fear", *New York Times*, 24 March. nytimes.com/2019/03/24/world/middleeast/gaza-protests-hamas.html

Al-Rayes, Salem 2019, "Between a rock and resistance: how Hamas crushes dissent in Gaza", *Raseef22*, 8 April. https://raseef22.net/english/article/1072896-between-a-rock-and-the-resistance-how-hamas-crushes-dissent-in-gaza

Adam, Ali 2019, "Hamas crackdown on protests snuffs out a push for change in Gaza", *The National News*, 24 April. www.thenationalnews.com/world/mena/hamas-crackdown-on-protests-snuffs-out-a-push-for-change-in-gaza-1.839824

Baconi, Tariq 2018, *Hamas Contained: The Rise and Pacification of Palestinian Resistance*, Stanford University Press.

Caridi, Paula 2023, *Hamas: From Resistance to Regime*, Seven Stories Press.

Eid, Haidar 2021, "Palestinian elections: reconstructing the status quo", *Mondoweiss*, 11 February. mondoweiss.net/2021/02/palestinian-elections-reconstructing-the-status-quo/

Fanon, Franz 1963, *The Wretched of the Earth*, Grove Press.

Filiu, Jean-Pierre 2012, "The Origins of Hamas: Militant Legacy or Israeli Tool?", *Journal of Palestine Studies*, 41(3), pp.54–70.

Hamas 1988, *The Covenant of the Islamic Resistance Movement*. avalon.law. yale.edu/20th_century/hamas.asp

Hamas 2017, *Charter*, *Middle East Eye*, 2 March. middleeasteye.net/news/ hamas-2017-document-full

Hroub, Khaled 2010, *Hamas: A Beginner's Guide* (second edition), Pluto Press.

Humaid, Mariam 2019, "Gaza rights groups denounce Hamas crackdown on protests", *Al Jazeera*, 19 March. aljazeera.com/news/2019/3/19/ gaza-rights-groups-denounce-hamas-crackdown-on-protests

Human Rights Council 2019, *Report of the independent international commission of inquiry on the protests in the Occupied Palestinian Territory*, 25 February. https://www.ohchr.org/sites/default/files/Documents/HRBodies/ HRCouncil/CoIOPT/A_HRC_40_74.pdf

Inbar, Efraim 2018, "'Mowing the grass' in Gaza", *The Jerusalem Institute for Strategy and Security*, 25 June. jiss.org.il/en/inbar-mowing-the-grass-in-gaza/

Israel Ministry of Foreign Affairs 2013, "Victims of Palestinian Violence and Terrorism since September 2000". web.archive.org/web/20130703052746/ http://www.mfa.gov.il:80/mfa/foreignpolicy/terrorism/palestinian/pages/ victims%20of%20palestinian%20violence%20and%20terrorism%20sinc.aspx

Kear, Martin 2018, *Hamas and Palestine: The contested road to statehood*, Routledge.

Liebermann, Oren 2019, "Hamas accused of violent crackdown on Gaza protests", *CNN*, 19 March. edition.cnn.com/2019/03/19/middleeast/ gaza-protests-intl/index.html

Middle East Media Research Institute 2010, "The Islamists' Claims to Promote an Islamic Culture Are Hollow", Special Dispatch No. 3314, 22 October. https:// www.memri.org/reports/palestinian-researcher-islamists-claims-promote- islamic-culture-are-hollow#_edn1

Shikaki, Khalil 2024, "Palestine Report – Report 1 Domestic Balance of Power and Palestinian-Israeli Relations Before and After October 7th", *Arab Barometer*. arabbarometer.org/wp-content/uploads/Arab-Barometer-PSR- Palestine-Report-Part-I-EN-.pdf

Usher, Graham 2005, "The New Hamas. Between Resistance and Participation", *Middle East Report Online*, 21 August. merip.org/2005/08/ the-new-hamas/

Usher, Graham 2006, The Democratic Resistance: Hamas, Fatah, and the Palestinian Elections, *Journal of Palestinian Studies,* 35(3), pp.20–36.

Zilber, Neri 2023, "'Dead man walking': How Yahya Sinwar deceived Israel for decades", *Financial Times*, 6 November. ft.com/content/de78c7a0-f8f0-403e-b0db-eb86d6e76919

JORDAN HUMPHREYS

Palestine and the classless politics of settler colonial theory

Jordan Humphreys is a socialist activist who has written extensively on Indigenous oppression and working-class history. His book *Indigenous Liberation and Socialism* is available from Red Flag Books.

I SRAEL'S BRUTAL WAR on the people of Gaza, and the support this war has received from governments around the world, has once again shown that the modern Middle East is wracked by the violence of imperialism. A new generation of young people in the Western world have been shaken up by Israel's actions, and in the process have come to reject many of the Zionist myths that for too long have hidden Israel's crimes.

For many the oppression of the Palestinians seems similar to other examples of injustice that they care about, such as the treatment of African Americans, anti-migrant racism and the oppression of Indigenous peoples in Australia or the US. Israel is seen as another embodiment of white supremacy, colonialism and racism alongside Donald Trump, the police, Western corporations and the far right. This has given many the confidence to stridently reject the claims that criticising Israel is anti-Semitic and that the conflict is simply too complex to take a side.

Many of the young left-wing people grappling with these issues have adopted a framework for understanding them that is heavily influenced by the politics of settler colonial theory. This theory argues that many of the examples of racism and oppression seen in the world today are the products of colonialism, and often a particular form called settler colonialism. This colonialism is often seen as a product of "whiteness" and the inherent drive within Western culture to dominate other territories and peoples. Because of this, an anti-colonial struggle is needed that unites the Indigenous population and their potential allies against the settler population in a battle for decolonisation.

This is seen as being a useful framework for understanding not only the plight of the Palestinians but also other cases of oppression and racism. So the oppression of Indigenous people within Australia is said to be due to an ongoing process of colonisation that benefits all of settler society. The same is true in the US, with the addition that racialised minorities such as African Americans or Hispanic and Latino Americans are seen as members of internal colonies being exploited by the rest of the settler population of the United States.

For many, the politics of anti-colonialism has been a starting point for rejecting the racist lies of capitalist society and supporting the struggles of the oppressed. In this sense, it is a positive move away from the limitations of liberal multiculturalism and moderate centrism with its emphasis on gradually reforming capitalism into a supposedly "post-racial", "colour-blind" society.

However, there are also significant problems with settler colonial theory and the contemporary politics of anti-colonialism. Most importantly, it either discounts or heavily distorts the relationship between imperialism and racism, and abandons any serious understanding of class and capitalism more broadly. This has important implications for developing the kind of organisations and struggles we need to successfully confront racism and oppression in the Middle East and throughout the world.

In previous issues of the *Marxist Left Review*, I've explored the problems that arise when applying settler colonial theory to understanding Indigenous oppression in Australia. In brief, I argued that settler colonial theory is inaccurate because it presents Indigenous oppression in contemporary Australia as being caused by an ongoing colonial process rather than capitalism. This leads settler colonial theorists to place the blame for anti-Indigenous racism on the entirety of "settler society", including non-Indigenous workers. Settler colonial theorists argue that the mass of workers in Australia are essentially akin to the settler population in Israel. This ignores the history of non-Indigenous workers supporting the struggles of Indigenous people in Australia and absolves the Australian ruling class and capitalism of their role in oppressing Indigenous people.[1]

When it comes to Israel and Palestine, however, settler colonial theory can seem much more useful. After all, Israel most definitely is a settler colonial state and it is involved in an ongoing process of colonisation in which it seeks to dispossess the Palestinian population of their remaining control over sections of Gaza and the West Bank. Also, while reasonable people can debate exactly why this is the case, it is clear that orienting towards the Israeli working class as the key ally for the Palestinians is a dead-end strategy. There is also a long tradition of radicals and socialists arguing that Israel is a settler colonial state to rebut those who want to defend Israel's existence and its genocidal actions.

However, there are important limitations to the settler colonial theory analysis even in the case of Israel and Palestine. Here we must distinguish between the *analysis that Israel is a settler colonial state*, a position shared by revolutionary Marxists, Arab nationalists, anarchists, Stalinists, anti-Zionist liberals and others, and the broader *political framework of settler colonial theory*.

While it is absolutely correct to distinguish between the oppressors and the oppressed, this is only the beginning of any serious analysis of the oppression of the Palestinians. Unfortunately, the narrow framing of the question by settler colonial theorists as only being about settlers versus Indigenous people leaves essential questions unanswered. This article will hope to demonstrate that Marxism offers a much more sophisticated and deeper framework to understand Israel's oppression of the Palestinians and its relationship to broader dynamics of capitalism in the Middle East and globally.

---

1.   See Humphreys 2021 and chapter 3 in Humphreys 2023.

Colonialism, imperialism and capitalism in the Middle East

Control over the Middle East has long been an important project of various imperialist nations due to the region's central role in both global trade routes and the production of raw materials, particularly oil. The geopolitical structure of the modern Middle East is largely the product of various partition plans and occupations by the British and French empires during the early twentieth century, who sought to mould the region to suit their interests. Following the decline of the European powers the United States took a leading role in defending and entrenching the interests of Western capitalism in the region, from forging alliances with the Gulf states and Egypt to providing Israel with military funding and diplomatic support, and invading countries that were seen as bucking Western control, such as Afghanistan and Iraq in the 2000s. This is the historical context for both the creation of the Israeli state, the role it has played in the region and the continued support it has obtained from capitalist governments around the world. So understanding, and opposing, colonialism and imperialism are of course important for grasping the history and present nature of the oppression of the Palestinians and the situation in the Middle East more generally.

However, this is not the whole picture. While the Middle East has long been dominated by the interests of imperialist powers residing outside of the region, it would be wrong to present the situation as one of a homogeneous, undifferentiated "Middle East" dominated by foreign imperialism. As the Marxist writer Adam Hanieh has argued, "capitalist class formation in the Middle East has become increasingly tied to the ebbs and flows of accumulation at the global scale", and this has led to the creation of a "domestic capitalist class internal to the Middle East that is to a great extent aligned with the interests of global (imperialist) capital".[2]

Even before Western imperialism established a foothold in the region, the Middle East was dominated by class societies with long-established structures of inequality and exploitation. Since then capitalism has developed throughout the region, creating powerful

---

2.   Hanieh 2013, pp.13-14.

and wealthy ruling classes and states, and a mass of exploited workers. The modern Middle East is not simply dominated by imperialism, a system in which Middle Eastern ruling classes at any rate are complicit, it is also divided sharply by class. Challenging the class structure of the region and the capitalist system that underlies it must then be an essential part of any movement seeking to seriously combat imperialism in the Middle East.

It is precisely on this point that settler colonial theorists fall short. Because they treat colonialism as a discrete factor that should be analysed primarily on its own terms, these theorists cannot accurately explain the roots of imperialism and they have little appreciation of the role that class and capitalism play in the region. They tend to apologise, either explicitly or implicitly, for the crimes of ruling classes among the oppressed group. In both these senses, settler colonial theory is a contemporary variation of the third world nationalism of earlier generations.

Patrick Wolfe, the founder of settler colonial theory as an academic field of study, presents settler colonialism as a self-perpetuating political system in which settler societies are driven by a "logic of elimination" due to their desire for unrestricted control over land. Offhand references to capitalism aside, Wolfe spends little time looking at the material interests underlying this desire for land but rather focuses on its various ideological and cultural manifestations.[3] As critics have increasingly noted, Wolfe also created a highly rigid and abstract model of colonialism, in which settler colonies, as distinct from franchise colonies, had no interest in the Indigenous population bar wiping them off the face of the earth, a crude picture that doesn't fit with the concrete reality of settler colonial regimes across history.[4] Lorenzo Veracini, another influential academic in the field, is even more explicit in seeing colonialism as an autonomous force to be analysed in isolation from the rest of society, theorising settler colonialism as a distinct "mode of domination".[5]

---

3. See Wolfe 2006 for a classic statement of his theory of the logic of elimination.
4. See Davies 2023 and Ajl 2023; also Englert 2020 who is otherwise quite supportive of other aspects of settler colonial theory.
5. See Veracini 2016.

In response to criticism that they ignore the material aspects of colonialism, settler colonial theorists have tried to relate their analysis to capitalism. They can only do so by significantly distorting what the capitalist system is and how it works, in order to make it fit into their inaccurate understanding of colonialism.

So Veracini, drawing upon the economist David Harvey, argues that capitalism is defined by a constant and never-ending process of "accumulation by dispossession" or "perpetual primitive accumulation".[6] By this Veracini means that what drives capitalism is the system's need to steal land, resources and wealth by dispossession, force and theft. This then is supposedly the connection between settler colonialism and capitalism. Settler colonies like Israel are simply the vanguard of this process of dispossession, its most undiluted form. For Veracini settler colonialism even comes to "fundamentally define" the logic of modern capitalism. So the current workings of the financial institutions or the property market or the expansion of the fossil fuel industry are also said to be expressions of this "perpetual primitive accumulation" and bizarrely reveal that the whole world is a settler colony.

But this is very different from the traditional Marxist understanding of capitalism. Marx argued that what was at the core of the system was the exploitation of workers by bosses; it was this and only this that created the huge amounts of surplus wealth that the ruling class used to enrich themselves and create the whole modern industrial capitalist economy on a scale previously impossible. It is the exploitation of the working class, and the competition between bosses for control over the wealth this produces, that defines capitalism as a system. It is on this bedrock that the capitalist state system was constructed, to ensure the continued exploitation of labour power, to regulate the stability of capitalist society, and as the vehicle through which geopolitical competition between imperialist powers could play out. Dispossession, military conquest and outright theft of course occur, and have occurred under capitalism, but they happen within this broader context of the dynamics of capitalist society; they are not the driving feature of it.

---

6.   Piterberg and Veracini 2015, p.469 and Veracini 2021.

The settler colonial theory view of capitalism as driven by "accumulation by dispossession" or "perpetual primitive accumulation" echoes traditional liberal and reformist critiques of the system that see the problems of capitalism as due to its predatory nature rather than the production of surplus value through the economic exploitation of workers. As Jack Davies, a critic of settler colonial theory explains, for the settler colonial theorist:

> [t]he problem with capitalism is, as it has always been, that it is predatory; and predation, on capitalism's own ideology of justice and fairness, is immoral. This moralism evaporates the analytic distinctions that would specify the settler colony and acquits its theorist of historical study. Even the firm and gritty matter of land, settler colonialism's "irreducible element", is airily abstracted into phenomenological standpoint theories and metaphysical assertions about the "logic of elimination".[7]

It is unsurprising then that settler colonial theorists don't appreciate the importance of understanding how class and capitalism underpin and shape imperialism, colonialism and racism. In particular, they fail to grasp how capitalism, due to its drive to gain profits out of the exploitation of workers, also creates a working class with the potential power to challenge its rule. This is something that would not occur if capitalism was simply stripping the Middle East of its resources and leaving nothing behind but a network of military bases. Of course, economic development in the Middle East has not been some linear progression that follows earlier European models. It *has* been marked by the interventions of powerful imperialist states who have sought to shape the economic structures of the region for their benefit, but also the emergence of domestic class forces, both rulers and ruled. As you would expect, given these complex and evolving factors, the nature of this intervention has changed over time.

Before the Second World War economic development in the region was focused on supplying cotton, silk, wheat and olive oil to Europe,

---

7.   Davies 2023.

while the Middle East was seen as a market for some European goods such as textiles. During this period capitalist industry developed very slowly and the historian Anne Alexander argues that "the political and social institutions fostered by colonial-era capitalism were specifically designed to preclude" the development of domestic industry.[8]

Even during this period though there were exceptions that would have ramifications for the later history of the region. Alexander points out that Iran and Turkey, which did not experience direct colonial rule, were able to begin the process of capitalist transformation much earlier, in the process becoming powerful states in the region. Meanwhile much of the Gulf also didn't experience direct colonial control, because at first the economic value of the area was dismissed by the European powers. Once oil production entered the picture, the rulers of the Gulf were thrust into imperial relationships and capitalist development in a very different context from those countries that had suffered under decades of colonial occupation.

The 1940s and '50s saw explosive uprisings across the Middle East against colonial rule and economic inequality. Space opened up for greater economic development in the newly founded post-colonial states, albeit still shaped by the history of underdevelopment and hostility from rival imperialist powers. The second half of the twentieth century saw capitalist industry grow throughout the region and with it both industrial capitalist classes tied to various competing nation-states and working classes exploited by their rulers.

The contradictory dynamics of capitalist development in the Middle East is something ignored by settler colonial theorists. By seeing capitalism as essentially something external to the region parasitising it, rather than deeply embedded and constitutive of the social and political order of the region, is it little wonder then that the existence of Arab ruling classes and working classes is ignored by them?

---

8.   Alexander 2022, p.110.

The origins of Israel

Taking a closer look at how settler colonial theory analyses the nature of Israel and the oppression of the Palestinians – precisely the situation where it should be of most use – helps to clarify the pitfalls of their approach more concretely.

The origins of the Israeli state are commonly portrayed by settler colonial theorists as lying in the Jewish settlers making a pact with the West to serve its interests in the region and in the process transforming themselves into a "white" population. As academic Johannes Becke writes, "While American Jews became white by suburbanisation, Israeli Jews did so by colonization".[9]

This is a very reductive understanding of the origins of Israel on a number of levels.

First of all, it obscures the fact that imperialist nations came to support the Zionist state because it was perceived to be in the interests of their ruling classes and states to do so. It wasn't in the interests of the undifferentiated mass of people living in the Western countries, the vast majority of whom had no say in the matter anyway. Class divisions run through the so-called "West".

Secondly, settler colonial theorists see the similarities between the colonial ideologies of the Zionists and the West as key to explaining why Western governments supported the creation of Israel. However, the relationship between Western governments and the Zionist movement was complicated, tension-filled and evolved over time, undermining the idea that common cultural affinities between the two drove the relationship.

The British government, the key Western player in the region in the lead-up to 1948, was primarily concerned with entrenching its control over Mandate Palestine, not, at least initially, in supporting the narrow goals of the Zionist movement. There was considerable debate within the London colonial elite about the positives and negatives of the Zionist project. These debates were underpinned by discussions about what course would best serve the material interests of British imperialism first and foremost. While the British were happy to suppress

---

9.   Becke 2018.

the rights of the Palestinians, they were hesitant for a long time about unconditionally backing the creation of a Jewish state. They preferred to lord over the region themselves and play the Jewish and Arab populations off against each other, even while granting more concessions and privileges to the Jewish settlers. As the Zionist movement emerged as a powerful force, the British government came to endorse this project as seemingly the best way to stabilise Western influence over the Zionists and the region in the upheavals of the postwar world.

The United States, which would emerge in the postwar world as the major Western imperialist power, was also ambivalent about Israel for some time. It endorsed the establishment of Israel in 1948 but then opposed the failed 1956 invasion of Egypt by Israel, Britain and France. There was a strong "Arabist" wing of the American state department that worried that if the US backed Israel it would send Arab states into the arms of the Soviet Union. It was only after Israel had proven its military credentials in the 1967 war that American state officials swung around to build the tight alliance with Israel they have today.

Here it is also important to note that it was not only the traditional imperialist countries of the West that endorsed the establishment of Israel. The Soviet Union was the first country in the world to recognise Israel, and both the USSR and its satellite states in Eastern Europe supported the UN partition plan in 1947. Until the 1950s the Soviet Union either supported Israel or took a neutral position on conflicts between it and the Arab states. This further complicates the idea that Israel was simply created by the West. It was also a factor in British support for Israel – they were worried that otherwise it could fall into the Soviet camp.

Settler colonial theorists also tend to downplay the existence of class dynamics and capitalist relations within the Zionist movement and Israeli society. Patrick Wolfe, drawing upon another settler colonial theorist, Gershon Shafir, argues that the accumulation of capital was absent from Zionist settler society. Instead, the Zionist economy was based on "non-profit-seeking capital" organised in the collective organisations valorised by the "socialist" wing of the Zionist movement. In

Wolfe's eyes, the settler community was essentially a classless one, outside of capitalism.[10]

The ideological character of the Zionist movement, its focus on creating a separate Jewish state as supposedly the only way to escape European anti-Semitism, is of course essential to understanding why the movement decided to colonise Palestine. The Zionist colonisation of Palestine then wasn't driven crudely by profit rates; but that doesn't mean issues of class and capitalism were irrelevant to the situation.

To start with, contra Wolfe, by 1948, 60 percent of the Israeli economy was owned by private capitalists. As well, the capital invested into "collective" Zionist organisations such as the Histadrut was created via exploitation both among the Jewish diaspora and in the decades before and after the creation of Israel. As such, there were clear class divisions among the Jewish settlers, leading to strikes against Jewish bosses. More significantly Wolfe sidesteps the issue of why other capitalist nations would support the creation of the Zionist state and the disruption of an entire region. From a Marxist point of view, it can only be because of the material interests of those capitalist states in promoting the creation of a pro-imperialist enclave in the region.[11]

The argument that Jewish settlers transformed themselves into a "white" population and that Israel is an example of white supremacy is also dubious. There are indeed white nationalists like Richard Spencer who champion Israel. There are also certain similarities between how Zionism racialises the Arab world and racism in Western countries. And there is clearly discrimination against Jews from non-white backgrounds in Israel, such as those who arrived from the Middle East, North Africa or Ethiopia. However, as the Jewish anti-Zionist historian Tony Greenstein argues:

> [T]he major division within Israeli society is not between black and white, but between Jewish and non-Jewish, and in particular between Israeli Jewish and Palestinian... The Law of Return allows Jews of any colour to emigrate to Israel anytime they want. That is not a right which non-Jews – black or white – possess. Only

---

10. Quotes from Ajl 2023, p.270.
11. Ajl 2023, p.270.

> Jews can be nationals in Israel and some 93 percent of Israeli land
> is Jewish national land from which non-Jews are legally barred…
> Of course, the best land in Israel is reserved for the Ashkenazim.
> So yes, Zionism is certainly tainted by white supremacy, but this
> is a secondary, not primary, feature.[12]

The idea that Jewish settlers – including the many Black and Brown ones – became "white" springs from the illogical underpinnings of identity politics which is deeply embedded within settler colonial theory. It flows from the idea that imperialism, racism and colonialism are products of "whiteness" and Western culture, rather than something pursued by capitalist states and nationalist movements regardless of their race or ethnicity.

Are Hindu nationalists in Modi's India "white" because they organise violent attacks on Muslims and other minorities? Granted, these divisions have historic roots in the imperialist strategies of the old British Raj, but they continue today because of the political dynamics of contemporary Hindu nationalism. The reality is that violent oppression is something that all sorts of capitalist states, political parties and movements can participate in. As capitalist development has spread across the world, including into the Global South, more and more non-Western countries have become violent and oppressive capitalist states. To explain this reality by claiming that ruling figures in these societies have become "white" would mean describing large parts of Asia, the Middle East, Latin America and Africa as such.

Most of the current settler colonial projects in the world today are being carried out by "non-white" countries. China's ongoing push to replace Uyghurs with Han Chinese settlers in Xinjiang, India's colonisation of Kashmir and the genocide of the Rohingya by the military of Myanmar are just some of the most prominent examples. Most theorists of settler colonialism show little interest in this, presumably because it goes against the thesis that settler colonialism is a product of Western culture, and it cuts against the softness on non-Western governments notable in settler colonial theory circles.

---

12.   Greenstein 2019.

Finally, the settler colonial theory framework downplays how the class divisions within the Palestinian population and the broader Arab world facilitated the rise of the Zionist state. Absentee Palestinian landlords sold large tracts of land to the Zionist organisations, helping them gain a substantial foothold in the region. When Palestinian peasants and workers erupted into protest against Zionist attacks, some sections of the Arab elite helped the British crush these movements. King Abdullah I of Jordan, for instance, forged an alliance with the Zionists in the 1930s and received money from the Jewish Agency, a branch of the World Zionist Organization. When the revolt of 1936 began he helped Zionist and British forces isolate and eventually defeat the rebellion. At one point he even tried to encourage Zionist settlement in Jordan, a move blocked by the British government.

Palestinian elites, such as the al-Husayni family, held back the struggles of the Palestinians, instead placing their hopes in negotiations with the British government. This led to a series of tragic defeats for the Palestinians that paved the way for the victory of the Zionist forces in 1948. After the *Nakba*, Arab ruling classes treated the mass of poor Palestinian refugees disgracefully, shunting them away into refugee camps. It was a different story for the elite of Palestinian society, who quickly carved out a position for themselves within the Arab states as successful business owners and professionals.[13]

This history makes it clear that we can't have a simple picture of Indigenous people united against settler populations and imperialism. Like so many groups of people the category of Indigenous is divided by class, shaped by capitalism.

A common community of settler colonies?

Another example of the pitfalls of the settler colonial framework is the idea that the reason Western countries like Australia, the United States, Canada and New Zealand support Israel is because of their common heritage as settler colonial states. As Jewish Voice for Peace Deputy Director Cecilie Surasky puts it: "The 'special relationship' between

---

13.   Marshall 2023 [1989], pp.53–72.

Israel and the United States is rooted in our common national narratives and founding mythology".[14]

But this can't explain why governments that have suffered from colonialism such as Modi's administration in India or the Kenyan government are such strong supporters of Israel. Conversely, it cannot explain why countries like Indonesia that are currently engaged in colonisation are capable of opposing Israel's actions, even if only at the rhetorical level.

Even in the cases of the United States and Australia, the establishment's support for Israel has little to do with some shared history of settler colonialism. They support Israel because it is in the interest of their ruling classes to do so. They want to enforce their dominance over the global capitalist system by strengthening their hold over one of the key pillars of Western imperialism in the Middle East. If for some reason it was no longer in their imperialist interests to support Israel then the ruling classes of the West wouldn't do so, no matter what shared history they might have. This explains why neither the US or Australia are particularly supportive of Chinese colonisation of Tibet and Xinjiang.

The constant historical analogies and abstract categories of settler colonial theorists end up distorting how the world really works.

The idea that Western nations support Israel because of their common colonial history also repeatedly spills over into cultural explanations for imperialist backing of Israel rather than material ones. Surasky from Jewish Voice for Peace argues that:

> If the root of this special relationship is not as much AIPAC [American Israel Public Affairs Committee] and money, as much as it is our national narrative and the feelings it engenders – and an unquestioning belief that Israel has an infinite right to expand onto other people's land, then it is narrative that holds unconditional support in place, and our resistance must also be at the level of narrative.

---

14. Surasky 2015.

"All of us in this movement", Surasky concludes, "have to decolonize our minds".[15]

It is true that Western support for Israel isn't due to the influence of AIPAC. But nor is it simply rooted in "our national narrative and the feelings it engenders", as I've already made clear. Narratives can change, and feelings are fickle, but America's bipartisan support for Israel is grounded in material interests that are yet to be shaken.

The flipside of the argument that Western support for Israel is based on the common heritage of settler colonies also often goes along with the idea that there is also a group of nations that are leading an anti-colonial struggle against Israel, such as South Africa, Ireland, or one or another of the Arab states, particularly those outside the Western camp such as Iran or Syria. Some influenced by a more hardened Stalinist approach champion China or Russia as the saviours of the Palestinians.

This is based upon an extremely shallow and idealised picture of these nations, as well as a misunderstanding of the nature of modern imperialism.

Matt Kennard, a left-wing investigative journalist and founder of Declassified UK, has argued that not only is "solidarity with Palestinians...woven into the fabric" of the Irish nationalist party Sinn Féin but that "[e]very major political party in the Republic of Ireland now supports Palestinian liberation".[16]

The reality is quite different. While support for Palestine is quite high among the population, socialists in Ireland have repeatedly criticised the government of the Republic of Ireland, composed of Fianna Fáil, Fine Gael and the Green Party, of "paddy-washing genocide".[17] As they point out, the Irish government has refused to expel the Israeli ambassador and didn't even bring itself to openly support South Africa's case against Israel in the International Court of Justice (ICJ).

Sinn Féin is rhetorically more pro-Palestine, and there is considerable support for the issue among the party's membership. However, the pro-capitalist core of this party does not have any genuine commitment to fighting against imperialism in the Middle East or elsewhere. When

15. Surasky 2015.
16. Kennard 2023.
17. Uidhir 2024.

Joe Biden visited Ireland in 2023 Sinn Féin leader Mary Lou McDonald ruled out talking to him about Palestine, and instead focused on "Ireland-specific issues". In October 2023, after Israel's attack on Gaza had been going on for three weeks, Sinn Féin hailed the arrival of US Special Envoy to Northern Ireland, Joe Kennedy III. As the Irish socialist Somhairle Mag Uidhir explained:

> They wined and dined with him at Stormont and with city councillors in Belfast City Hall, got in multiple photo ops across the North, and defiantly trumpeted his presence. While thousands remained trapped under genocide's rubble, they didn't utter a peep about the US backing of the Israeli murder machine, much less challenge it. Joe Biden was never named publicly, his main man in the North, Joe Kennedy, given a hero's welcome when he should have been shunned as a Zionist villain.[18]

The government of South Africa also attracted a lot of support from pro-Palestine activists when it brought Israel before the IJC on the charge of genocide. However, we should be clear that South Africa is not leading an alliance of anti-colonial states in a struggle against imperialism. It is itself a regional capitalist power that seeks to project its influence across Africa while shooting down striking workers and building strong economic ties with the West. The South African ruling class may see in this crisis an opportunity to create some space for itself on the global stage. But it does so not to challenge global inequalities but to enrich and empower itself. Domestically, Ramaphosa's government remains committed to entrenching privatisation, anti-poor and anti-worker policies, and a reactionary social agenda.

Even on the question of Israel, there is much hypocrisy in the South African government's positioning. In 2021 trade between South Africa and Israel was valued at $285 million, a third of all trade between Sub-Saharan Africa and Israel. In 2022 53 percent of South African coal exports went to Israel, as did a quarter of its diamonds. Despite significant public pressure South African companies have refused to cut

---

18. Uidhir 2024.

economic ties to Israel since the outbreak of the current war in October last year, and the president of South Africa defied a parliamentary vote to expel the Israeli ambassador.[19]

Class divisions among the Palestinians

Settler colonial theory also significantly downplays, and often totally ignores, the class dynamics within the Palestinian population. As noted earlier, this was a feature of Palestinian society from the very beginning. Since the *Nakba* the class divisions among Palestinians have continued to be an important issue. The hundreds of thousands of Palestinians expelled from Palestine were integrated into the class structures within the surrounding Arab states which if anything exaggerated the already-existing class differences among Palestinians.[20]

Wealthier Palestinians were more insulated from the worst effects of the expulsion. Many Palestinian merchants, bankers and entrepreneurs already had well-established links with capitalists and markets in Arab countries, and transferred what movable assets they could. They then quickly merged into the broader Arab ruling classes, their sons and daughters marrying the children of the Jordanian, Lebanese and Saudi elites. By the 1960s there were hundreds of Palestinian millionaires throughout the Gulf states.

Middle-class Palestinians suffered more but most were able to find employment as professionals or at least skilled workers. Many Arab regimes seeking to modernise became reliant upon the more educated Palestinian middle classes to serve as government administrators, educators and the like.

Eighty percent of the Palestinian refugee population, however, were former peasants and unskilled workers who were viewed as unwelcome and potentially rebellious visitors by the Arab governments. Despite incredible difficulties, this population became more and more integrated into the working class of the Arab world, often forming a particularly radical wing of the workers' movement. So Palestinian workers played a key role in unionising the oil, construction and transport industries in Kuwait, Qatar and Saudi Arabia. In Jordan, the

19. Rawoot 2023 and Mkokeli 2024.
20. The following draws from Marshall 2023 [1989], pp.97–115.

Palestinian population became a large section of the working class and helped form left-wing unions and organisations.

It is these class divisions that lay behind many of the political debates within the Palestinian national movement. The disastrous concept that the PLO should look primarily to the Arab states for support didn't come out of nowhere, but reflected the fact that the upper sections of the Palestinian population were deeply connected materially to the Arab regimes.

Patrick Wolfe has defended the absence of any discussion about the class divisions within nationally oppressed groups such as the Palestinians by stating that: "I have regularly been accused of binarism – though not once by a Native".[21] Without accepting the identitarian assumptions behind this ridiculous response, it is worth quoting at length from Tunisian writer Max Ajl:

> "Native peoples" do not speak with one voice... The class character of national liberation movements or their antagonists or half-hearted supporters are absent [in Wolfe's writings]... Class conflicts riddle populations. Some are keen to preserve the occupation/colonialism... For some, "elimination" means enrichment through settler-capitalist domination and its stabilization of neo-colonial domination in the West Bank and the tendrils of finance linking that to Gulf capitalist class formation, while for some, displacement has meant immiseration in the Gaza Strip.[22]

Some anti-colonial theorists can acknowledge divisions within national movements but they see elite layers within nationally oppressed populations as simply sellouts putting their own narrow interests above that of the national movement as a whole, rather than a class pursuing its own class interests. They also often underestimate the problem of

---

21. Quoted in Ajl 2023, p.274.
22. Ajl 2023, p.275. Ajl's insightful criticism of settler colonial theory is unfortunately marred by his campist politics, notably in his defence of Iran, Syria, Hezbollah and even China and Russia; see pp.277–8 of the same essay.

middle-class layers within these movements having different class interests from the mass of workers.

This echoes the political framework of Arab nationalists and the Stalinist left who draw a distinction between sections of the Arab elite, or particular leaders or governments, who have become pawns of imperialism, and the "patriotic bourgeoisie" and supposedly anti-imperialist states. However, as Adam Hanieh argues, "it makes little sense to identify a 'national' bourgeoisie whose interests are somehow counterposed to those of large international or regional capital"; and

> it is a fantasy to hold out the possibility of convincing a "patriotic bourgeoisie" to act in the interests of the majority and build "social democratic" capitalist states in the Middle East. These capitalist classes are part of the problem, not the solution.[23]

The role that the Palestinian Authority has played in working with the Israeli state to suppress any genuine resistance to Israeli rule is often seen as an example of a small section of elites selling out the nation's cause. Hanieh explains though how the actions of the Palestinian Authority are only explicable from an analysis of the class structure of Palestinian society. Since Israel occupied it in 1967 the economy of the West Bank has transformed from a mainly rural one dominated by structures of traditional village life into "an incorporated, dependent, and subordinated appendage of Israeli capitalism". This shift saw the mass of the Palestinian population dispossessed of what little land they still controlled and proletarianised while at the same time there developed "a tiny layer of Palestinian capital that articulates Israeli rule and whose accumulation is dependent on that meditating position".[24]

The Palestinian writer Toufic Haddad similarly writes about how the basis for the Palestinian Authority was constructed through an "interpermeation of interests" between Palestinian diaspora capitalists in the Arab states and domestic Palestinian capitalists in the West Bank, with the aim to "consolidate a strata of political and economic elites in the West Bank tied to the political economy of neoliberal state

23. Hanieh 2013, p.174.
24. Hanieh 2013, p.100.

building"; meanwhile of course "the majority of Palestinian society remained disenfranchised politically and economically".[25]

The focus that settler colonial theorists have on how settler colonies like Israel are motivated by a desire to eliminate Indigenous populations rather than exploit them also reinforces this tendency to ignore questions of class among the Palestinian population. As a number of scholars critical of settler colonial theory argue:

> [T]he prevailing scholarly emphasis on the elimination of the native, at the expense of labor exploitation, not only is an analytical shortcoming but also obscures the link between the political, economic, and military violence of the occupation and the extraction of Palestinian labor-power by different means.[26]

It is true that since 1993 in particular Israel has sought to largely exclude the Palestinian population from as much of the Israeli workforce as possible, in order to marginalise their potential economic and political power. Historically though this was not always the case, and the integration of Palestinians into the Israeli economy was an important factor behind the First Intifada. The more important problem here however is that simply stating that Israel has no need for Palestinian workers and therefore issues of class and exploitation are irrelevant in the case of settler colonialism ignores how these issues are very relevant for the Palestinians who live and work in the broader region. Finally, the logic of elimination tells us nothing about who and how we can resist the undeniable genocide that Israel is carrying out. Only a Marxist assessment of the issues brings to the fore the exploited classes across the Middle East as a whole which are key to liberating Palestine.

Anti-colonial struggle?

Another feature of settler colonial theory is the inaccurate way it presents "anti-colonial" or "anti-imperialist" struggle. The academic founders of settler colonial theory were in fact deeply ambiguous about the possibility of struggle against settler colonialism, or at

25. Haddad 2016, p.263.
26. Davies et al. 2023.

least anything anyone left-wing would recognise as struggle. So Patrick Wolfe argues:

> In the settler colonial economy, it is not the colonist but the native who is superfluous. This means that the sanctions practically available to the native are ideological ones. In settler colonial formations, in order words, ideology has a higher systemic weighting – it looms larger, as it were – than in other colonial formations.[27]

Thus it is only on the ideological terrain that Palestinians can hope to perhaps disrupt settler colonialism, presumably by exploiting the contradiction between public endorsements of human rights, equality, etc. with the reality of oppression. As one critic explains, "Wolfe's reversion to ideology as the level of struggle in the settler colony is a desperate move" that "would appear to suggest that what we might call 'real conditions' in the settler colony do not admit the possibility of other forms of struggle for the native".[28]

More seriously minded settler colonial theorists are more likely to look towards military actions such as those carried out by Hamas in October 2023, Houthi attacks on Red Sea shipping, or at best armed struggle like that engaged in by the old Palestine Liberation Organization. While armed action against imperialist forces and the violent ruling classes of the region can hardly be ruled out by any movement seeking to transform the Middle East, to elevate this particular form of action is to drastically distort what it will take to liberate Palestine and indeed the broader region.

Imperialism and capitalism in the region is underpinned by multiple powerful ruling classes, both foreign and domestic, with substantial financial and military resources and a proven track record of unleashing violence against any serious signs of opposition. No armed force not connected to one or another of these ruling classes has the capacity to defeat such an extensive system of power and control. And those that

---

27. Wolfe 1999, p.3.
28. Davies 2023.

are well funded and armed, such as the Saudi and Emirati militaries, do not wish to see imperialism defeated because they are part of it.

In this situation, Marxists look towards the potential power of a mass working-class movement as the only solution. The classic features of such a movement through history – grassroots workplace activism and organisation, general strikes, and eventually mass insurrections in major urban centres – places in it a unique position to challenge the ruling classes and states of the Middle East. And we have seen examples of exactly this kind of struggle in the region before. During the 1940s and '50s there was a wave of mass working-class revolt in many Middle Eastern countries.

In Egypt an independent workers' movement arose that challenged not just colonial rule but capitalist exploitation, culminating in a massive strike movement erupting in February 1946. The anti-Zionist Jewish socialist writer Tony Cliff captured some of the key features of this huge strike:

> In Alexandria the students turned towards the workers and arranged a large demonstration together with them. A few days later – on the 21st. February, "Evacuation Day" – about 100,000 workers and students made a strike and demonstration in Cairo. The spirit of the demonstrators was clearly revealed in the fact that none of the traditional parties had any sway over them… The solidarity of Moslems, Christians and Jews was an oft-repeated slogans [sic] throughout the demonstrations. Sudanese students studying in Egypt who called for a common struggle against British imperialism were carried shoulder high.[29]

Cliff explains that the demonstrations and strikes were organised by a workers' and students' committee which was "democratically elected" and truly "representative of the masses", whose "members were chosen in democratic elections from each faculty and trade union" and in "every quarter of Cario special local quarter committees were also elected" with worker activists in the "big foreign companies" having a

---

29. Cliff 2011 [1946], chapter 23.

"decisive influence on the direction of the movement". In Alexandria, it was anti-Stalinist activists who had a majority on the city-wide workers' and students' committee.[30]

Such scenes were repeated in Iraq, which was shaken by huge protests and general strikes that fused together anti-colonial and class demands. In 1948 a mass urban rebellion erupted against the killing of student protesters, with striking oil workers in Kirkuk playing a key role in radicalising the movement. The rebellion was suppressed but followed by a new uprising in 1952. Even after a group of nationalist military officers took power in 1958, strikes continued and Communists could reportedly bring over 1 million people onto the streets in demonstrations.[31]

More recently the revival of strike action by key sections of workers was a crucial factor in the outbreak of the Arab Spring, and the lack of a sizeable socialist workers' movement to build upon such action was key to its eventual defeat.[32]

The class basis of anti-colonial politics

The politics of settler colonial theory are not simply ill-thought-out ideas. If taken seriously as a guide to action they would be disastrous for building a movement that can actually challenge imperialism and capitalism.

In South Africa, the theory that Africans suffered from "internal colonisation" was developed by primarily white intellectuals around the South African Communist Party. They used the theory to justify the pro-capitalist strategy of the African National Congress, which sought to narrow the radicalism of African workers around a program of simply replacing the racist apartheid regime with a new capitalist government controlled by a Black elite. In the United States, Black Power activist Stokely Carmichael (Kwame Ture) and political scientist Charles V Hamilton used the theory that African Americans were a colony within the US to argue for building up a Black political power bloc. This

---

30. Cliff 2011 [1946], chapter 23.
31. Alexander 2003.
32. See chapter 9 in Alexander 2022 for a discussion of the revival of the workers' movement before the Arab Spring.

ultimately primarily benefited the layer of Black mayors, congressmen and police chiefs who were elected to supposedly decolonise urban spaces. In Australia anti-colonial rhetoric is just as often used to argue for more Indigenous-owned businesses, NGOs and government bureaucracies as it is to argue for any genuine struggle against racism, let alone capitalism.

Throughout the twentieth century, we saw anti-colonial movements win across Africa, Asia and the Middle East. While socialists celebrated the end of direct colonial rule, we need to be clear that in none of these cases did anti-colonial revolutions lead to societies based on equality and justice. Instead new capitalist states were created, with continued exploitation and oppression the result.

Ironically the classless politics of anti-colonialism actually has a class basis. It represents the interests of all those social layers – middle-class intellectuals, state bureaucrats and aspiring politicians from oppressed backgrounds – who might oppose racism, or war or a particular national oppression but don't want the capitalist system to end. Instead, they want a new nation-state or business or bureaucracy in which they or someone from their background are in control.

There are of course those on the left who adopt the politics of settler colonial theory but consider themselves to be fighting for something more radical than the examples raised above. But the problem is that the logic of anti-colonial politics inevitably leads towards pro-capitalist so-called solutions to the issues of racism and imperialism. Its very framing reinforces the idea that the key division in the world is different national groups rather than classes, and that the problems of the world are due to things external or secondary to capitalism, rather than the fundamental nature of the system itself.

Sai Englert, a socialist writer, argues that one of the benefits of settler colonial theory is that it can provide a framework for a struggle for liberation that can foster "unity across different sections of the Palestinian people". But unity with whom and on what political basis? Englert's *Settler Colonialism: An Introduction* discusses many examples of movements against national oppression, including in Palestine, but at no point even acknowledges, let alone discusses, the different class forces within them, opting for uncritical veneration instead.[33]

Many of the people protesting for Palestine today are doing so at least in part because of these anti-colonial ideas, which make sense as a starting point given the weakness of class struggle and the left. But if we are to begin to build the kinds of organisations we need to actually defeat capitalism and imperialism then as many people as possible need to go beyond the limits of these politics.

Throughout the twentieth and twenty-first centuries we've had all sorts of very radical, even revolutionary-sounding anti-racist and anti-imperialist theories: racial-capitalism, revolutionary black nationalism, dependency theory, third-worldism, Guevarism and so forth. But when put into practice they all ended in disaster. The uncritical championing of Indigenous nationalist movements by settler colonial theorists echoes the problems of third worldism that influenced much of the radical left in the second half of the twentieth century.

Faced with another century of brutal wars and vicious oppression we need clear Marxist politics that emphasises the necessity of confronting the underlying structures of capitalism through the immense potential power of the working class.

References

Ajl, Max 2023, "Logics of Elimination and Settler Colonialism: Decolonization or National Liberation?", *Middle East Critique*, 32:2, pp.259–83.

Alexander, Anne 2003, "Daring for victory: Iraq in revolution 1946–1959", *International Socialism*, 2:99, Summer. https://www.marxists.org/history/etol/newspape/isj2/2003/isj2-099/alexander.htm

Alexander, Anne 2022, *Revolution is the Choice of the People. Crisis and Revolt in the Middle East and North Africa*, Bookmarks.

Becke, Johannes 2018, "Dismantling the Villa in the Jungle: Matzpen, Zochrot, and the Whitening of Israel", *International Journal of Postcolonial Studies*, 21(6), pp.874–91.

Cliff, Tony 2011 [1946], *The Problem of the Middle East (Egypt, Palestine, Syria, Lebanon and Iraq)*, *Marxists' Internet Archive*. https://www.marxists.org/archive/cliff/works/1946/probme/index.html

---

33. Englert 2022, p.13.

Davies, Jack 2023, "The World Turned Outside In: Settler Colonial Studies and Political Economy", *Historical Materialism*, 31(2&3), January. https://www. historicalmaterialism.org/index.php/articles/world-turned-outside

Davies, Jack, Muriam Haleh Davis, Martin Devecka, Robin Jones, Thomas Serres and Becker Sharif 2023, "Translators' Introduction to *The Palestinian and Jewish Working Class and Its Organisations 1918–1939 by Omar Talibi*", *Critical Ethnic Studies Journal*, 8(1), Minnesota University Press. https://manifold.umn.edu/read/ces0801-03/section/ f4b677a6-25b4-4b9e-9738-1b10ccb6c6c4

Englert, Sai 2020, "Settlers, Workers and the Logic of Accumulation by Dispossession", *Antipode: a Radical Journal of Geography*, 52(6), July, pp.1647–66. https://onlinelibrary.wiley.com/doi/epdf/10.1111/anti.12659

Englert, Sai 2022, *Settler Colonialism: An Introduction*, Pluto Press.

Greenstein, Tony 2019, "Why Israel is a Jewish, not a white supremacist state", *Al Jazeera* 7 February. https://www.aljazeera.com/opinions/2019/2/7/ why-israel-is-a-jewish-not-a-white-supremacist-state

Haddad, Toufic 2016, *Palestine LTD.: Neoliberalism and Nationalism in the Occupied Territory*, I.B Tauris.

Hanieh, Adam 2013, *Lineages of Revolt: Issues of Contemporary Capitalism in the Middle East*, Haymarket Books.

Humphreys, Jordan 2021, "Capitalism, colonialism and class: A Marxist explanation of Indigenous oppression today", *Marxist Left Review*, 21, Summer. https://marxistleftreview.org/articles/Indigenous_oppression/

Humphreys, Jordan 2023, *Indigenous Liberation & Socialism*, Red Flag Books.

Kennard, Matt 2023, "The anti-imperialist movement that supports Palestinian liberation and runs part of the UK", *UK Declassified*, 19 October. https://www.declassifieduk.org/the-anti-imperialist-movement-that-supports-palestinian-liberation-and-runs-part-of-the-uk/

Marshall, Phil 2023 [1989], *Intifada: Zionism, imperialism and Palestinian resistance*, Red Flag Books.

Mkokeli, Sam 2024, "South Africa's Gaza stance threatens trade ties with Israel" *Semafor*, updated 31 January. https://www.semafor.com/ article/01/30/2024/south-africas-gaza-stance-threatens-trade-ties-with-israel

Piterberg, Gabriel and Lorenzo Veracini 2015, "Wakefield, Marx, and the world turned inside out", *Journal of Global History*, 10(3), November, pp.457–78.

Rawoot, Ilham 2023, "South Africa's perplexing relationship with Israel", *The New Arab*, 11 December. https://www.newarab.com/analysis/south-africas-perplexing-relationship-israel

Surasky, Cecilie 2015, "Settler colonialism, white supremacy, and the 'special relationship' between the U.S. and Israel", *Jewish Voice for Peace*, 24 February. https://www.jewishvoiceforpeace.org/2015/03/10/settler colonialism-white-supremacy-and-the-special-relationship-between-the-u-s-and-israel/

Uidhir, Somhairle Mag 2024, "Paddy-Washing Genocide? The case for boycotting the White House", *Rebel News*, 24 January. https://www.rebelnews.ie/2024/01/24/paddy-washing-genocide-the-case-for-boycotting-the-white-house/

Veracini, Lorenzo 2016, "Introduction: settler colonialism as a distinct mode of domination", *The Routledge Handbook of the History of Settler Colonialism*, Routledge.

Veracini, Lorenzo 2021, *The World Turned Inside Out: Settler Colonialism as a Political Idea*, Verso.

Wolfe, Patrick 1999, *Settler colonialism and the transformation of anthropology*, Bloomsbury Publishing.

Wolfe, Patrick 2006, "Settler colonialism and the elimination of the native", *Journal of Genocide Research*, 8(4), pp.387–409. https://www.tandfonline.com/doi/full/10.1080/14623520601056240

LIZ ROSS

Nuclear war – "I am become Death, the destroyer of worlds"[1]

Liz Ross has written extensively on a range of issues including women's and gay liberation, the environment and the Australian union movement. Her most recent book is *Stuff the Accord! Pay Up! Workers' resistance to the ALP-ACTU Accord*.

THE OBLITERATION OF the Japanese cities of Hiroshima and Nagasaki at the end of World War II signalled the final barbarity of this imperialist war; and hurtled the world into the nuclear era, where the brilliance of scientific endeavour was converted into an apocalypse, showing how the ruling class could indeed "become Death, the destroyer of worlds".

Imperialist war is the most barbaric of wars, justified by the drive to maintain capitalism and its destructive profit-seeking rationale, regardless of the human cost. From the trench warfare and mustard gas of World War I to the Nazi holocaust and nuclear bombs of World War II, millions of workers' lives have been lost or irreparably damaged. Earlier, the Roman historian Tacitus described such wars for empire, writing: "They ravage, they slaughter, they seize by false pretences and all of this they hail as the construction of empire. And when in their wake nothing remains but a desert, they call that peace".[2]

But what became possible in a capitalist world was the creation of the working class, the only majority class which could halt this deadly construction of empire. The first imperialist world war was supposed

---

1. Bhagavad-Gita, 11:32, as quoted by Robert Oppenheimer, leader of the US Manhattan Project, many months after the Hiroshima and Nagasaki bombings.
2. Tacitus 96.

to be the war to end all wars, and now life would be better for all. But workers, having suffered the barbarity of the trenches, had little trust in their leaders to deliver. They rose up, determined to overthrow their bloodthirsty rulers in revolutions from Russia to Germany and in mass strikes and major upheavals throughout the world.

However, the defeat of these inspirational struggles meant the re-assertion of the capitalist dynamic. After a temporary economic boost at the end of conflict, the world was plunged into the 1930s Great Depression. Though it devastated the working class, this economic catastrophe didn't revive the dropping rate of profit, so the ruling class once more turned to war. To gain mass support for yet another war, the naked grab for profits and imperialist gain was hardly a winning strategy. Each war, as Rosa Luxemburg wrote, finds a more ideological, nationalist rationale for the slaughter. "Each and every belligerent party...with heavy heart, draw[s] the sword from its sheath for the single and sole purpose of defending its Fatherland and its own righteous cause from the shameful attacks of the enemy. This legend is inextricably a part of the game of war as powder and lead".[3]

And so it was in WWII. Described as a war for democracy, a war against fascism, it was nothing more than a war for empire, the inevitable outcome of capitalist competition. In a recent *Red Flag* article, Tess Lee Ack writes:

> World War Two is best understood, as historian Richard Overy put it, as one between "incumbent" and "insurgent" imperialist powers – primarily Britain, France and the US (the Allies) on one hand, and Germany, Japan and Italy (the Axis) on the other. The Allied powers held fifteen times more colonial acreage than the Axis states. As the head of Britain's navy candidly observed in 1934, "We have got most of the world already, or the best parts of it. We...want to keep what we have got and prevent others from taking it away from us". The Axis powers sought to redivide the world and grab a bigger share for themselves.[4]

---

3.   Luxemburg 1915.
4.   Lee Ack 2023.

By 1945, with Germany surrendering in May, Japanese cities firebombed and then Hiroshima and Nagasaki flattened, the war was ended, the Allies victorious over their Axis enemies.

Despite the fanfare of the declaration of peace, arms production continued apace, but with the new deadlier nuclear arsenal. It was the basis for a new arms race, where the USA and its Western allies jostled for domination against its former WWII allies, the USSR and its satellite Eastern Bloc countries. For the British, having their own nuclear weapons was a way of boosting Britain's credibility as a postwar participant in world affairs, a way of reclaiming its status as empire. "The Bomb was also recognised as being chillingly economic", explains Tim Sherratt. "In the financially difficult post-war years, where a full-scale military force was difficult to maintain, the cost-effective A-bomb was an attractive proposition to British military planners."[5]

The Cold War, which quickly followed, witnessed proxy South-East Asian hot wars against "communism" and saw the world teetering on the brink of total annihilation as Russia and the US faced off in the 1962 Cuban missile crisis. After this, Armageddon, the prospect of "mutually assured destruction" aptly known as "MAD", was held off with international agreements. Nonetheless, despite various nuclear non-proliferation treaties and self-imposed limitations, the number of countries with nuclear weapons increased from the initial US monopoly to include Britain, France, Israel, India, Pakistan, North Korea, Russia and China, all of which have exploded devices in tests.[6] The US remains the only country to have used atomic bombs in war. Though not considered a nuclear weapon, depleted uranium warheads have been used the US and UK in a number of recent wars, including currently providing them to Ukraine, while Russia's deployment is suspected but unconfirmed.[7]

Nuclear weapons sharing expands this deadly accumulation.

5. Sherratt 2003, p.7.
6. South Africa disassembled its nuclear force before joining the Non-Proliferation Treaty. The former Soviet republics of Belarus, Kazakhstan and Ukraine transferred the weapons to Russia. In 2023 Russia transferred nuclear warheads back into Belarus. Israel has never acknowledged its nuclear arsenal, signed the Non-Proliferation Treaty, nor allowed scrutiny by international inspectors.
7. Physicians and Scientists for Global Responsibility New Zealand 2012.

America, for example, has arms stores, B52 planes and the like in Belgium, Germany, Italy, the Netherlands and Turkey, and formerly in Canada and Greece.[8] For Russia, with its borders on Europe, the strategic placement of weapons plays the same role. Countries such as Libya, Iran and Iraq have developed or are accused of developing weapons-grade uranium and delivery devices, but so far appear not to have produced or exploded actual weapons.

These nine nuclear warhead-armed countries have, according to the Stockholm International Peace Research Institute, an estimated total of 12,512 weapons as of January 2023, with 90 percent owned by either Russia or the US. This is down slightly on the 13,080 in 2021, cold comfort given that only a fraction of this number would be needed to annihilate the world. And that could happen in an instant with around nine and a half thousand weapons in military stockpiles and two thousand on high operational alert in the US and Russia. A total of $82.9 billion was spent by the nine countries on those deadly arsenals in 2022 alone, with the US spending $43.7 billion.[9] Between 1940 and 1996 American spending on nuclear weapons totalled $5.5 trillion, 30 percent of the total $18.7 trillion military spend.[10]

The more recent development of nuclear arsenals to include less powerful or "low-yield" nukes, so-called tactical or non-strategic nuclear weapons, has lowered the threshold for nuclear weapons use – and alarmingly raised the potential for global nuclear war. And willingness to actually go to war has shifted. The Biden administration, for example, is preparing to rebuild the entire US nuclear arsenal and since October 2022 has threatened first use of nuclear weapons in a variety of scenarios, instead of the "nuclear deterrence or retaliation-only" policy.[11] China has significantly increased its nuclear arsenal, but still

---

8.   NATO's policy of nuclear deterrence allows member nations without nuclear weapons to participate in the planning for the use of nuclear weapons, including the use of their armed forces to deliver them. It also means maintaining technical equipment, such as nuclear-capable planes and storage of weapons on their territory. Earlier the US stationed nuclear weapons in Japan, South Korea and Taiwan, removing all by the 1990s.

9.   Montague 2023.

10. Montague 2023.

11. Johnson 2022.

maintains its "no first use" policy, even urging other nuclear states to restate their commitment to this policy. However, with some recent defence personnel changes, *The Economist* speculates that China is moving towards a "launch on warning" of incoming nuclear missiles.[12] Russia's policy allows for the use of so-called tactical smaller nukes to defend the country. *The Age* commented: "Russian policy states that 'in an escalating military conflict, demonstrating readiness and determination to use force using non-strategic nuclear weapons is an effective deterrent', which has been interpreted by some analysts as describing a single nuclear detonation or launch". Since the war in Ukraine Russia has increased its nuclear submarine drills and deployment of mobile missile launchers.[13]

The US and UK have used depleted uranium warheads, including most recently in Ukraine, while Russia's deployment is suspected but unconfirmed. Inexplicably these are not recognised as nuclear weapons, so are not covered by non-proliferation treaties.

Though not usually included in arms assessments there are also the 440 nuclear power plants scattered around 31 countries, plants that generate one key ingredient for many nuclear weapons – plutonium.[14] Given the reliance on plutonium by the modern nuclear weapons industry and space propulsion, it is disingenuous to say the least to claim that nuclear power plants are just a source of peaceful power, especially considering the increasing weaponisation of space. In reality, the keen support for nuclear power is based on the understanding that these power plants can also be converted for nuclear weapons manufacture, as well as producing plutonium. Just as concerning is the vulnerability of nuclear power plants themselves in war, as the Russian control of the Ukrainian power plant in Zaporizhzhia has demonstrated. Or their vulnerability in a world of increasing climate instability to weather events such as happened at Fukushima in 2011.

In 2024 we live, as Alex Callinicos points out, in a "new age of catastrophe" as we face not only nuclear annihilation, but also

---

12. *The Economist*, 3 August 2023.
13. Groch and Zappone 2022.
14. World Nuclear Association 2024. Plutonium has occurred naturally, but except for trace amounts is not found in the earth's crust: World Nuclear Association 2023.

economic crises, pandemics and climate collapse, with 2023 the hottest year in recorded history. Some suggest that the Anthropocene, the time of major human impact on the world's climate, actually began with the first atom bomb test, Trinity, at Los Alamos on 16 July 1945.[15] And rather than an easing of imperialist rivalries, these factors, as well as the much feted "competition busting" globalisation, turbocharge capitalism's underlying characteristics of economic crisis and imperialist geopolitical competition.

According to the *Financial Times* a second global arms race, the remilitarisation of industry, is already under way. In 2022 well over $2 trillion globally was spent on defence spending, trending higher in 2023.[16]

It is a highly volatile and unpredictable time. Just witness the recent sudden rise of the COVID-19 pandemic and its devastating impact, or the Ukraine-Russia war and Israel's genocidal war on Palestinians in Gaza, leading to rising instability. Russia remains a rival, but is no longer America's foremost imperialist challenger, with the US recently making a highly public "pivot to Asia" to take on China. Portrayed as "Western freedoms" versus "Chinese authoritarianism", in fact it is about the world's leading imperialist power, the US, trying to contain the world's second-biggest economy, China, and keep it out of the Indo-Pacific, now the main hub of global capitalism, representing about 40 percent of global Gross Domestic Product (GDP).

As Callinicos argues, the rivalry between the US and China is no simple confrontation between declining and rising powers:

> Both rivals have pursued mutually dependent debt-driven accumulation strategies whose limits are now very visible. These economic difficulties could of course encourage the political leaderships on both side of the Pacific to beat the nationalist drum in order to focus discontent outwards. This is, in essence what Trump did, with great political success. Thus, as in the 1930s, economic crisis can fuel geopolitical antagonism.[17]

---

15.   Callinicos 2023. Anthropocene description in Physics arXiv Blog 2023.
16.   Haldane 2023.
17.   Callinicos 2023, p.99.

Imperialism and capitalist competition didn't end with WWII; the world just launched the latest iteration, armed this time with the ultimate in destructive weaponry, nuclear bombs. Australian nuclear scientist Mark Oliphant wrote: "It is the impersonal killing, by remote control, which makes modern war the most degrading activity of man".[18]

From Trinity to Nagasaki and the ongoing nightmare

Foreseen first by HG Wells, his 1914 novel *The world set free* describes planes dropping an "atomic" bomb of infinite power, continuing to explode once it hit the ground. A military future for atomic energy was science fiction at the time, but with breakthroughs in understanding atomic structure occurring through the 1930s such a use was soon discussed as much as peaceful power generation. Now out of the realms of science fiction, nuclear weapons represent more like science apocalypse scenarios. Most recently romanticised by the Hollywood blockbuster *Oppenheimer*, the path to the first nuclear bomb is more a horror-filled, sordid, grubby grab for world domination and profit than the film – a shameless apologia for US imperialism – portrays. It is a highly secretive story, laden with lies, cover-ups, thousands of dead, injured and irradiated people, polluted water, air and land – a war crime from the start.

At the beginning of WWII several countries appeared on the verge, albeit still somewhat theoretical, of unleashing the compressed power of the atom as a destructive force. Three imperialist powers – the UK, US and Germany – had the scientific research facilities, scientists and knowledge available to consider further development. By the end of the 1930s the science and technological know-how was there. The Nazis didn't follow through, focusing more on conventional warfare, but the UK and US went ahead with feasibility studies.

In 1939 physicists Albert Einstein and Leo Szilard warned the US of the possibility of a German bomb, encouraging Roosevelt to urgently expand US research and development. Somewhat cautiously, the President set up an advisory Uranium Committee in October 1939, which by June 1942 became the secretive Manhattan Project. Similarly

---

18. As quoted in Holden 2019, p.225.

in the UK, in March 1941, their scientific working group, the MAUD Committee, released two reports detailing the uses of uranium for weaponry and as a source of power. Britain's resultant covert nuclear bomb project, codenamed Tube Alloys, was set up in August 1941, with the clear objective of making bombs in Britain.[19] With its far greater resources and distance from the major war zones, however, it was America which was to become the world's first nuclear weapons manufacturer and warrior.[20]

It was not so much science as the politics of empire that were very much at the forefront for some of the scientists involved, equally so with the politicians and defence forces. Australian nuclear physicist Mark Oliphant, leading research at Birmingham University and on the MAUD Committee during the 1930s, urged his colleagues in the US to promote bomb production. In a note to Robert Oppenheimer he wrote:

> Whichever nation is first to succeed in this quest will undoubtedly be master of the world. If peace were to come tomorrow it would still be necessary to obtain the answer first, at all costs, for in the hands of a resentful or unscrupulous nation such power would be dangerous.[21]

While Oppenheimer continued to support the use of the bomb, he did campaign against proliferation in later years. Afterwards Mark Oliphant called himself a "belligerent pacifist" and took part in anti-nuclear campaigns as well as marching against the Vietnam War. But the damage was done; they were among the leading scientists at Los Alamos who enabled the bombing of Japanese cities. Environmental scientist Brendan Montague notes that, by the end of WWII, "The

---

19. Sherratt 2003, p.7. MAUD was not an acronym, the name is attributed to the Danish physicist Niels Bohr, referring to his housekeeper. In November 1945 Winston Churchill stated in parliament: "This I take is already agreed, we should make atomic bombs". One of the industrial facilities constructed to service the Tube Alloys program was given the remit to produce plutonium for military purposes.
20. Scientists involved in nuclear research in the US and UK, and sympathetic to Russia, passed on the MAUD Committee reports and US details of the bomb's development, enabling Russia's postwar weapons production and their own bomb in 1949.
21. As quoted by Holden 2019, p.87.

American state, as imperialist and murderous as any, ensured that the weapon was tightly gripped in its fist".[22]

That was achieved through the Manhattan Project. With unlimited money and resources 6,000 scientists, including world leaders in atomic research and military experts, were marshalled under the leadership of nuclear physicist Robert Oppenheimer and US Lieutenant General Leslie Groves. It was a highly secretive project, not just in the way it was initially conducted, but also in the deliberate withholding of information from those affected by the whole process of research, production, testing and use of these devices. The "forever" waste from these projects was similarly minimised, ignored or hidden. This has remained the case, thwarting any attempt to make accountable, regulate or ban any aspect of the nuclear industry, peaceful or military.

The Manhattan Project incorporated four separate sites and ultimately employed half a million people, at a cost of $21.5bn in today's dollars. The most famous was Los Alamos in New Mexico, the Oppenheimer-led scientific centre which designed and built the bomb. The second was Oak Ridge in Tennessee which refined uranium to weapons-grade level; the third was Red Gates Wood, Cook County where a nuclear reactor was built. The fourth, and one of the most polluted sites, was Hanford in Washington state, producing plutonium.

Los Alamos was also the site for the experimental explosions needed before a fit-for-purpose bomb could be successful. The project developed three bombs at over $5bn each, as well as trialling various separate pieces of equipment and materials. The first, on 7 May 1945, tested a device with 100 tons of TNT spiked with plutonium. It was a callously inept test using tethered rats, a total disaster delivering no information at all and leaving plutonium scattered to the winds. The first fully radioactive bomb, a plutonium weapon codenamed Gadget, was tried in the Trinity test on 16 July 1945 in New Mexico. The next two were dropped on cities of hundreds of thousands – the uranium-based "Little Boy" over Hiroshima on 6 August 1945 and the plutonium-loaded "Fat Boy" on Nagasaki, 9 August 1945.

Trinity's impact on surrounding areas and peoples was never

---

22. Montague 2023.

properly measured in New Mexico, but later studies indicate fallout across much of America, even reaching Canada and Mexico by 20 July, causing generations of cancers, deformities and environmental damage. The two bombs dropped on the Japanese cities killed hundreds of thousands and have left an everlasting radioactive legacy.[23]

While some of the generals demurred, it was the scientist Oppenheimer who insisted the bombs be tested on highly populated cities, not to end the war but to measure the bomb's effectiveness. After all the Los Alamos tests had *only* impacted a relatively small, scattered population and he knew no proper pre- or post-explosion studies were undertaken. It fell to Admiral Chester Nimitz, the commander-in-chief of the US Pacific fleet and certainly no pacifist, to raise even a glimmer of dissent: "The Japanese had, in fact, already sued for peace. The atomic bomb played no decisive part, from a purely military point of view, in the defeat of Japan". Showing more concern for civilian lives than Oppenheimer, Nimitz added: "I felt that it was an unnecessary loss of civilian life… We had them beaten. They hadn't enough food, they couldn't do anything".[24]

In the aftermath of the bombing, however, ending WWII became the Allies' public justification for such pointless carnage. The use of nuclear weapons to defeat Japan wasn't the point for Truman and his government, nor for many in the military. It was about securing the spoils of war and a pre-eminent postwar imperialist role for the US, sending a political message to its former ally Russia to back off from asserting any expanded claims in a postwar settlement. As one commentator wrote, the dropping of the bomb was "the first major operation of the diplomatic war with Russia".[25]

The recurrent lie that bombing Japan had ended the war exists alongside the equally criminal abdication of post-bomb responsibilities and the recurring nightmare of nuclear waste. Ever since Trinity the

---

23. Wheeler 2023.
24. Montague 2023. The Japanese had approached the Russians in the last months of the war, seeking talks to end the conflict. Stalin ignored them, but both the Americans and British knew the Japanese were suing for peace. At least five other military leaders, including Chief of Army Douglas MacArthur, disagreed with nuclear bombing the two Japanese cities.
25. PMS Blackett, physicist and advisor to Churchill, quoted in Tanaka and Zinn 2010.

massive impact of these weapons of mass destruction on both people and the environment has been minimised, covered up, lacked treatment, clean-up or remediation, called enemy propaganda or outright lied about by authorities.[26]

Both North Korea and Russia have detonated missiles as late as 2023, but from Los Alamos, through Hiroshima and Nagasaki and until 1996, atmospheric and underground explosions by the British, French and Americans as well as Russia, China and North Korea, have exposed civilians and military personnel to highly dangerous levels of radiation and destruction of their lands, air and water.[27] One such example is the Bikini and Eniwetok atolls in the Marshall Islands, where 67 detonations occurred almost constantly from 1946 to 1996, leading to massive contamination which has forced many from their lands. So-called peaceful nuclear energy production is just as capable of long-lasting damage, as the 2011 Fukushima disaster has shown.

Overwhelmingly too, nuclear weapons testing has been a story of racism by largely white colonisers further dispossessing indigenous populations they'd already robbed. Test sites around the world have been declared empty deserts or uninhabited islands, despite well known facts of occupation.[28] In the case of Japan, there was no denying the large population, nor was there colonial dispossession; so anti-Japanese sentiment was whipped up in the US during the war. Magazines such as *Time* wrote: "The ordinary unreasoning Jap is ignorant. Perhaps he is human. Nothing indicates it". Meanwhile the government sent 120,000 Japanese-Americans to concentration camps within the US. It was anti-Japanese racism that fuelled responses to surveys showing that between 1944 and 1945 a growing number of Americans (up to 85 percent in one questionnaire) wanted to see Japanese cities destroyed and their populations wiped out.[29] The US, backed by major-

---

26. Ramirez 2020. It has been estimated that the US Army disposed of 29 million kilograms of mustard gas and nerve agent and 454 tons of radioactive waste in the Pacific – excluding that left on the remains of islands such as the Marshall Islands, where 70,000 square metres, maybe as much as 3.1m cubic feet, of radioactive debris is "stored" in the Dome on Runit Island.
27. Sauer 2023.
28. Bullimore 2023.
29. Tanaka and Zinn 2010.

ity American opinion as late as the 2000s, has never apologised, nor paid compensation for WWII bombing of the Japanese – whether from nuclear weapons or fire-bombs. A small measure of justice however was achieved when, after years of campaigning, President Reagan signed the 1988 Civil Liberties Act which offered every interned Japanese-American a formal apology and $20,000 in compensation.[30]

In Los Alamos after Trinity the local peoples also got short shrift. Trinity was supposedly dropped on empty land, a desert of sand and cacti. But authorities knew there were people in the New Mexico area, largely poor agricultural workers, many Hispanic or Indigenous members of the Apache and Navajo nations. Some, closest to the test site, they had already evicted. Other nearby populations, an estimated total of 13,000 within a 50-mile radius, were left on the land, lacking any warning of the coming test and its dangerous plutonium-laden fallout. Afterwards there was little to no post-test monitoring or care and without pre-testing, claims of harm could be easily dismissed. As one doctor in charge of safety commented about those exposed to radiation: "they couldn't prove it, we couldn't prove it, so we just assumed we got away with it". The chief Manhattan Project medical adviser Stafford Warren said: "The army and the government lawyers wanted to put it all out of sight and mind as quickly as possible".[31]

The authorities have only been partially successful in Trinity's cover-up, thanks to the determination of the original Pueblo peoples to expose the facts, but the full story remains hidden, permanently filed away under national security measures or destroyed. After the white-washing film *Oppenheimer* screened in 2023, cancer survivor Tina Cordova, whose family lived in Tularosa just 50 miles from Trinity in 1945, spoke up:

> The Manhattan Project was an invasion of our land and lives. And the film feels like that too. Without all the Hispanic and Native

---

30. Yoshida 2021; Tasevski 2020.
31. Wheeler 2023. The Manhattan Project, with the approval of Oppenheimer, authorised doctors to secretly inject hospital patients with plutonium to test its effects. These tests lasted till 1947. President Clinton later apologised.

people...Los Alamos doesn't exist...and the Manhattan Project
doesn't happen...but we don't think they'll ever tell that story.[32]

To add insult to the injury of barely mentioning the local people,
Oppenheimer was actually filmed in part at Los Alamos.[33]

The pressure to stay quiet about radiation exposure in New Mexico
continues to this day. The state has what could be called a cradle-to-
grave industry of uranium mining, weapons manufacture and waste
storage; no-one is encouraged to stand up for their rights, let alone
shut the whole industry down. In 2003 the American news analysis site
Democracy Now estimated that if New Mexico seceded it would be the
third-biggest nuclear power in the world.[34]

In 1990, nearly five decades after the tests, the US federal government finally introduced a Radiation Exposure Compensation Act
(RECA), an act more noted for its miserliness and restrictions than its
benefits. One-time payments of $50,000 or $100,000 were available
for those exposed to atmospheric nuclear tests or workers in uranium
mining or the nuclear weapons industry. But only a small proportion of
those affected by the tests are actually covered, and despite attempts to
extend the Act it is due to expire permanently in July 2024. The RECA
has paid out about $2.5bn, about 0.0005 percent of the estimated $6
trillion the US has spent on nuclear weapons. As the funding for
weapons continues to increase, the compensation amount will effectively amount to zero.[35]

Another scandalous legacy of the Manhattan Project was the pluto-
nium-producing town of Hanford.[36] From 1943 around 5,500 workers
operated the nine nuclear reactors and two weapons facilities and the
underground waste storage tanks. The town produced most of the US
war-time plutonium, starting with the first plutonium bomb dropped
on Nagasaki, finally supplying over 21,392 nuclear warheads. When
Nagasaki was hit the local paper proudly exclaimed: "PEACE! OUR

32. Wheeler 2023.
33. Taylor 2023.
34. *Democracy Now*, 2003.
35. Wheeler 2023.
36. All information about Hanford is from Frank 2022 and Wheeler 2023.

BOMB CLINCHED IT!" The War Department applauded the Hanford employees; *Time* magazine and Portland's *Oregonian*, too, voiced appreciation for their efforts. The "peaceful" atom bomb was being celebrated across the country.

Shuttered in 1987, Hanford is now "a sprawling wasteland of radioactive and chemical sewage...[recognised by the federal government] as the most contaminated place on earth", holding two-thirds of America's high-level radioactive waste. The figures are mesmerisingly frightening. There are 56 million gallons of nuclear waste in this abandoned site, about a third of the 177 storage tanks are leaking into the ground water and into the Columbia River; the soil is contaminated by billions of gallons of waste, from radioactive elements to hazardous chemicals such as mercury, PCBs and sulphuric acid. From 1947 to 1951 two hundred different radioactive nuclides, including the dangerous iodine-131, went airborne during production at the plant, spreading over at least 75,000 square miles of land.

Horrifyingly, you can actually visit Hanford's B Reactor where the guide will tell you: "It was the perfect marriage of science and engineering. The brave men that built this left us a history we should not ever forget".[37]

But the government is trying its best to forget Hanford. There are currently attempts in Congress to downgrade its classification from a high- to low-grade waste site. As of 2020, the latest of a number of companies employed to clean up the town is Bechtel, quoting a finish date of 2080 and a cost of $550bn, greatly exceeding all previous plans. While they haven't actually started the clean-up, a monstrously difficult project, they have already been paid millions. "Hanford has become the epitome of the US government's permanent war economy – in this case, not by making weapons but by cleaning up the aftermath of their production. The problem, of course, is that they aren't cleaning it up at all".[38] But even if they had we probably wouldn't know, as the remediation of nuclear waste is classified, meaning accidents, radiation exposure, worker injuries rarely, if ever, get public scrutiny.

In this context it's worth a quick look at Bechtel. It is one of the

37. Frank 2022, p.10.
38. Frank 2022, p.69.

largest US companies with a long history of underperforming, not finishing or botching projects during US military operations, covert and otherwise, in Iraq, Yemen, Syria, Iran, Palestine, Lebanon and Libya. It is a company, says Sally Denton, that has, "pioneered the revolving door system that now pervades both US politics and the American economic system – a door that came to shape foreign policy not always in the interest of the nation and its citizens, but for the interests of multinational corporations".[39]

The Hanford area was previously home to the Wanapum and Nez Perce nations and the Yakama and Umatilla tribal confederations, situated along the Columbia River. In 1943 they were unceremoniously forced off the land and relocated 40 miles northwest with no compensation. Told at the time that: "[T]his would just be for the war, that in order to protect the United States of America, they were going to do something here," they have never been allowed to return except for occasional visits. The people were expendable, say the indigenous groups, and "the environment was sacrificed in the name of global power".[40] Across the Manhattan Project as a whole, as well as the postwar Nevada tests, while some from the original tribes were offered low-paying jobs, the displacement from their lands and disruption of their culture have been overwhelmingly negative. In Hanford in particular the environmental damage has been savage; the tribes' removal from the lands is now effectively permanent because of the failures of remediation and has led to a justifiable bitterness. Now the groups have mobilised to sue the Department of Environment over the continued contamination and injustice. The Department's response has been to stall and claim it's too soon to assess the environmental impact.[41] There are other organisations along the length of the Columbia River who have joined this ongoing fight for justice.[42]

39. Quoted in Wheeler 2023.
40. Atomic Heritage Foundation 2016.
41. Dininny 2004.
42. Columbia River Keeper; Hanford Challenge.

Peace in our time – or never-ending war?

Peace in our time, declared the victors of war! Barely refraining from announcing that the spoils would go to them, after WWII the Western nations turned to rebuilding a shattered Europe and Japan – and reaping the profits that flowed primarily to the US.

It was a highly contradictory time. On the one hand it was to be a world full of promise, a world of the peaceful atom, a world of plenty for all, or so it was claimed. On the other, arms spending not only continued but escalated and even more countries acquired nuclear weapons. As Noel Sanders writes about the model towns built for the white workers in the uranium mine in Australia: "modernity as the hope for the future life and the threat to such life combined in a cultural double bind... The promise and the threat were inextricably interwoven: the promise was there only under the conditions as threat".[43]

The hot war was succeeded by the repressive Cold War that demonised and jailed dissent, launched a war on workers and became ever more secretive. Capitalism, meanwhile, entered its longest economic boom lasting until the early 1970s, paradoxically underpinned by what has been called the "permanent arms economy".[44]

At the same time as America was building a huge nuclear arms stockpile, bomb shelters and running nuclear attack drills for school children to huddle under their desks, governments and nuclear agencies were lauding the prospects of nuclear-enabled homes and townships. As Utah-based Chip Ward explained: "Back then, 'the peaceful atom' was being plugged as a miracle answer to any problem. Energy 'too cheap to meter'? You bet. Harbors constructed by detonating atomic bombs? Sure thing".[45] Disney released films like "Our Friend the Atom" where you could "view animated farm animals and plants sparkling like so many Tinkerbells with irradiated promise; or you might play with your H2O Missile, a water-powered 'ICBM'". A US-led campaign in Japan in 1955 avoided any mention of military use and

---

43. Sanders 1986, p.163.
44. See Kidron 1967. Recently William Hartung has argued that we are now in a "permanent war economy" where there has been little benefit for workers but a bonanza for the top one percent of capitalists. Hartung 2021.
45. Ward 2008.

instead highlighted the peaceful applications for generating electricity, treating cancer, preserving food, controlling insects and advancing scientific research.

But as the veil over nuclear warfare lifted, Tom Engelhardt remembers:

> It was I who watched the irradiated ants and nuclearized monsters of our teen-screen life stomp the Earth. It was I who went to the French film *Hiroshima Mon Amour*, where I was shocked by my first sight of the human casualties of the A-bombing, and to *On the Beach* to catch a glimpse of how the world might actually end. It was I who saw the mushroom cloud rise in my dreams, felt its heat sear my arm before I awoke.[46]

And within a year of a 1955 campaign to build a nuclear power plant (see below) 60 percent of Japanese still believed nuclear energy would prove more of a curse than a boon. In Australia opposition to nuclear power rose, forcing the ALP to end the bipartisan party support for nuclear power and weapons and adopt a non-nuclear policy at its national conference in 1977.

Instead of turning away from building a nuclear arsenal the ruling class sought to mask the negatives with the promise of a peaceful atom, as Peter Kuznick describes in *The Bulletin of the Atomic Scientists*. On December 8, 1953, newly elected US President Dwight D Eisenhower delivered his "Atoms for Peace" speech at the United Nations. He promised that the United States would devote "its entire heart and mind to find the way by which the miraculous inventiveness of man shall not be dedicated to his death, but consecrated to his life".[47] He pledged to spread the benefits of peaceful atomic power at home and abroad.

But the horrors didn't abate and in March 1954, the US tested a hydrogen bomb, *Castle Bravo*, on the Marshall Islands, the fallout contaminating 236 islanders and 23 Japanese fishermen. When the irradiated fish were sold in Japan, long suppressed rage over the 1945

---

46. Engelhardt 2004.
47. Kuznick 2011. Quotes in this and the following five paragraphs are from Kuznick.

bombings erupted. In response to these protests the National Security Council suggested that the US wage a "vigorous offensive on the non-war uses of atomic energy", including an offer to build an experimental nuclear reactor in Japan. Thomas Murray from the US Atomic Energy Commission condescendingly advised:

> Now, while the memory of Hiroshima and Nagasaki remain so vivid, construction of such a power plant in a country like Japan would be a dramatic and Christian gesture which could lift all of us far above the recollection of the carnage of those cities.

The Washington Post editorialised: "How better, indeed, to dispel the impression in Asia that the United States regards Orientals merely as nuclear cannon fodder!"

Unsurprisingly many in Japan didn't exactly buy this "white man's" promise. The *Mainichi* newspaper blasted the resulting campaign: "First, baptism with radioactive rain, then a surge of shrewd commercialism in the guise of 'atoms for peace' from abroad". The newspaper called on the Japanese people to "calmly scrutinize what is behind the atomic energy race now being staged by the 'white hands' in Japan".

More widespread international condemnation of *Bravo* shocked the White House. Eisenhower told the National Security Council in May 1954: "Everybody seems to think that we are skunks, saber-rattlers, and warmongers". Secretary of State John Foster Dulles complained: "Comparisons are now being made between ours and Hitler's military machine".[48] Before becoming president, Eisenhower had opposed using atomic bombs against the Japanese, even advocating international control of atomic energy and turning the existing US stockpile over to the UN. Once in power, however, he turbocharged the military-industrial complex, turned control of atomic energy over to the military and went on to threaten nuclear war against Korea, the Suez Canal and twice over islands in the Taiwan Strait. Instead of weapons of last resort, under Eisenhower nuclear arms became the foundation of US

---

48. Maley and Hohan 2001.

military strategy and he oversaw the biggest expansion of nuclear hardware development.

As Kuznick concludes, atoms for peace were buried in radioactive ash.

And the dumping of waste and the building and testing thousands of weapons in a growing arms race continued apace. In all, 1,030 nuclear arms tests were conducted by the US military and its contractors, 215 in the air and 815 underground, from 1945 to September 1992.

The history of the US bombings of the Marshall Islands on the Bikini and Eniwetok atolls is just one of many horrendous examples of devastation.[49] With soft-sounding names such as Butternut, Holly and Magnolia that hid their deadly purpose, a total of 67 bombs were detonated in the sky, underwater and on the islands themselves. In 1958, with growing concern about the possible banning of above-ground tests, the US dropped nearly half of that arsenal, 33 bombs, between 28 April and 18 August. But this was not the end for the Islands. No sooner was the nuclear test program dropped after the 1958 non-proliferation agreement than the US used these same atolls for biological and chemical warfare experiments.

As a result of the nuclear tests, hundreds of islanders have been forced to evacuate and thousands more have suffered life-long health impacts, let alone the continuing environmental damage. In the now radioactive waste-filled bomb craters on the atolls America has also dumped 130 tons of nuclear waste from its Nevada test sites. One infamous nuclear waste burial site, the dome or "Tomb" on Runit Island on Eniwetok, is leaking into a surrounding lagoon. When the Marshallese demanded it be dealt with they were informed that the lagoon was so contaminated that added radioactive waste from the Tomb would be virtually undetectable there or in the wider ocean waters! In Rongelap the fallout from the 1954 Bikini Atoll *Castle Bravo* test led to residents' evacuation, albeit 12 hours later; they were encouraged to return after three years. Hidden from the people was that the US wanted to allow researchers to study the effects of lingering radiation on the peoples of Rongelap. In 1956, Merrill Eisenbud from

---

49. Rust 2019; Maclellan 2017 and 2023.

the US Atomic Energy Commission justified the return, claiming that "Data of this type has never been available. While it is true that these people do not live in the way that Westerners do, civilized people, it is nonetheless also true that they are more like us than the mice".[50]

In their attempts to get compensation Marshall Islanders have been denied standing to sue the US courts and while an independent US-Marshall Islands Nuclear Claims Tribunal did award $2 billion in damages, only $4 million of that has been paid. In 2023 US stalling on aid to the Islands was quickly reversed when neighbours Kiribati and Solomon Islands developed ties with mainland China. Former US Secretary of State Mike Pompeo was dispatched to Micronesia, promising a secure military presence and working rights for Marshallese in America, as well as renewing an economic pact that was due to expire.

Black mist, burnt country: Australia's nuclear role
Unspeakable horrors also occurred in Australia where British nuclear tests left a legacy of destruction for local Aboriginal groups. Between 1952 and 1963 Britain held twelve weapons and components trials – Operation Hurricane and the Mosaic series at Monte Bello Islands, the Totem series at Emu Field and Buffalo and Antler trials at Maralinga. The last test was at Maralinga in 1963.[51]

In 1953 Indigenous activist Jessie Lennon, her family and many others were suddenly exposed to fallout from the Totem I nuclear blast. In her book *I'm the one that know this country!* she recalls the horror, the bewilderment, the sicknesses, miscarriages and cancers that followed – and the ensuing anger and activism in the fight for compensation. "The bomb caught us then at Twelve Mile... 'Something **wrong!**'... bluish smoke rolled over...filled up the hills, the holes – rolled along the ground – to the tree tops... Right over the top of us".[52]

"The wrenching irony and tragedy of Totem", Elizabeth Tynan reveals in her exposé of the Emu Field tests, "for both the Aboriginal people and the military personnel caught up in the tests were that the

---

50. As quoted in Rust 2019.
51. For a comprehensive expose of the nuclear testing fallout from these sites see Tynan 2016 and 2022.
52. Lennon 2011, p.88–9. Emphasis in the original.

harm was caused in pursuit of technology that was soon to become obsolete".[53] Attempts to obtain compensation or ensure clean-up and remediation, either from British or Australian governments, have been delayed and inadequate. In Maralinga and Emu Field the land was grudgingly handed back in 1984 and 1996, effectively minimising government responsibility.

Once again, these tests were done in the interests of empire – for both Britain and Australia – with next to no concern for local populations, or for workers involved in production or testing. Britain was close to bankruptcy at the end of the war, but the imperialist imperative to become the third nuclear superpower was clear. Foreign secretary, Labour's Ernest Bevin said: "We've got to have this thing over here whatever it costs... We've got to have the bloody Union Jack on top of it".[54] Refused closer ties with the US and denied access by Canada, in 1950 Britain turned to Australia for testing grounds, attracted by the "vast, empty spaces" and availability of uranium. It was a win for Australia too, as one local paper editorialised: "Almost overnight we have emerged as a prospective major supplier of the precious and coveted ore, source of the military power in the present and of industrial power in the not distant future".[55]

Immediately postwar in Australia, Labor as much as Liberal wanted nuclear bomb capabilities, though it was to be the Menzies Liberal-Country Party coalition that oversaw Australia's attempt at atomic engagement. Protecting the nation from the postwar "communist threat" – by enabling a superpower's nuclear arsenal through testing and building supporting infrastructure in Australia – was to be Menzies' justification for this escalation in military expansion.[56]

In one of his weekly "Man to Man" radio talks, Menzies played down any notion of danger from radioactive contamination, while stoking fears about Russia and China.

---

53. Tynan 2022, p.4; p.63.
54. Tynan 201,6 p.115.
55. *The Rockhampton Morning Bulletin*, 15 October 1953, quoted in Tynan 2016, p.235. Wayne Reynolds' important analysis expands on the expected industrial bonanza the Australian ruling class planned for. Reynolds 1997.
56. Reynolds 1997.

> There is tremendous public interest in Atomic Bombs...
> Unfortunately there are scare stories, wild allegations and
> between you and me, a good deal of nonsense... But we must
> face the facts. And they are that the threat to the world's peace
> does not come from the Americans or the British, but from
> aggressive Communist-Imperialism. In this dreadful state of
> affairs, superiority in atomic weapons is vital. To that superiority
> Australia must contribute as best she can.[57]

Postwar most nations saw nuclear war as the way of the future and
wanted to develop their own industries. Such a move could, as Wayne
Reynolds in his book *Australia's bid for the atomic bomb* points out,
also be an economic boost. To have a nuclear state required a major
reorienting of industry, building a strong academic base in science
and technology and significant investment in military hardware – the
aircraft, naval and land-based rocket launchers necessary to deliver
the weapons. In Australia the Snowy Mountains Scheme, a secure
water and power source, the development of a strong research base
at the Australian National University and other major projects were
harnessed for this future state.[58]

In comparison to such major outlays to nuclearise defence, little
attention was paid then or since to dealing with the "eternity" waste
left by both power plants and weapons. At Emu Field, for example,
the area was barely touched in the so-called clean-up, though some
equipment was removed at the time, including a tank used on site to
measure exposure to radiation. Still radioactive, the vehicle was sent to
the Puckapunyal army base then shipped to Vietnam for the war there.
Hundreds of thousands of radioactive trinitite glass fragments, buried
vehicles and other decaying structures litter the area still. There are
almost no living creatures to be seen in the area to this day.[59]

And today, governments whether Labor or Liberal are adopting

---

57. Tynan 2022, p.200.
58. Reynolds 1997. See also Walsh 1997.
59. Trinitite contains trapped radioactive materials including plutonium; Tynan 2022,
    pp.84-5. The "minor" Kitten tests at Emu Field caused chemical and radioactive
    contamination.

the same Orwellian double-speak, the same repressive legislation, the same disregard for clean-up or remediation and war preparedness in the latest imperialist posturing. The current AUKUS nuclear submarine deal, an eye-watering $368 billion spend, has no feasible plans for waste storage to protect us from contamination. This is despite the agreement binding Australia to dispose of the spent fuel, a deal which can only be made possible by overriding the various federal and state laws which have a variety of prohibitions on travel, disposal or use of radioactive materials.[60]

The 2023 Defence Strategic Review has fuelled the ALP's march to war in more conventional hardware. Military spending must be a priority, Treasurer Jim Chalmers told *The Australian*, because "when we look out to the region, we see intensifying great power competition, rising tensions, military build-up".[61] In mid-January 2024 acting Defence Minister Paul Conroy described Australia's newest $37 million long-range missile purchases from Lockheed Martin, a company that openly profiteers from wars (for example, its fighter jets currently bombing Gaza), as "contributing to peace and stability in the Indo-Pacific".[62] Corporate vultures (venture capitalists) in the three AUKUS countries are already circling, looking to profiteer out of the massively expanded military spend, both nuclear and conventional. Heather Jo Richman, chair of the newly formed AUKUS Defense Investor Network, boasted about the "really ripe opportunities" from Australia's rare earth and mineral deposits that Network members could expedite getting "into the hands of the warfighters".[63]

Modernisation and expansion of nuclear arsenals by the world's nine nuclear-armed nations continues despite the newest Treaty on the Prohibition of Nuclear Weapons.[64] The treaty prohibits all aspects of nuclear weapons, from development and deployment to stockpiling and even the threat of use. Australia, while signing the Treaty, has left

---

60. These include the federal Environment Protection and Biodiversity Conservation Act and the Australian Radiation Protection and Nuclear Safety Act, as well as other restrictions in every state and territory's legislation.
61. Benson 2024.
62. As quoted in Wareham 2024.
63. Nilsson 2024.
64. United Nations Treaty Collection 2024.

the door wide open for the expansion of nuclear weapons capability with its AUKUS deal on submarines and providing harbours for US nuclear-fuelled and armed submarines, in addition to the long-standing spy bases at Pine Gap and Nurrungar (effectively American-controlled) and expanded stationing of US troops and nuclear weapons-armed B52 bombers in northern Australia.

The warmongers are, as one writer argues, exacting a high price on most of us just to "keep the factories of the merchants of death humming and the generals and admirals happy".[65] Armageddon is coming closer, warns the Bulletin of Atomic Scientists, as it moved the Doomsday Clock to 90 seconds to midnight.

Over 100 years ago, in the midst of the first imperialist world war, Rosa Luxemburg wrote that the international working class faced a future of either barbarism or socialism. Today the possibility of nuclear war has brought us ever closer to barbarism.

References

Astore, WJ 2023, "Talking and writing honestly about war", *Bracing Views*, 8 September. https://bracingviews.com/2023/09/08/talking-and-writing-honestly-about-war/

Atomic Heritage Foundation 2016, "Native Americans and the Manhattan Project", 28 June. https://ahf.nuclearmuseum.org/ahf/history/native-americans-and-manhattan-project/

Bhagavad-Gita, 11:32, attributed to Krishna Dvaipayana (also called Veda-Vyasa), https://www.holy-bhagavad-gita.org/chapter/11/verse/32

Benson, Simon 2024, "Anthony Albanese on the frontline to fast-track defence fix", *The Australian*, 20 January. https://www.theaustralian.com.au/nation/politics/anthony-albanese-on-the-frontline-to-fasttrack-defence-fix/news-story/f572e74c44580073866b7fab6376061c

Bullimore, Kim 2023, "Imperialism, racism and the atomic bomb", *Red Flag*, 21 August. https://redflag.org.au/article/imperialism-racism-and-atomic-bomb?fbclid=IwAR1BBT_A_OacnP5S42GVgcUcolrAa8NmhnrENYkkAAQpJL40pq8uxOomNBk

Callinicos, Alex 2023, *The new age of catastrophe*, Polity.

---

65.   Astore 2023.

Columbia River Keeper, "Cleaning up Hanford", viewed 21 February 2024. https://www.columbiariverkeeper.org/about-us/strategic-plan/cleaning-hanford

Democracy Now 2003. https://www.democracynow.org/2003/1/21/if_new_mexico_seceded_it_would

Dininny, Shannon 2004, "Umatilla tribes say they'll sue over environment at Hanford", *Seattlepi*, 6 October. https://www.seattlepi.com/seattlenews/article/umatilla-tribes-say-they-ll-sue-over-environment-1156031.php

The Economist 2023, "What to make of a surprise shake-up in China's nuclear force", 3 August. https://www.economist.com/china/2023/08/03/what-to-make-of-a-surprise-shake-up-in-chinas-nuclear-force

Engelhardt, Tom 2004, "Hiroshima Story", *TomDispatch*, 5 August. https://tomdispatch.com/three-characters-no-dialogue/

Frank, Joshua 2022, *Atomic Days: The untold story of the most toxic place in America*, Haymarket.

Groch, Sherryn and Chris Zappone 2022, "Who has nukes, and what do Russia's nuclear threats mean?", *The Age*, 3 April. https://www.theage.com.au/national/who-has-nukes-and-what-do-russia-s-nuclear-threats-mean-20220330-p5a9an.html

Haldane, Andy 2023, "The global industrial arms race is just what we need", *Financial Times*, 26 June. https://www.ft.com/content/45f57bc8-d2b2-4a23-88aa-b04d290b54a8

Hanford Challenge, viewed 21 February 2024. https://www.hanfordchallenge.org/

Hartung, William D 2021, "The profits of war: How corporate America cashed in on the post-9/11 Pentagon spending surge", *International Socialism Project*, 30 September. https://internationalsocialism.net/author/william-d-hartung/

Holden, Darren 2019, *Mark Oliphant and the Invisible College of the Peaceful Atom*, PhD thesis. https://researchonline.nd.edu.au/theses/270/

Johnson, Jake 2022, "'A terrifying document': Critics say Biden nuclear policy makes the world more dangerous", *Common Dreams*, 27 October. https://www.commondreams.org/news/2022/10/27/terrifying-document-critics-say-biden-nuclear-policy-makes-world-more-dangerous

Kidron, Michael 1967, "A permanent arms economy", *International Socialism*, 1:28, Spring 1967, pp.8–12. https://www.marxists.org/archive/kidron/works/1967/xx/permarms.htm

Kuznick, Peter 2011, "Japan's nuclear history in perspective: Eisenhower and atoms for war and peace", *Bulletin of the Atomic Scientists*, 13 April. https://thebulletin.org/2011/04/japans-nuclear-history-in-perspective-eisenhower-and-atoms-for-war-and-peace-2/

Lee Ack, Tess 2023, "Why the US bombed Hiroshima and Nagasaki", *Red Flag*, 6 August. https://redflag.org.au/article/why-us-bombed-hiroshima-and-nagasaki

Lennon, Jessie 2011, *I'm the one that know this country!*, Aboriginal Studies Press, 2nd edition.

Luxemburg, Rosa 1915, *The crisis of German Social Democracy. The Junius Pamphlet*. https://www.marxists.org/archive/luxemburg/1915/junius/index.htm

Maclellan, Nic 2017, "Grappling with the Bomb. Britain's Pacific H-bomb tests", ANU Press. https://press.anu.edu.au/publications/series/pacific/grappling-bomb

Maclellan, Nic 2023, "Preserving nuclear memories", *Inside Story*, 20 November. https://insidestory.org.au/preserving-nuclear-memories/

Maley, Leo III and Uday Hohan 2001, "Hiroshima: military voices of dissent", *Origins*, Ohio State University, July. https://origins.osu.edu/history-news/hiroshima-military-voices-dissent?language_content_entity=en

Montague, Brendan 2023, "Oppenheimer will blow you away", *Ecologist*, 20 July. https://theecologist.org/2023/jul/20/oppenheimer-will-blow-you-away?fbclid=IwAR11WhDFzXVhZVlLopjYpnQJjAiAuB3tY5_1TKK-2ejKVYr-jkQBH-NVJQ4

Nilsson, Anton 2024, "AUKUS will be a feast for US venture capitalists – but will Australian firms get a slice of the cake?", *Crikey*, 18 January. https://www.crikey.com.au/2024/01/18/aukus-usa-venture-capitalists-australian-firms-defence/

Physics arXiv Blog 2023, "The Trinity nuclear test spread radioactive fallout across America", *Discover*, 27 July. https://www.discovermagazine.com/planet-earth/how-the-trinity-nuclear-test-spread-radioactive-fallout-across-america?utm_campaign=organicsocial&utm_content=%F0%9F%92%A5%E2%98%A2%EF%B8%8F_the_trinity_nuclear_t&utm_medium=social&utm_source=facebook&fbclid=IwAR1avF7IYOoaeFyKU0Q2OpxunYxaHYrzRm-dTQolHVVNyvyudM8SOdlwRrU

Physicians and Scientists for Global Responsibility New Zealand 2012, "Depleted Uranium. Why depleted uranium should be banned from New Zealand". https://psgr.org.nz/component/jdownloads/send/5-depleted-uranium/52-psgr-2012-depleted-uranium

Ramirez, Rachel 2020, *"Poisoning the Pacific*: New book details US military contamination of islands and ocean", *Guardian*, 11 October. https://www. theguardian.com/world/2020/oct/11/poisoning-the-pacific-new-book-details-us-military-contamination-of-islands-and-ocean

Reynolds, Wayne 1997, *Australia's Bid for the Atomic Bomb*, Melbourne University Publishing.

Rust, Susanne 2019, "How the U.S. betrayed the Marshall Islands, kindling the next nuclear disaster", *LA Times*, 10 November. https://www.latimes.com/projects/marshall-islands-nuclear-testing-sea-level-rise/

Sanders, Alan 1986, "The hot rock in the Cold War: uranium in the 1950s", in Ann Curthoys and John Merritt (eds), *Better Dead than Red. Australia's first Cold War: 1945-1959*, Vol.1, pp.155–69, Allen & Unwin.

Sauer, Pjotr 2023, "Vladimir Putin escalates nuclear rhetoric with threat to resume testing", *Guardian*, 6 October. https://www.theguardian.com/world/2023/oct/05/vladimir-putin-escalates-nuclear-rhetoric-with-threat-to-resume-testing

Sherratt, Timothy Paul 2003, *Atomic Wonderland: science and progress in twentieth century Australia*, PhD thesis. https://openresearch-repository.anu.edu.au/handle/1885/146417?mode=full

Tanaka, Yuki and Howard Zinn 2010, "Hiroshima: Breaking the silence", *The Asia-Pacific Journal*, 21 June. https://apjjf.org/-Yuki-Tanaka/3375/article.html

Tacitus, Caius Cornelius 96, "The life of Cnaeus Julius Agricola", in *The Germany and the Agricola of Tacitus*. https://www.gutenberg.org/files/7524/7524-h/7524-h.htm

Tasevski, Olivia 2020, "'Hey, let's forget that': No apology for the atomic bombings of Hiroshima and Nagasaki", *The Diplomat*, 25 August. https://thediplomat.com/2020/08/hey-lets-forget-that-no-us-apology-for-the-atomic-bombings-of-hiroshima-and-nagasaki/

Taylor, D 2023, "Oppenheimer: an American Stalinist tragedy", *Red Flag*, 19 July. https://redflag.org.au/article/oppenheimer-american-stalinist-tragedy

Tynan, Elizabeth 2016, *Atomic Thunder: the Maralinga Story*, New South Books.

Tynan, Elizabeth 2022, *The secret of Emu Field. Britain's forgotten atomic tests in Australia*, New South Books.

United Nations Treaty Collection 2024, Chapter XXVI, Disarmament, 9, "Treaty on the prohibition of Nuclear Weapons", 7 July 2017. https://treaties.un.org/pages/ViewDetails.aspx?src=TREATY&mtdsg_no=XXVI-9&chapter=26

Ward, Chip 2008, "Big bad boom. Radioactive Déjà Vu in the American West", *TomDispatch*, 19 June. https://tomdispatch.com/chip-ward-uranium-frenzy-in-the-west/

Walsh, Jim 1997, "Surprise Down Under: the secret history of Australia's nuclear ambitions", *The Nonproliferation Review*, Fall. https://www.nonproliferation.org/wp-content/uploads/npr/walsh51.pdf

Wareham, Sue 2024, "We're being sold a false choice on war", *Pearls and Irritations*, 24 January. https://johnmenadue.com/were-being-sold-a-false-choice-on-war/

Wheeler, Joshua 2023, "In the shadow of Oppenheimer", *Distillations Magazine*, *Science History Institute*, 16 July. https://www.sciencehistory.org/stories/magazine/in-the-shadow-of-oppenheimer/

World Nuclear Association 2023, "Plutonium", August. https://world-nuclear.org/information-library/nuclear-fuel-cycle/fuel-recycling/plutonium.aspx#ECSArticleLi

World Nuclear Association 2024, "Nuclear power in the world today", March. https://world-nuclear.org/information-library/current-and-future-generation/nuclear-power-in-the-world-today.aspx

Yoshida, Helen 2021, "Redress and reparations for Japanese American incarceration", National WWII Museum, 13 August. https://www.nationalww2museum.org/war/articles/redress-and-reparations-japanese-american-incarceration#:~:text=This%20law%20gave%20surviving%20Japanese,the%20redress%20movement%20into%20legislation

ELEANOR MORLEY

The assault on workers in Australia

Eleanor Morley is a socialist activist in
Sydney and an editor of *Red Flag*.

A USTRALIAN WORKERS HAVE been hit with the biggest drop in
living standards in half a century. Since the end of 2021, real
household disposable income has fallen from $62,000 a year
on average to $56,000, according to Australian Bureau of Statistics data.
And little is being done to alleviate the hardship.

In the 2010s, living standards didn't increase much. But they
jumped during the pandemic because of increased financial support
from governments and the inability of households to spend much
under the lockdowns. However they've been rapidly falling in recent
years, for several reasons.

First is rising consumer prices. Over the past three years,
prices have risen by more than 16 percent, according to the latest
quarterly consumer price index figures from the Bureau of Statistics.
Non-discretionary items (things you generally *must* pay for, such as
food, electricity and rent) have gone up by nearly 20 percent. While
headline inflation has dropped in recent months, things aren't getting
cheaper – prices are just rising at a slower pace than they were twelve
months ago.

With rising food prices, more people are relying on charity to get
by. One-third of households experienced moderate or severe food
insecurity in 2023, meaning they compromised on their meal choices

or skipped whole meals or days of eating, according to the latest Foodbank Hunger Report. Three-quarters of those experiencing food insecurity did so for the first time that year.

Inflated prices have been blamed on supply chain disruptions, Russia's invasion of Ukraine and catastrophic weather events. But another major factor has been the opportunistic profiteering of business owners. An Australia Institute report found that in 2022, Australian companies increased prices by $160 billion above their increased costs for wages, taxes and other inputs. That's an extra $160 billion taken from consumers and pocketed as profits. The banks, supermarkets, energy companies and airlines are all in on it, recording record profits and payouts to shareholders. For instance, Woolworths' net profit increased by 4.6 percent to $1.2 billion in the last financial year; the big four banks have recorded higher profits in the last couple of years than their 15-year average; and Origin Energy announced an 84 percent surge in annual profit in August last year (while energy prices were basically doubling).

Second is the housing crisis. Twenty-five years ago, the average house was worth nine times the average disposable household income; now it's sixteen and a half times, according to data from the Bureau of Statistics. Prices have risen astonishingly in some cities: 57 percent in Adelaide since the end of 2019, 51 percent in Brisbane and 38 percent in Sydney. Sydney's median house price is now $1.6 million.

So a lot of people are taking on a lot more debt, which has become more expensive to service. The average new mortgage nationally is about $620,000. Increasingly, young people can't buy into the market without help – parental assistance for new home purchases is up from 12 percent in 2010 to 75 percent today.

Repayments on expiring fixed rate mortgages taken out before interest rates started rising in 2022 have increased by an average of 64 percent. Average monthly mortgage repayments now range from $2,855 in the Northern Territory to $5,118 in New South Wales, according to calculations by Forbes Advisor Australia. To take a whole set of averages, a single person with an average mortgage on the average income would need to spend 3.6 weeks of every month's wage on mortgage repayments – this is clearly impossible.

What do you do if you can't buy a house? You rent, of course. But there's serious trouble there as well. On average, rents have gone up by about one-third since mid-2020, and this trend is accelerating. In the first three months of this year, capital city rents rose faster than any other three-month period for the last 17 years, according to a report from property website Domain. And forking out a significant chunk of your income to a landlord is now a perverse privilege; rental vacancies are at a record low of 1 percent.

Again, this is a crime with a culprit. Decades of Labor and Liberal housing policy have encouraged speculative investment in housing. Extensive tax concessions have helped a small minority purchase an increasing share of dwellings, while public housing stock has been annihilated, forcing an upward trend in prices for the rest of the housing market.

Third, wages have not kept up with inflation. Rising prices wouldn't be such an issue if wages were keeping pace. But since March 2021, wages have risen on average by 9 percent, while inflation rose 14.6 percent. The last three years have wiped out more than a decade of wage growth. As house prices jumped 30–50 percent over the last five years, wages rose only 12 percent.

Real wages (wages adjusted for inflation) started to rise a little last year: the wage price index rose 4.2 percent while inflation rose 4.05 percent. But there are caveats to this. Wages have not risen more than inflation on non-discretionary items (which is basically all that lower-income households are currently buying), and they have not risen for all workers.

Consequently, household savings are rapidly being depleted. Many households built savings buffers during the lockdowns, which helped to soften the financial blow of the last few years. But a report by comparison website Finder estimates that almost half of all households have less than $1,000 saved, and one in five have nothing at all. Only the top 20 percent of households have maintained their savings – these are people who earn so much that they are relatively unscathed by the cost-of-living pressures.

The one small solace of the last few years has been that unemployment has not risen sharply. When interest rates started to rise in

2022, many economists assumed that this would force a recession and push up unemployment. This hasn't eventuated – for now at least. Nevertheless, unemployment is slightly ticking up from 3.5 percent in March 2023 to 3.8 percent this March, and is rising faster for young people (youth unemployment is often a bellwether for broader unemployment trends). Also, many people *with* a job do not get paid enough to make ends meet – more than a half of those suffering from food insecurity have at least one family member in paid work.

The only options available to people to deal with these financial pressures are to reduce their standard of living by reducing consumption, work more or take on debt.

According to the Bureau of Statistics, household spending plateaued late last year, rising only 0.1 percent, while spending on discretionary items fell by 0.9 percent compared to the same period the previous year. In the December quarter, businesses ran down the amount of stock they had on shelves and in storage: why stock items no-one can buy?

The number of people working more than one job has increased to a record high of almost 1 million, and credit card debt (which has an average interest rate of 18 percent) is up 17 percent since September 2021, according to Reserve Bank figures.

That's the statistical round up of where things are at, but to simplify the picture: over the last few years prices have gone up, real wages have gone down and people are taking on larger amounts of debt. Life is getting a lot tougher for millions of people.

Meanwhile, the total wealth of Australia's billionaires increased by 70 percent in the first three years of this decade, according to the latest Oxfam Inequality Report, and fully doubled for the richest three Australians – two mining barons and a property developer.

The Labor government has done little to ease the cost-of-living crisis. This is not surprising, considering the message they took into the 2022 federal election. When Albanese replaced Bill Shorten as party leader in 2019, he axed Labor's mild program of wealth redistribution that included tackling generous tax concessions to the middle class and wealthy. Just days before the election, Jim Chalmers, the soon-to-be

Treasurer, told the National Press Club: "We want to be a pro-business, pro-employer Labor party".[1]

Albanese tried to be a little more balanced on election night, saying: "We can work in common interests with business and unions to drive productivity, lift wages and profits".[2] But in order to provide relief for the millions of people struggling with rising costs, the government needs to make capital pay in one way or another: price caps, a super profits tax, restricting property investment. Capitalism is a zero-sum game between bosses and workers, particularly when the economy is in trouble. But Labor is first and foremost the "pro-business" government.

It has claimed the tiniest of measures as great victories, for instance a $40 increase to fortnightly welfare payments and $500 energy subsidy for very-low-income households. But these are measly figures, and the households that receive them are still worse off than they were three years ago. They also only apply to a minority of people, welfare recipients, which holds to the neoliberal idea that government assistance should only happen on a small scale and only for the very poorest, rather than expansive policies that would benefit the working class as a whole.

Labor has trumpeted the Housing Australia Future Fund (HAFF) as a major step in tackling the housing crisis. But when you crunch the numbers, the new funding is enough to build around 6,000 homes a year. There are currently 175,000 people on the social housing waitlist, and it's increasing by 10–15,000 a year – so this policy won't even keep pace with the rate in which the waitlist is *increasing*, let alone start to reduce it.

In January, Labor announced changes to the deeply unpopular Stage 3 tax cuts, a Liberal government policy that was set to give the rich an extra $9,000 a year, while taxes on middle-income earners would increase. That Labor felt compelled to amend the policy after defending it for years reflects mounting popular pressure about the cost-of-living crisis and a dip in opinion polls for the government at the end of last year. But the new version is still a regressive tax policy. Those in the top income bracket (who earn more than $190,000 a year)

1. Chalmers 2022.
2. Albanese 2022.

will receive a $4,500 reduction in their tax bill, while middle income earners will receive only a $780 benefit. The lowest 40 percent of income earners will receive less than 10 percent of the total benefits.

In response to growing pressure about supermarket prices, the government commissioned a review headed by former Labor minister Craig Emerson. But the findings, which were handed down in April, will, if anything, raise prices for consumers. The inquiry focused on the relationship between the major supermarkets and their suppliers, and recommended a series of measures that would improve the bargaining power of suppliers. The supermarkets can then simply pass on any extra costs to consumers. Emerson tried to square this circle in an opinion piece for the *Financial Review*, arguing that suppliers would be better able to invest in "innovation and equipment that would enable them to offer better-quality products at lower prices".[3] This argument exists in the same fantasy land as trickle-down economics.

It's easy to think of policies that would *actually* ease the burden. In addition to those listed above, the government could substantially lift welfare payments and public sector wages, build more public housing and cap rents.

And it's not as though Labor isn't spending any money. It has committed $370 billion to purchasing nuclear-powered submarines, provides more than $11 billion a year in subsidies and tax breaks to the fossil fuel industry, forgoes $50 billion a year with its property investor tax incentives and is cutting income taxes to benefit high income earners disproportionately.

The Greens under the leadership of Adam Bandt have taken something of a social democratic turn. Their strategy in the last election was less about challenging the Liberal Party in some inner-city blue-ribbon seats (a mantle taken up by the Teal independents), and more about relating to young people and those frustrated by Labor's right-wing politics.

Since Labor took office, the Greens have publicly criticised some of the worst aspects of the government, most recently its response to the genocide in Gaza. They have positioned themselves as the party of

3. Emerson 2024.

renters, opposed the regressive Stage 3 tax cuts and called for Labor to raise the rate of welfare to $88 a day.

But political parties must be judged not just by what they say, but by what they do. And the Greens have done little. Despite holding the balance of power in the Senate, the Greens have not used this to force substantial concessions out of Labor. After criticising key policies like the HAFF, they have folded and ended up voting them through. This is no way to mount a challenge to a right-wing government.

For years, the primary strategy of the Greens has in effect been to hold the balance of power during a Labor government, and then negotiate from this position of strength. They have achieved this twice, from 2010 to 2013, and again at the last election. But this strategy has borne no fruit for progressive social change. In 2010, all the Greens achieved was the establishment of the Parliamentary Budget Office – a measure that is unlikely to make it to the history books. They are failing even on their own terms.

The party's glaring weakness is its commitment to electoral politics as the main, even only, way to change society. The Greens still occasionally refer to their activist roots, and some Greens politicians will speak at rallies or share activist events on social media. But they are not trying to mobilise their membership or support base to rebuild social movements or a combative union movement. This has been notable at the weekly demonstrations in solidarity with Palestine in Melbourne and Sydney, where at best only a handful of Greens flags can be spotted in the crowds.

Like all political parties, their strategy flows from their analysis of the world: that capitalism is not in and of itself the problem, it just needs to be better regulated by intelligent politicians. Bandt spelled this out in an interview with *The Monthly* in 2020, arguing he would rather his daughters "live a long life under Green capitalism than a short, nasty, brutish life facing climate collapse".[4] But the Green capitalism Bandt longs for is another fantasy – one only need look at the escalating carbon emissions, deforestation and rising temperatures.

---

4.   Simons 2020.

Having a few extra Greens MPs sitting in Canberra has done precisely nothing to turn the situation around.

More recently, the Greens have embraced the supposed power of competitive market forces as a tool to tackle rising supermarket prices. In March, they introduced a bill seeking to introduce divestiture powers into Australian competition law to allow regulators to break up the supermarket duopoly. As though opening more IGAs or bringing back Franklins is going to lighten the load.

Nevertheless, the Greens are widening their support base, particularly among young voters. At the last election, they secured 12.2 percent of the general vote, but won a third of 18- to 34-year-olds. This likely reflects a new generation of voters who feel little hope about a future of skyrocketing housing costs and runaway climate change. It's an important shift among young people, which hopefully can be funnelled into a more fruitful political project in the future.

The other institution one might expect to fight for workers in a time like this is the trade union movement. Again, things have been sadly lacking on this front. Union density is at an all-time low of 12.5 percent – which drops to 5 percent for workers in their early- to mid-20s – but there are still around 1.4 million union members in Australia. If mobilised, this power would be formidable.

But the approach of the Australian Council of Trade Unions has not been to organise and fight. Instead, it has pumped out endless surveys, inquiries and press releases. This is an elaborate way of doing nothing.

It's been a long time since there was a genuinely combative union movement in Australia, but it's even worse under an ALP government. The union leaders are structurally and politically tied to the Labor Party and basically function as a wing of the government when Labor is in office. The unions talk a lot about the cost-of-living crisis, but their fire is aimed solely at major corporations, without a peep about the government. This is an utter betrayal of the union membership considering the scale of the assault on workers in Australia.

Looking at how union politics have played out on a state level in recent years is instructive. There was an uptick in the number of workers going on strike in 2021 to 2022, largely due to a few big public sector strikes such as those by teachers and nurses in NSW when

Dominic Perrottet's Liberal government was in office. But the outcome was dismal. The unions wrapped up their campaign in the lead-up to the 2023 NSW state election and jumped on board Chris Minns' Labor campaign. Only the teachers won a pay rise above inflation, which was partly reflective of the fact they were the worst paid teachers in the country and there were serious concerns that too many would leave the state during a teaching crisis.

Meanwhile, in Victoria the situation was even worse. The Australian Education Union signed with the Daniel Andrews Labor government to accept a 1.5 percent pay cap while inflation was already running above 5 percent.

All of this could very well amount to a potential opportunity for the right. The European far right, and Trump, surged in popularity following the economic devastation of the Global Financial Crisis and austerity. While the same phenomenon is yet to gain prominence in Australia, we're starting to get a whiff of it.

Peter Dutton is trying to make a running from right-wing attacks on the Labor government and a series of racist scare campaigns. This is partly just reverting to the traditional Liberal party playbook, and partly because Dutton has little else to offer. The Liberals – who remain Australian capitalism's A team – will not introduce sweeping economic reforms, even if they take the occasional populist potshots.

Last year, Dutton argued that a surge in migration was responsible for the housing crisis. For the last 18 months, there has been a recurring hysteria about Indigenous children in Alice Springs, culminating in an evening curfew for under-18-year-olds in March and April. More recently, refugees have been in the firing line.

The Liberals are not the only ones fanning the flames. The mainstream media has predictably amplified every racist comment and fed the moral panics. Labor has either capitulated or been a willing participant in all these issues – it's a Labor government in the Northern Territory that has swelled the number of cops on the streets of Alice Springs, and the Albanese government that is trying to imprison refugees who do not comply with their own deportation and to deny visas to residents of entire countries.

While Labor continues to do nothing to address the cost-of-living crisis, more people could be open to such arguments. After all, immigrants and refugees have long been a useful scapegoat for the neoliberal hellscape. Migration is at the centre of right-wing politics in the UK, US and Europe.

On the whole, it is a bleak time for Australian workers and politics. But there are some bright spots. That thousands of people have rallied week in and week out against a genocide happening on the other side of the world is cause for hope; as is the growing youth dissatisfaction with the state of society and mainstream political parties. Polling indicates that millennials are not following the well-trodden path of shifting to the right once they hit their mid-30s.

Dissatisfaction and despair can head in several different directions: depressed resignation, a right-wing backlash that picks the wrong targets to blame, or progressive movements that fight to make the world a better place. Politics and organisation determine how people respond at a time like this. We need to rebuild a genuine fighting left, in politics and in the unions. A left that won't capitulate, compromise and sell out.

References

Albanese, Anthony 2022, "Prime Minister-elect Anthony Albanese's victory speech in full", *The Sydney Morning Herald*, 22 May. https://www.smh.com.au/politics/federal/prime-minister-elect-anthony-albanese-s-victory-speech-in-full-20220522-p5andv.html

Chalmers, Jim 2022, "National Press Club Q&A", 5 April. https://jimchalmers.org/latest-news/transcripts/national-press-club-q-a-05-04-22/

Emerson, Craig 2024, "Compulsory grocery code strikes right balance", *Financial Review*, 7 April. https://www.afr.com/companies/retail/compulsory-grocery-code-strikes-right-balance-20240407-p5fhx6

Simons, Margaret 2020, "Adam Bandt, the personable hardliner", *The Monthly*, May. https://www.themonthly.com.au/issue/2020/may/1588255200/margaret-simons/adam-bandt-personable-hardliner#mtr

LIAM KRUGER

Green growth, degrowth and a humanist Marxism

Liam Kruger is a socialist activist and has
been involved in campaigns for climate
justice, Palestine and against the far right.

Capital...allows its actual movement to be determined as much
or as little by the sight of the coming degradation and final
depopulation of the human race, as by the probable fall of the
earth into the sun. ...everyone knows that some time or other
the crash must come, but everyone hopes that it may fall on the
head of his neighbour, after he himself has caught the shower of
gold and placed it in his secure hands. *Après moi, le déluge!* (After
me, the flood!) is the watchword of every capitalist and of every
capitalist nation.

– Karl Marx[1]

Marx says that revolutions are the locomotive of world history.
But perhaps it is quite otherwise. Perhaps revolutions are an
attempt by passengers on this train – namely, the human race – to
activate the emergency brake.

– Walter Benjamin[2]

1.   Marx 1976, pp.380–1.
2.   Benjamin 2003, p.402.

C APITALISM IS DESTROYING the planet. A climate report released at the end of 2023 emphasises that "we are entering an unfamiliar domain regarding our climate crisis, a situation no one has ever witnessed firsthand in the history of humanity".[3] Despite the propaganda in the capitalist press green energy is not being taken up fast enough to prevent catastrophes, and the elevated threat of extreme weather events can already be seen.[4]

Responding to the climate crisis and related environmental destruction is urgent, but politically contested. At the centre of this lies the key question: can the capitalist system be restructured to enable a sustainable future, or indeed any future for humanity at all? The climate movement is divided on this point. Advocates of green growth assert that the system merely needs to be responsibly managed – that with the right policies the economy and environment can be balanced. In contrast are those who argue that a change in the system of production is needed to solve the climate crisis. They understand, albeit to varying degrees, that it is the normal functioning of capitalism that results in climate change and environmental degradation. Within this anti-capitalist camp, however, there is no single coherent program for changing the world. Many have taken up degrowth theory, which insists that the economy must be shrunk to ensure it remains within environmental limits.

This article will engage with various green growth, degrowth and ecosocialist thinkers to try to construct a Marxist approach to these issues. Key questions relating to the nature of growth will be drawn out, as well as an understanding of science, and of labour as a means by which humans relate to the natural world. Given that most degrowth theorists base their assumptions on the creation of a post-capitalist society, issues arise surrounding the animating forces of such a society, such as what would drive it and, more fundamentally, how it can be achieved.

One question I want to address now is whether Marxists have anything to gain from engaging in debates on the nature of post-capitalist societies. A common, and not at all incorrect, response from

---

3.   Ripple et al. 2023.
4.   Ripple et al. 2023.

revolutionary socialists is to assert that the solution to the climate crisis is a socialist revolution. And given the challenges to achieve such a feat, speculating about how to organise a post-revolutionary society is futile. However, through this article I hope to show that there is a lot to be gained by applying the Marxist method and historical approach to contemporary environmental debates, including on the nature of a social organisation under a speculative communist society. Doing so can shine light on key assumptions and conclusions of Marxism. These include the necessary distinction between universal and historically contingent human social relations, the nature of the forces of production, the ever-evolving relationship of human society to nature through changes in labour and science, and a Marxist understanding of growth.

I will begin by arguing why green growth is impossible under capitalism. Degrowth and its history will then be discussed, before I move on to some direct debates between socialist green growth and degrowth advocates and a critique of the attempted synthesis of Marxism with degrowth in the works of Kohei Saito. I will argue for the fundamental incompatibility of degrowth with Marxism, concluding with an analysis of science and labour under capitalism, and why a Marxist vision for a communist future is one motivated by freedom, not degrowth.

Green growth: Why capitalism cannot be sustainable

The vast bulk of organisations advocate a "green growth" perspective.[5] This includes the OECD, the United Nations Environment Program and World Bank, as well as many groups on the broad left. Despite their differences, green growth advocates tend to argue that there is nothing fundamentally incompatible between economic growth and environmental sustainability. Instead, they argue that it is a matter of proper policy and management as to whether a sustainable ecology can be maintained. Theoretically, green growth depends upon both significant government intervention into the economy to invest and regulate as required, but also the market mechanisms of capitalism encouraging

---

5. Li, Dong and Dong 2022.

new sustainable technologies.[6] Governments and corporations around the world claim to be growing sustainably, or at least suggest that they will transition to environmentally friendly practices over time as they invest in green technology.

However, the kinds of actions required for sustainable growth have not been undertaken.[7] The UN's Sustainable Development Goals are "far off track", according to an official report.[8] No international agreement on climate emissions has been able to abate the steady increase in atmospheric carbon dioxide concentrations. Green New Deal (GND) policies amount to social democratic measures which seek to manage capitalism's most destructive tendencies while maintaining profitability and capital expansion.[9] This basic fact – that capitalism is not sufficiently responding to the climate crisis – is no surprise when you consider the essential logic of the system.

Capitalism is a form of society which is characterised by a class of labourers who have no control over the means of production and must sell their labour power to survive. The class system is based on accumulation,[10] crises, commodity production and the production of surplus value by exploiting the working class.[11] For a capitalist firm to survive, it must not simply make a profit, but reinvest that profit back into production; to grow each year so as to keep up with new advances in the industry, speed up the rate of turnover[12] and enter new markets before its competitors.[13] When capital isn't in the process of circulation or reinvestment it is reducing in value due to inflation or the depreciation of machinery. Because of these factors, both individual capitalist firms and even the total economies of countries must grow at a steady rate in order to be healthy. This growth is dependent on the exploitation

---

6. For a history of green growth and how it is a distinct phase of political discourse from sustainable development (they are collapsed together for the purposes of this article), see Dale 2015.
7. Vogel and Hickel 2023.
8. UN DESA 2023.
9. Saito 2024a, pp.31–2; Garnham 2020.
10. Hickel 2022, pp.84–88.
11. Marx 1981, pp.1019–21.
12. Marx 1978, pp.200–29.
13. D'Amato 2014, pp.51–80.

of both labour power and the Earth's natural resources.[14] It is also important to understand that capitalism isn't just a system of private ownership of production, but one defined essentially by the relationship of the mass of the population to production.[15] It follows that an economy centrally planned by the state does not itself transcend capitalism if the relationship of the mass of the population is still that of exploited proletarians.[16]

Growth is a central feature of capitalism, and our institutions and economy are geared towards maximising it. This "growth paradigm" is a focus of the degrowth criticism of green growth. Degrowth advocates see the growth paradigm, "growth ideology", or "growth imperative"[17] as the major barrier to a sustainable transition. This can take extremely idealistic forms, in that it is simply the Western ideology of growth or consumerism which must be combatted. On the other hand, some criticism of the growth imperative can take a systematic approach and point towards growth being essential to capitalism. In this form it is a critique which can point to and combat the source of the climate crisis – the global system of waged labour, competition, private accumulation and exploitation.[18] Degrowthers also argue that Gross Domestic Product (GDP) – a measure of the monetary value of everything a country produces – is a key part of growth ideology, as it reduces all the different measures of a society's functioning to a single number which values only the expansion of the economy, especially finance and extractive industries.[19] In addition, current growth has exceeded many of the limits corresponding to environmental and planetary boundaries.[20]

Because capitalism cannot exist without expanding and there are limits related to planetary materials and pollution, whether or not green growth is possible depends upon growth being decoupled from

14. Marx 1976, pp.636–639.
15. See Chapter 1, "Socio-economic relations in Stalinist Russia", in Cliff 1964.
16. D'Amato 2014, pp.171–174; see also Binns, "The Theory of State Capitalism" in Arnove et al. 2017.
17. Delves 2021.
18. Dale 2015.
19. Hickel and Hallegatte 2021; Klitgaard 2023; Roberts 2020.
20. Persson et al. 2022; Rockström et al 2009; Nebel et al 2023.

resource use and carbon emissions.[21] While some wealthy developed countries have achieved or are in the process of achieving decoupling of carbon emissions from GDP, this is only possible through the export of manufacturing and investment in renewable energy made possible through imperialism.[22] At a global scale, there is zero evidence that absolute decoupling of resource use from GDP is being achieved, and certainly not at the pace necessary to avoid climate destruction.[23]

One of the hopes of green growth advocates is that as new technologies develop, they will decrease the resource and energy cost of production as a whole. However, because of the logic of the capitalist system such hopes are ill-fated. The Jevons paradox is the phenomenon whereby increases in the efficiency with which a resource is used in production results in no change, or even an increase, in the rate at which that resource is consumed.[24] In degrowth literature this is known as a rebound effect.[25] The Jevons paradox reflects the contradictory functioning of capitalism, and is informed by the same logic as the tendential fall in the rate of profit.[26] When some new development makes production more efficient it becomes incumbent upon a capitalist firm not just to adopt the development, but exploit it to the fullest, buying new machinery, working labourers harder and so on. They must do this because of competition; if they do not adopt new technology and expand they risk losing market share and going out of business. New technologies have always resulted in an increase in resources use, in productivity and the destruction of nature.[27]

The other means by which new technologies are supposed to save capitalism from the climate crisis is through some breakthrough development which can solve some issue of unsustainable production or global warming. Proposed routes for these developments include nuclear energy, expanding recycling to encourage a more circular economy, carbon capture and storage, or forms of geoengineering.

21. Parrique et al. 2019.
22. Hickel et al. 2022a; Saito 2024a, pp.14–15, 42–43.
23. Hickel et al. 2022a.
24. Saito 2024a, pp.43–4.
25. Saito 2024a, pp.43–4.
26. Marx 1981, pp.317–48.
27. Hickel 2022a, pp.154–7.

Nuclear energy is no environmentally friendly or sustainable solution, requiring immense resources use and producing a toxic byproduct.[28] Recycling, despite its potential, does little more than encourage the expansion of plastics.[29] And while carbon capture and storage – including sequestering excess carbon dioxide from the atmosphere and BECCS (Bioenergy with carbon capture and storage) – will probably play some role in a sustainable transition,[30] the technology is largely unproven. For now, an over-reliance on BECCS in climate change mitigation targets tends to be an excuse to postpone action, leaving the problem for future generations to solve.[31] This is the basic logic behind most of green growth; do everything to keep the system running as normal, pushing action further and further into the future when supposed rapid advances in technology, aided by good government policy, will solve the crisis.

Finally, geoengineering, which refers to methods which alter the Earth's energy balance, is the most potentially disastrous. Geoengineering includes projects which could increase the reflectivity (albedo) of the Earth so that the amount of incoming solar radiation which reaches and heats up the surface of the planet is reduced. It includes things like whitening clouds or building massive mirrors to put into space or cover the surface of the ocean. These methods would mask the damage that carbon dioxide emissions are having on the atmosphere by counteracting the impact on heating, but they would do nothing for other effects such as ocean acidification and would have to be continually scaled up with atmospheric carbon dioxide. Even more dangerous is the sending of aerosols into the stratosphere to increase its reflectivity, which is also the geoengineering method most accepted by the Intergovernmental Panel on Climate Change (IPCC).[32] Stratospheric aerosols don't just mask the effects of carbon dioxide and require constant upkeep to do so, they also could have a slew of other impacts on atmospheric chemistry and cloud formation.[33] Capitalism, a

---

28. Williams 2016; Garnham 2020.
29. Hasselbalch et al. 2023.
30. Fajardy et al. 2021.
31. Hickel and Kallis 2020.
32. Masson-Delmotte 2018.
33. Cziczo et al. 2019.

system driven by competition and prone to crises, cannot be trusted to maintain the massive feats of geoengineering which would be required to mitigate global warming.

It's clear that green growth or sustainable development is impossible under capitalism, and that therefore, a solution to the climate crisis must radically challenge the logic of the system and do more than reform it. Degrowth purports to be one such radical challenge.

Degrowth as an alternative

As an area of academic development, degrowth is presently in a state of flux and evolution, with a few tendencies vying for influence. For the purposes of this article, only the more left-wing versions of degrowth will be addressed. Jason Hickel is the foremost representative of what can be termed socialist-technocratic degrowth. In his highly influential book *Less is More*, Hickel defines degrowth as "a planned downscaling of energy and resource use to bring the economy back into balance with the living world in a safe, just and equitable way".[34] However, disagreements exist on the source of the growth problem, the exact form that degrowth takes, and how it can be achieved. To discuss this requires first outlining the history of degrowth.

For most of its history degrowth existed as an economic perspective prevalent only in academic circles. *Décroissance* (degrowth) was first used by the French intellectual André Gorz in a debate with Herbert Marcuse and others in 1972 to counter a government conference on economic growth.[35] From this first mention degrowth was counterposed to capitalist growth, questioning whether the system is compatible with a balanced Earth.[36] However, despite the term arising in the radical atmosphere after May 1968, it failed to develop into a coherent critique of capitalism and was limited to a counter-position to economic growth.[37] It wasn't until a re-emergence in late 2001 that degrowth took on its modern definition with a special issue of the periodical *L'*écologiste (The ecologist) titled *Défaire le développement,*

---

34. Hickel 2022a, p.29.
35. Parrique 2020, p.172.
36. Saito 2024a, pp.77–78.
37. Parrique 2020, p.176.

refaire le monde! (Unmake development, remake the world).[38] It was specifically the work of Serge Latouche which brought degrowth from mere economic decline into a more holistic questioning and restructuring of society.[39] However Latouche was no anti-capitalist.[40] He argues that degrowth is possible under capitalism as the drive to growth was a recent development after Fordism and Keynesianism, not an inherent feature of the system.[41] For the next decade, degrowth theory spread throughout European academic circles and developed theoretically,[42] only breaking out beyond the continent and the halls of universities from 2008–2018.[43] Many of the developments up to that point were then synthesised and popularised by Jason Hickel in *Less is More*, and subsequently there has been further attention to degrowth in the works of Kohei Saito, which will be discussed later.

Socialist-technocratic degrowth recognises the need to move beyond capitalism, but fails to articulate the form this transition could take beyond a set of radical policy measures. But before extrapolating this key criticism, there are a few weak arguments against this form of degrowth that should be clarified.

The most popular rejoinder to degrowth proposals is the truism that there are places in the world which do not bear significant responsibility for the climate crisis, and where a decrease in the scale of the economy would result in a large portion of the population not having their needs adequately met. However, degrowth asserts that while a net decrease in global resource use is required, not every society, nor every individual in the most affluent societies, need consume less. Hickel in particular[44] has placed great emphasis on decolonisation and how degrowth policies could allow for historically colonised nations to wipe away predatory debt arrangements with, and develop unhindered by, the West.[45] And for the developed world, while there would be a net

38. Parrique 2020, p.176.
39. Flipo 2008.
40. Bellamy Foster 2011a.
41. Bellamy Foster 2022a, pp.363–72.
42. Parrique 2020, p.207.
43. Parrique 2020, pp.220–1.
44. Hickel 2021a.
45. Hickel 2021b.

decrease in material throughput and energy use, through redistributive measures the poorest should see an increase in their standard of living.[46]

This also addresses a second common challenge – that degrowth is another form of austerity that would decrease the living standard of working-class people. While empirically this is untrue with regard to the kind of degrowth argued for by Hickel, it still stands as a propagandistic barrier to degrowth being popularly accepted. Some degrowthers welcome this response, as it shows that degrowth is a term which cannot be coopted by capitalism, unlike something like "sustainable development" or a "just transition".[47] Elsewhere degrowth is talked of less as a propagandist term and through a more scientific lens. But most interestingly degrowth is used as a wedge to push against the capitalist ideology of growth,[48] and if degrowth is seen as austerity then capitalist ideology still maintains too tight a hold for any slogan to really break capitalism in the first place. This is part of a broader strategy whereby degrowth, along with other appealing anti-capitalist policies, develops into a counter-hegemony to neoliberal capitalism, *à la* a particular reading of Italian communist Antonio Gramsci.[49] However, under capitalism the reality of degrowth – economic contraction – will always be against the basic interests of the working class, which is to increase their material standard of living, and so is effectively limited as a popular slogan.[50]

Finally, it's argued that degrowth does not mean a return to primitive forms of technology but would in fact require widespread adoption and development of new, truly environmentally friendly techniques and machinery.[51] While these clarifications make degrowth less disagreeable, it is unclear what it adds to a revolutionary socialist strategy beyond an empirical argument for decreasing total resource and energy use in the immediate transition away from capitalism. This

46. Millward–Hopkins 2020.
47. Kallis and March 2015.
48. Hickel 2021c.
49. Hendrickx 2023.
50. Molyneux 2022.
51. Hickel et al. 2022b; Hickel 2023a.

is especially true when considering the major proposed methods of application are technocratic and idealist.

In chapter 5 of *Less is More*, Hickel outlines "Pathways to a Post-Capitalist World".[52] His proposals are based on an understanding that "capitalism is a system that's organised around exchange-value, not around use-value"[53] and that therefore if society were more rationally organised it wouldn't be directed at profit but fulfilling needs. Firstly, he that argues in order to rapidly slow down the rate of resource and energy use the global economy needs to end planned obsolescence and advertising, shift from ownership to usership, end food waste and decrease the size of environmentally destructive industries.[54] Then addressing the political problems such challenges to the current capitalist order would entail, Hickel resorts to explaining how the policies would rationally work. He argues that a degrowth transition would be accompanied by a jobs guarantee, while also reducing work hours.[55] Also, he contends, there would be a radical redistribution of wealth[56] and "decommodifying basic goods and expanding the commons".[57] And finally Hickel utilises another tool of left-wing intellectual policy-making – Modern Monetary Theory (MMT)[58] – to answer potential questions about how degrowth projects will be funded.[59]

While Hickel recognises that there are forces in society with an interest in preventing these reforms, he appeals to an idealised democracy in which, because degrowth is in the interests of most people, it will be adopted despite the protests of the minority.[60] This is what separates Hickel's perspective from a Marxist one. Hickel and other writers from his intellectual milieu see the problems of society as technical, and while they agree that there are systemic issues in the way society is organised, they believe these can be changed by properly outlining a

---

52. Hickel 2022a, p.205.
53. Hickel 2022a, p.208.
54. Hickel 2022a, pp.205–22.
55. Hickel 2022a, pp.223–6.
56. Hickel 2022a, pp.227–31.
57. Hickel 2022a, p.231.
58. See Kelton 2020 for an overview of MMT.
59. Olk et al. 2023.
60. Hickel 2020a, pp.245–50.

more logical way of running things which benefits most people and will for this reason be possible.[61] He implicitly argues for the possibility that the system could be reformed away from its dependence on growth. For Marxists, the illogical organisation of production under capitalism is tied to the fact that society is not democratic, and that the capitalist class rules in their own interest, disregarding damage to the environment, or the will of the majority of working-class people. The only way to enact the kind of radical and anti-capitalist policies Hickel and other degrowthers advocate is through the self-activity of the working class, and a revolution which overturns the capitalist relations of production.

Hickel's formulation of degrowth is one of the more serious in that it not only recognises the scale of change necessary to solve the climate crisis but also attempts to deal with the challenges of bringing about this change. However, the lack of a Marxist understanding of capitalism and the limit to reforms means that it cannot be anything more than a series of technocratic solutions to the ecological crisis. So socialist-technocratic degrowth does not offer a convincing alternative to capitalist green growth, but the empirical argument for the need to degrow generally is compelling, and degrowth advocates have not limited their arguments only to capitalist green growth.

Degrowth vs socialist green growth

This section explores the debate between *Jacobin* contributor Matt Huber, representing a socialist perspective of green growth, and a number of degrowth proponents, most notably Giorgos Kallis. Kallis' critique is targeted at socialists who accept capitalism's deleterious impact on the natural world but suppose that if the growth were to happen under socialism it would, by some mechanism, be sustainable.[62] He also problematises growth as something with a quantitative meaning in a post-capitalist society, as a socialist economy would seek to maximise use-value, rather than having any measure of exchange

---

61. While Hickel does advocate for mass activity, as in Hickel 2022b, it is clear that the bulk of his work is oriented towards providing solid policy proposals that convince regular people, rather than the self–activity of workers being the solution.
62. Kallis 2019a.

value (GDP, typically).[63] A final key intervention is the argument that growth requires accumulation through exploitation; that a socialist society wouldn't accumulate as it wouldn't take surplus value from its workers.[64]

Matt Huber has long argued that the climate movement must appeal to and base itself in the working class.[65] His 2022 book, *Climate Change as Class War*, is a polemical work largely directed at the middle-class climate movement, and argues for a turn away from emphasising climate policies and towards empowering the working class as the solution to the climate crisis. He emphasises that the dominant discourse wrongly centres individual consumption choices rather than capitalism-enforced production, and that what is needed is not the utopian solutions of many climate-minded academics, but class war which puts power in the hands of the global proletariat.[66] While some degrowth advocates attempt to grapple with the political problems which stand as roadblocks to social transformation, much of what is published is unashamedly utopian.[67] Huber responds to these by invoking Friedrich Engels' *Socialism: Utopian and Scientific*, arguing against any utility to the imaginative futures described in works such as *Half Earth Socialism* by asking rhetorically: "[d]oes this utopianism yield a strategy to confront the political and economic power of the planet's opponents – in the first instance, key sectors of the American ruling class?"[68] Adopting the label of a "socialist eco-modernis[t]",[69] Huber confronts the charge that all growth is unsustainable by appealing to the creative power of the proletariat, arguing that "solving climate change requires new social relations of production that would develop the productive forces toward clean production".[70] On this essential

63. Kallis 2019a.
64. Kallis 2019a. Here Kallis has an interesting discussion of Marxist terminology as historically specific to analysing capitalism, while the terms "accumulation" and "surplus" are more universal. A similar discussion will occur later in this article.
65. Huber 2019a.
66. Huber 2022a.
67. See Vettese and Pendergrass 2022 for the most overt example of this tendency.
68. Huber 2022b.
69. Huber 2022b.
70. Huber 2022b.

point Huber is correct – as will be expanded upon in the final sections of this article.

As for the other arguments Kallis makes of socialism requiring degrowth, Huber is consistent in mischaracterising the latter.[71] Huber's primary issue with degrowth is that it is seen as a politics of less, whereas socialism must be emphasised as a politics of more.[72] To Hickel's assertion that degrowth would mean shorter working hours, public wealth and a greater fulfilment of people's need despite less stuff produced,[73] Huber sees that there will be less stuff and dismisses it as austerity.[74] However, Huber makes many useful criticisms of degrowth, powerfully demonstrating how degrowth makes a fetish of growth and in doing so hypostasises the concrete capitalist class into an abstract system rather than a concrete collection of companies, governments, and so on.[75] Huber also rightly argues that the decolonial emphasis territorialises responsibility for degrowing and hides the decisive class element, so that degrowthers see the world primarily in terms of Global North and Global South, rather than workers and bosses.[76] And it's absolutely true that – in the words of degrowth proponent Timothée Parrique – "degrowth as a political movement has failed".[77] This failure is primarily due to failing to move beyond its support base among middle-class intellectuals.[78] Despite these potent critiques, when dealing with the essence of degrowth Huber is arguing with a straw man.[79] By reducing degrowth to eco-austerity in strategy and therefore a political non-starter he is ignoring the relevant questions that the theory brings up, most importantly the nature of growth, which was the key question of Kallis' criticism.[80]

Degrowthers' responses to Huber's criticisms were varied. The strategic problems in particular which are Huber's main focus are

---

71. Ahern 2022.
72. Huber 2023a.
73. Hickel 2019.
74. Huber 2022a, p.119.
75. Huber 2022a, pp.120–1.
76. Huber 2022a, pp.121–2.
77. Parrique 2020, p.204.
78. Huber 2022a, pp.114–6, 120, 124–6.
79. Suzelis 2022.
80. Kallis 2019b.

well recognised,[81] as is the problem of degrowth only appealing to intellectuals and the middle-class.[82] The sharpness with which Huber emphasises the necessity of the working class for a radical transformation is also nominally accepted, as well as that of combatting capitalism in the realm of production.[83] However, Huber has been harshly criticised for his failure to truly engage with degrowth,[84] especially where there could be great agreement.[85] The potential for this is seen in a response to an earlier article against degrowth,[86] explaining that the "more" he is advocating for is not just material stuff, but more community and meaningful social interaction.[87] Also, despite his harsh criticism of degrowth for the same weakness, Huber fails to produce a strategy beyond vague allusions to class struggle and strikes. In the end he proposes many of the same policies as degrowthers,[88] as well as advocating for a Green New Deal.[89] While Huber speaks favourably of revolutionary transformation,[90] the maximum program he espouses is merely the state ownership of production.

Despite Huber's green growth perspective being fundamentally correct – that the collective creativity of workers could allow for a sustainable development of production – his lack of a clear revolutionary perspective means he fails to articulate a method of achieving this. So his advocacy of green growth fails to break with the fundamental problems of sustainable development under capitalism. He also fails to articulate what this growth-based future society could look like.

While degrowth theory has moved closer towards socialism, with many advocates today being explicit about combining the two,[91] it is clear that these debates sorely need a clear revolutionary Marxist

---

81. Huber 2023a.
82. Pineault 2019.
83. Maher and McEvoy 2023.
84. Parrique 2021; Holgersen 2023.
85. Maddrey 2022; Katz-Rosene 2023a.
86. Huber 2019b.
87. Huber 2019c.
88. Maddrey 2022.
89. Huber 2022a, pp.137–66.
90. Katz-Rosene 2023b.
91. Löwy et al. 2022; Murphy and Spear 2022; Löwy 2020; Miller-McDonald 2021.

intervention. To date, the most significant intersection of degrowth theory and Marxism came with Kohei Saito.

Marx and degrowth communism

Marxist terminology and concepts are present throughout much of the degrowth literature, and a Marxist understanding of class was dominant in the socialist articulation of green growth, but neither make full use of the Marxist tradition in responding to the problem of climate change and ecological destruction. For much of the late twentieth and twenty-first centuries Marxism was not widely considered conducive to an ecological understanding. This was due primarily to hostility to a class analysis from ecological thinkers in this period, reinforced by the productivist perversion of Marxism prevalent in the Soviet Union and China, and the abandonment of a dialectics of nature by the Western Marxist tradition after Lukács. In recent years however, there has been a resurgence and rediscovery of the Marxist ecological tradition, primarily through the works of John Bellamy Foster, in particular his 2000 book *Marx's Ecology*, along with Paul Burkett's Marx and Nature from 1999.[92] They form much of the basis for Kohei Saito's degrowth communism.

Saito's works have drastically changed the terrain of degrowth politics, popularising a form of Marxism among advocates of degrowth theory. His book *Slow Down: How Degrowth Communism Can* Save the Earth sold over half a million copies within a year of publication in Japan; its most theoretical sections were adapted and expanded in the 2023 *Marx in the Anthropocene* (hereafter referred to as *MitA*), to immense praise. Jason Hickel stated that the work is "A masterpiece... herein lies the secret to post-capitalist transition... it will change [socialism and environmentalism] forever". The attempted synthesis of Marxism with a degrowth perspective is the most controversial and noteworthy aspect of *MitA*.

Saito wants to establish Marx as a degrowth communist as the basis for theorising a future society which can reverse climate change and maintain sustainability. He argues that capitalism can no longer be

---

92. The 2014 edition will be cited in this article.

seen as progressive as it destroys rather than develops the foundation for socialism, and that Marx recognised this late in life and began to reformulate his theory. It follows from this that the post-capitalist society would much more likely be a return to steady-state communes rather than an expansive productive society that has come to dominate the Marxist understanding of communism.

According to Saito, the case for Marx adopting a degrowth perspective develops from his study of natural science and primitive human societies after the publication of the first volume of *Capital* in 1867.[93] On some fronts the argument is waged successfully, with Saito's deep reading of Marx and Engels showing a serious transformation in Marx's conception of history and society from unilinear, productivist and Eurocentric in his very early writings to one more thoroughly dialectical, ecological and most importantly for Saito, multilinear.[94]

Marx moving on from Eurocentrism is based on him not viewing colonisation as a barbaric yet progressive process which brings less developed societies closer to those of Europe,[95] and rejecting the "unchangeability of Asiatic societies".[96] Productivism, for Saito, broadly characterises how the early Marx saw the forces of production developing within an old society, coming into contradiction with that society, and driving change towards a new one. But Saito sees this understanding as untenable today, as "the acceleration of productive forces will sooner or later make most of the planet uninhabitable before the collapse of capitalism",[97] and argues that Marx himself "[abandoned] his celebration of the increasing forces of production [and] came to recognise that the sustainable development of the productive forces is not possible under capitalism".[98] Marx's transcending of a unilinear history is incontrovertible, as in *MitA* Saito develops Marx's rejection of his earlier position that "the country that is more developed industrially only shows, to the less developed, the image of its own future",[99]

93. Saito 2023a, pp.171–7.
94. Saito 2023a, pp.177–90.
95. Saito 2023a, pp.182–5.
96. Marx in *Capital*, Volume I, cited in Saito 2023a, p.184.
97. Saito 2023a, p.172.
98. Saito 2023a, p.181.
99. Marx in *Capital*, Volume I, cited in Saito 2023a, p.184.

to one that allows for multiple routes of development.[100] Ultimately for Saito's argument, Eurocentrism, productivism and a unilinear history are all inextricably connected, and combine to mean that "Marx must have completely parted ways with 'historical materialism' as it had been traditionally understood".[101]

To make this case, which is essential to claims about Marx's degrowth communism as it argues that progress is not tied up with productive power,[102] Saito has to invoke an extremely strict and inflexible definition of historical materialism in which the relations and mode of production in a society are mechanically driven by changes in the forces of production, and that there are therefore definite stages of society that must be passed through.[103] Thus, when developments in production are destructive – as is seen with anthropogenic climate change – and a more developed class society is not necessarily more progressive than what came before, historical materialism no longer holds. In contradistinction to this crude conception, historical materialism must be understood not only in the brief ways which Marx and Engels spoke of it,[104] but as the method of dialectics applied to history. Understood this way historical materialism is not incapable of such recognitions as a multilinear history or contradictions in productive development and the social relations or ecological damage they engender, but centres such discoveries and correctly emphasises them as the driving forces of change through history.[105]

Saito's main evidence for Marx abandoning historical materialism is in applying his reading of early human societies and confronting the problem of development in Russia; it is through this process that Marx supposedly comes to a new conception of communism.[106] In his unsent correspondence with Russian socialist Vera Zasulich, Marx argues

---

100. Saito 2023a, p.186.
101. Saito 2023a, p.182.
102. Saito 2023a, p.209.
103. Saito 2023a, pp.171–3.
104. The context Marx was writing in meant that his emphasis when speaking of historical materialism was on the forces of production as the basis for a materialist conception of history contra the idealist historiography of his various bourgeois and utopian contemporaries.
105. Novack 2002, pp.211–28.
106. Saito 2023a, pp.190–6.

that Russia can skip the capitalist phase of development through the pre-capitalist commune formations and adopting the advances from the West. In his own words from the first draft of the letter:

> [T]hanks to the unique combination of circumstances in Russia, the rural commune, which is still established on a national scale, may gradually shake off its primitive characteristics and directly develop as an element of collective production on a national scale. Precisely because it is contemporaneous with capitalist production, the rural commune may appropriate all its positive achievements without undergoing its [terrible] frightful vicissitudes. Russia does not live in isolation from the modern world, and nor has it fallen prey, like the East Indies, to a conquering foreign power.[107]

Saito interprets the letter and drafts not only as Marx articulating a new means of advancing towards communism, but necessarily because of this a new form of communism which supersedes the productivist ideas he held previously and can be based on communal peasants instead of the working class.[108] Rather, what Marx is attempting to do here is to apply historical materialism to a very peculiar historical circumstance in which a primitive mode of production prevails in a society while not being under the control of a more advanced power. Zasulich was directly appealing to Marx to answer whether Russian socialists should accept capitalist development, with all the exploitation and expropriation of primitive accumulation,[109] or whether they can skip to socialism. Marx responds, invoking a primitive form of the historical materialist concepts of combined and uneven development and permanent revolution,[110] that Russia can skip capitalist development only if aided by revolution in Western Europe and by adopting the "positive achievements" of capitalism already developed there. What these positive developments refer to is not in the text itself, and Saito limits them to

---

107. Marx 1881.
108. Saito 2023a, pp.199–210.
109. Marx 1976, pp.874–95.
110. Novack 2002, pp.75–105; originally Trotsky 1906 and Trotsky 1931.

productive technologies;[111] but applying a robust historical materialism makes it clear Marx also means the cooperative relations of production that the capitalist mode of production induced.[112] With this reading the conclusion no longer follows that Marx comes to a different conception of communism: it is still fundamentally based on socialised production and the working class. In addition, it is also clear that the development of the forces of production is still required for moving beyond capitalism, and that they will be harnessed by the collective working class to meet human needs. In fact, Marx's limited and unpublished analysis was proven wrong less than 30 years later in 1905, when the working class played the dominant political role despite still being a tiny minority. Although it is also true that in those years between Marx's draft letters and the revolution Russia underwent dramatic changes in the forces of production and the development of capitalism.

Finally, we come to the case Saito makes for Marx being a degrowth communist, which similarly relies upon a particular interpretation of the late Marx. Saito can point to no direct evidence that Marx advocates a "steady-state economy",[113] the necessary formulation to have a degrowth vision for communism.[114] While Marx's understanding of primitive steady-state societies had shifted since his negative comments on the unchangeability of the Asian communes, as Saito argues,[115] there is no indication that Marx thinks Western economies "consciously need to 'return'"[116] to the archaic equality of steady-state communes in a higher form. Simply put, in *MitA* Saito shows that Marx developed an appreciation for the stability of archaic societies, including the rural communes of Russia, but the link from this to adopting a steady-state economy as the basis for communism is missing.[117]

An additional part of Saito's project is providing an answer as to why

---

111. Saito 2023a, p.208.
112. For more evidence of Marx not abandoning historical materialism late in life, see the final paragraph of chapter 51 of Marx 1981, pp.1023–4 (*Capital*, Volume III), where he discusses with much nuance how production is essential to the transformation of the social form of production.
113. Saito 2023a, p.208.
114. Hampton 2023.
115. Saito 2023a, p.208.
116. Saito 2023a, p.208.
117. Gibson and Empson 2023.

Marxism has not been seen as ecological; why the USSR and China have had such a devastating environmental record, and why many Marxist theoreticians adopt a productivist view in which the goal of socialism is to expand humanity's productive power and that this itself would solve any ecological problems. He argues that the USSR and China were always going to develop into state capitalist nations because the form their Marxism took was one based on increasing material abundance. This is stated clearly in *Slow Down*, along with an incredibly apologetic tone in his application of Marxism.[118] Saito wants to make use of a particular interpretation of the late Marx, while rejecting much of his early writings and that of the tradition after him. To do this, Saito invokes a rift between Marx and Engels in which Engels' negative influence on the subsequent socialist movement is to blame.[119] Saito bases this on Engels' vision of post-capitalism being one of exponentially expanding and effectively infinite production, which Marx supposedly distanced himself from and "pointed to the need for social equality and sustainability".[120] It is then Engels' version which is taken to be orthodox Marxism because of the understanding that Engels was responsible for natural science in their division of labour[121] and suppressing Marx's ecological thinking in favour of his own dialectics of nature.[122]

This is not a unique argument;[123] many different left-wing traditions trace some theoretical failure to Marx's greatest collaborator. But Saito is particularly sharp in making his case that it was Engels' crude application of dialectics to nature that resulted in him missing Marx's more empirically derived conclusions on the concept of metabolism.[124] While it can be reasonably argued that there were differences between Marx and Engels,[125] on the question of the dialectics of nature,

---

118. See Saito 2024a, pp.88–9 for an example of this.
119. Bellamy Foster 2023a.
120. Saito 2023a, p.209.
121. Saito 2023a, pp.45–51.
122. Saito 2023a, pp.61–8.
123. Sheehan 2017, pp.53–60.
124. Saito 2023a, pp.65–6.
125. See Roso 2023, Dunayevskaya 2018, pp.241–76 and Blackledge 2020 for a discussion of some of these.

communism[126] and philosophy they were in fundamental agreement.[127] Saito's argument culminates with Engels' editing of the third volume of *Capital* to remove any reference to natural metabolism,[128] a weak basis for claims about the supposed wholesale suppression of Marx's ecological thinking.[129] Further, the claim that Marx had a different vision of communism than Engels rests on the conclusion that Marx was a degrowth communist. If this assertion, lacking any textual evidence, is rejected, all that is left is differences in emphasis which do not constitute a break between the two thinkers. As for explaining why the nominally Marxist USSR and China have poor ecological records, it is because they are simply capitalist states beholden to the same logic of accumulation and exploitation of nature and the working class. They took this particular form of state capitalism not because of a particular form of Marxism as Saito argues, but because the basis for working-class democracy was destroyed in Russia.[130]

In his attempt to green Marxism Saito seeks to go beyond the pragmatic adoption of degrowth and heavy emphasis on planning by the likes of Bellamy Foster[131] to a more theoretical synthesis of the two, rooting it in the supposed adoption of degrowth communism by the late Marx. But Saito cannot show any direct evidence for Marx as a degrowth communist. Nor does he fully apply the total breadth of Marxist theory to questions of degrowth and ecology. And in doing so, Saito invalidates the vast majority of Marx and Engels' intellectual output, as Matt Huber and Leigh Phillips argue: "All that's left in its ashes are idiosyncratic readings of *Capital*, some sparse notebooks copying disconnected passages from agricultural texts, and the letter to Zasulich".[132]

---

126. Engels read Marx drafts of his *Anti-Dühring* and Marx contributed a chapter to it; see Bellamy Foster 2022c.
127. Sheehan 2017, pp.48–53.
128. Huber and Phillips 2024.
129. See the postscript in Bellamy Foster 2023b.
130. See Harman, "How the revolution was lost" in Arnove et al., 2017.
131. Bellamy Foster 2023b.
132. Huber and Phillips 2024.

Humanist Marxism

For the purposes of this article humanist Marxism does not mean any particular tendency, but an emphasis on alienation and freedom that is for some only associated with the early Marx but is actually present throughout his late works. Humanism is the belief in the potential for a united human race and the ability for us to work collectively towards united interests.[133] This starting point is compatible with the Marxist argument that the proletariat has the potential to develop into the universal class which embodies the interests of all humanity.[134] Humanism can be the basis to reject responses to the climate crisis which assert that humanity will always be divided, or that certain forces such as an innate sense of competition will preclude collective efforts. But Marxism can take humanism further, transcending the liberal enlightenment humanism[135] through a dialectical materialist understanding of humans' nature to labour; to consciously, creatively and collectively change our environment.[136] Contra Hegel, Marx located alienation and its solution in the material world, and it is only through transforming the way that labour is performed that people can be truly free.[137]

Labour being the basis for Marxist theory contributes to the depth of the ecosocialist theory of the metabolic rift[138] – it is because labour is alienated under capitalism that the relationship between humanity and nature is not rationally managed by the former, and that there is an "irreparable rift in the interdependent process of social metabolism".[139] This brings into question exactly how labour will change post-capitalism, and answering this invokes the topic of universal and historically specific human relations. Simply, this distinction refers to whether relations in human societies apply to every form of social organisation, and are in this case universal, or whether they are limited to a particular

133. Fromm 1966, pp.vii–xiii.
134. Lukács 2017, pp.123–74.
135. Bellamy Foster 2023c.
136. Novack 1973, pp.39–56.
137. Dunayevskaya in Fromm 1966, pp.68–83; Dunayevskaya 1975, pp.53–66; Novack 1973, pp.81–103.
138. Bellamy Foster 1999; Bellamy Foster 2000, pp.155–63.
139. Marx 1981, p.949.

social formation and are historically specific. The distinction permeates any discussion of human essence and the form of future socialist or communist societies but is rarely directly addressed. To start with, it is clear that through the discussion of the human relationship with nature that metabolism is a universal condition of human existence – that is, that producing and reproducing social life will occur under every form of human social organisation. It also follows then that labour, the means by which humans interact with nature, is historically non-specific and essential to being human.[140] On the other hand, relations such as commodities, capital, exchange value, the division between mental and manual labour and many more are products of class society and liable to be sublated or abolished in post-capitalist societies. The most important historically universal social relation for the potential for a degrowth Marxism is that of necessary and "free" labour. A lengthy exposition comes late in *Capital*, Volume III:

> [T]he realm of freedom really begins only where labour determined by necessity and external expediency ends; it lies by its very nature beyond the sphere of material production proper. Just as the savage must wrestle with nature to satisfy his needs, to maintain and reproduce his life, so must civilized man, and he must do so in all forms of society, and under all possible modes of production... Freedom, in this sphere, can consist only in this, that socialised man, the associated producers, govern the human metabolism with nature in a rational way, bringing it under their collective control instead of being dominated by it as a blind power; accomplishing it with the least expenditure of energy and in conditions most worthy and appropriate for their human nature. But this always remains a realm of necessity. The true realm of freedom, the development of human powers as an end in itself, begins beyond it, though it can only flourish with this realm of necessity as its basis. The reduction of the working day is the basic prerequisite.[141]

---

140. Engels 1876.
141. Marx 1981, pp.958–9.

This quote contains many of the main arguments of this article: that humans are a part of nature with a unique relationship to it managed by labour; that properly managing this human social metabolism with natural metabolism requires rational organisation through socialised work; that the "development of human powers" is the goal of human society and an end in itself; and finally that achieving this end means decreasing the realm of necessity and maximising the realm of freedom;[142] practically through the reduction of the working day. Saito also uses this quote in *Slow Down* as a means of counterposing a Marxist understanding of freedom to a bourgeois one,[143] but in doing so he removed the line "accomplishing it with the least expenditure of energy and in conditions most worthy and appropriate for their human nature". In context, this sentence clearly indicates that the realm of necessity must be achieved with as little energy – labour time – as possible, so that freedom can be expanded. This a significant example of Saito wilfully misreading and misinterpreting Marx's revolutionary humanism to come to his degrowth communist conclusion. However, as useful as the Marx quote is to expand some of these ideas surrounding freedom, it does not directly refute Saito's case for a transformation of Marx's thought. What it does do is provide a counterposition to Saito's interpretation of the late Marx, in which he adds nuance and transcends some of the crudeness of his earlier productivism but maintains and strengthens his notion of freedom.

In every human society there will be a section of the day which consists of *necessary* labour, that which is directed towards reproducing society (food, clothes, waste, the means of subsistence), and a section which is *free*, which could be scientific, artistic, etc. and is the true location of our species being. Regardless of the fact that labour will become "life's prime want",[144] such a division will still remain and be the primary contradiction by which a communist society continues to develop, in that it works to decrease time spent on necessary labour and expand the time that is truly free. The point that the proletariat

---

142. Novack 1973, pp.136–50.
143. Saito 2024a, pp.173–4.
144. Quoted in the first section of *The Critique of the Gotha Programme*, in Marx and Engels 1949, p.23.

works to expand its own freedom is a consistent emphasis in Marx, not some abstract goal, but imputed from the self-activity of the working classes as they take steps towards realising their humanity.[145] This, and the further development that sees workers not just fighting quantitatively to decrease their working day but qualitatively to change the nature of work to better suit their needs, are the humanism at the heart of Marxism.[146] People would work both to expand truly free labour and transform necessary labour to be as dignified and "appropriate to (our) human nature" as possible. Expanding the realm of freedom is the driving force of a socialist transformation and communist society which values not labour power, but free time.[147]

With a humanist understanding of what motivates the working class, or associated producers under communism, Saito's attempt to synthesise Marxism with degrowth can be rejected. This is because unlike Bellamy Foster, who adopts degrowth as a mere practical necessity,[148] Saito makes a principle out of the potential necessity and develops a position in which Marxism envisions a society motivated not by freedom, but by maintaining a steady-state economy so as to be in harmony with nature.[149] While Saito and Hickel maintain that their visions of degrowth would result in decreased labour time, this is a product of ending capitalism generally. In *MitA*, Saito echoes Hickel when making the case that his vision of degrowth communism doesn't limit but fully realises freedom through the transcendence of artificial scarcity and people being "free from the constant pressure to earn money thanks to the expanding common wealth".[150] It is inarguable that relative to capitalism people would have greatly expanded individual wealth and freedom by any measure, but their degrowth societies would still require more labour than a more traditionally understood socialism or communism. For instance, Bellamy Foster accepts that

145. Dunayevskaya 1975, pp.87–91; Burkett 2014, pp.133–43.
146. Phillips and Dunayevskaya 1984; Dunayevskaya 1975, pp.266–87.
147. Hägglund 2020, pp.212–69.
148. Bellamy Foster 2023b.
149. This reading is derived from much of the second half of *Marx in the Anthropocene*, but primarily parts III and IV of the concluding chapter, "The Abundance of Wealth in Degrowth Communism"; Saito 2023a, pp.226–44.
150. Saito 2023a, p.234.

labour would have to substitute for fossil fuel-derived energy,[151] greatly increasing the necessary labour society would need to perform. And Saito's steady-state formulation has no interest in expanding the freedoms people could enjoy under communism, whether by investing in production towards making necessary labour more "worthy and appropriate for human nature" or decreasing the necessary labour required at all.

The failure of writers mentioned in this article to realise some aspect of Marxist theory is because many are not revolutionary Marxists, instead being various flavours of Marxian economists, post-Marxist world systems theorists, or academics using Marxology to attempt to develop a solution to the climate crisis, but missing the theory of international working-class revolution which is what really defines Marxism.[152] Therefore, attempts to combine Marxism with degrowth typically come with a revision of the orthodox Marxist understanding of class, such as Bellamy Foster's reclassifying the working class as an "environmental (or ecological) proletariat".[153] His attempt to include such groups as youth, women, indigenous populations and peasants as necessarily proletarians transforms the working class into a populist morass with no unifying social relation to production.[154]

While Saito never concretely advocates a political program in *MitA*,[155] his activism amounts to lifestylism, having used the money from his book sales to purchase land and do degrowth work on it.[156] In *Slow Down*, however, Saito is much clearer in advancing his reformist politics. Through the book Saito advocates for municipalism and cooperatives, with multiple references to "mutual aid and trust".[157] While workers are mentioned, ultimately for Saito it is a disambiguated citizenry which is the agent of change. His decentring of the working class shows that he is not thoroughly applying Marxism to the climate crisis, but rather a narrow sliver, improperly interpreted. In the

---

151. Bellamy Foster 2023b; Huber 2023b.
152. Molyneux 1983.
153. Bellamy Foster 2022c.
154. Molyneux 2022.
155. McNeill 2023.
156. Saito 2023b.
157. Saito 2024a, pp.212–4, 216–7, 232–3.

conclusion of *Slow Down* Saito invokes the idea that only 3.5 percent of a population is needed for major social change,[158] and goes on to explain that this percentage can be achieved through:

> A workers' co-op, a school strike, an organic farm – it does not matter the form it takes. You might run for office to become a part of the municipal government. You might act as part of an environmental NGO. You might join with your neighbours to start a citizen-run electric company. It would be a major step to demand that the enterprise that employs you put in place strict environmental policies. Bringing about the democratisation of production and the shortening of work hours, for example, must include the participation of labour unions. Signature-collection actions should be started that lead to more declarations of climate emergency; movements must be developed to demand that the richest elites pay their fair share. So doing, mutual aid networks will arise and be forged into something truly mighty.[159]

As this quote shows, where these authors do deal with the working class directly, it is often in an extremely limited way. Hickel advocates an alliance between environmentalists and the working class, as the latter have "much more political leverage".[160] Bellamy Foster's overwhelming emphasis is on planning,[161] rather than the self-activity of the working class (informed by his position that China is a fundamentally different kind of society to capitalist).[162] And Saito lacks a Marxist analysis when it comes to questions of trade unions and cooperatives, among other things.[163] For many of these writers, the revolutionary role of the working class is lost, reduced to the need for the mass of the population to be won over to the idea of degrowth so that it can be passed democratically.[164]

158. Saito 2024a, p.236.
159. Saito 2024a, p.237.
160. Hickel 2023b.
161. Bellamy Foster 2023b.
162. Bellamy Foster 2022c.
163. Dale 2023.
164. Gibson and Empson 2023.

The next step is to discuss the concept of growth and how production can be expanded without environmental destruction.

Growth and the forces of production

Up until this point growth has basically referred to material throughput, and for discussing growth under capitalism this has been sufficient. However, the definition is unscientific and circular in how it can actually be applied to an understanding of degrowth. For an economy to grow sustainably it must be able to decouple resource use from GDP, or the scale of the economy must be able to increase without a corresponding increase in resources. It therefore follows that an economy can grow only when it does not grow. One recourse to this problem is to limit growth to a measure effectively of exchange value under capitalism (GDP) and concede that no quantitative measure of growth exists post-capitalism in an economy directed towards the production of wealth or use value. Such an approach effectively gives up on answering the legitimate challenges degrowth poses as to the limits and source of growth under communism. Against this position, Marxism offers a transhistorical and scientific understanding of growth, rooted in the humanism and ecological theories discussed in this article. This understanding can then be developed and solidified through a Marxist conception of science and its practical embodiment in the forces of production,[165] made fully realisable through unalienated labour and making possible a growth-based communist society.

Capitalism is not the first society to grow. However, in all pre-capitalist societies, class-divided or not, which are driven only by meeting the needs of subsistence of the masses and potentially of luxury consumption for the ruling class and their armies, growth could not expand in the explosive, exponential way it does under the present social system. This is due to the fact that the surplus was not systematically reinvested into production, and therefore growth of an economy was dependent upon growth of the population. Capitalism is different because the surplus is put back into production, to increase the productivity of labour through investment in constant capital. Through this analysis

---

165. Bernal 2010 (1905), pp.24–9.

a number of factors in growth can be distinguished: population, labour hours and labour productivity. It is clear that if any country grows a greater population, has its citizens work more hours, or improves its process such that it is more productive, all else remaining the same, it has grown in all three instances.

Just as Marx had a specific and scientific analysis of value under capitalism, but at times hinted at the possibility of a transhistorical conception of value,[166] a transhistorical notion of growth can be grasped based on a function of labour hours (which also embodies population size and is itself the locus of value) and that labour's productivity. This is also the essence of the forces of production; that they are past labour, and the appropriation of natural resources, embodied in some form which increases the productivity of future labour. The forces of production are therefore the concrete form of one half of the growth equation. In this way growth is not just based on labour, but also on nature, in that the way productivity increases is through nature being used in the labour process to augment the work itself. Growth is therefore intimately linked to natural and social metabolisms,[167] with all forms of unsustainable growth being predicated on using nature to bolster labour productivity beyond the rate at which nature can reproduce itself; in producing a metabolic rift. We then return to the problem of sustainable growth requiring decoupling from resource use.

Every form of human social organisation has had some limit to its growth, often framed historically as a maximum population or holding capacity. Throughout history each of these has been surpassed due to advances in class society, the corresponding forces of production, and a greater understanding of science or humans' relationship with nature. The limits to growth under capitalism are the same as previous limits in that they are not absolute, but relative and dialectical. While the sustainable level of atmospheric carbon dioxide does present itself as a breakpoint beyond which the Earth's natural metabolism would be disrupted, or that there is a limit to the land which can be transformed for human use, these are not limits to growth universally, but in

166. Henderson 2013, pp.89–97.
167. Saito 2017, pp.63–79, 99–137.

particular.[168] Under capitalism, with its metabolic rift and competitive drive precluding serious counteraction, these limits can and certainly will prevent further growth. What is unique about capitalism is that its scale of production pushing up against these limits is threatening more than just stagnating growth, but utter collapse. However, if society were reorganised around collective ownership, the associated producers could realise the relativity of these limits, growing through other means. Where practical they could actively counteract the damage done by capitalism to the planet. These limits include those associated with being confined to planet Earth. Key to the conception of the malleability of limits to growth is expanding the forces of production.

Expanding here cannot just be quantitative, but qualitative. Contrary to the crude understanding of Marx's historical materialism, in which each form of class society is surpassed when it becomes a fetter on the scale of production, the humanist reading of Marx makes it clear that the sense in which capitalism is a fetter on production is through the alienation of the labourer; separating humans from the product of their labour and their species being. This is also the way that Marx advanced upon basic productivism in which the "domination over nature to achieve an abundance of wealth"[169] is celebrated. A number of counterpositions can be confronted with this interpretation.[170] Firstly, Bellamy Foster asserts that the quantitative side of production no longer needs to be developed as it did in Marx's age,[171] but that to meet human needs in today's age requires massive investment of labour and resources into actively combating climate change.[172] In the *Communist Manifesto*, Marx and Engels wrote that the working class will seize "all capital from the bourgeoise...to increase the total of productive forces as rapidly as possible".[173] Saito would say that this is an example of Marx's early productivism, but interpreted through a humanist lens and in a broader context, Marx and Engels' argument here is primarily about meeting our species being through the expansion of production.

168. Huber and Phillips 2024.
169. Saito 2023a, p.231.
170. Hughes 1995.
171. Bellamy Foster 2023b.
172. Huber 2023b.
173. Marx and Engels 1962, p.53.

Society's problems will be solved by mobilising our collective creative power through productive labour. Marx's early writings can fall into productivism because the expansion of productive powers appears as both the teleological goal of society and therefore the measure by which one society is more progressive or advanced than another, making it possible to read him as approving colonialism in some instances. However, it is clear that the late Marx recognises the contradictory nature of capitalist development and values productivity only insofar it is a necessary component to expanding human freedom; humanism – but only when free of the limitations of capital.

Degrowth also rests on an assumption that human needs are finite,[174] but Marx argued that after meeting human necessity, the goal of human society is to continue to expand the realm of freedom indefinitely. As for Kallis' argument that growth would require exploitation,[175] this fails to appreciate how a socialist or communist society would be fundamentally different from capitalism, as people would freely contribute their surplus labour towards increasing the common wealth after labour has become life's prime want – there would be no motivation nor possibility for exploitation without private ownership and appropriation. Capitalism has exploitation and surplus value or profit, communism has free time or surplus labour which would be willingly "reinvested" towards bettering society.

Finally, Saito makes a compelling case that the forces of production developed under capitalism cannot be completely subsumed into socialist or communist society,[176] given that certain techniques and entire industries are unsustainable or contrary to the goals of a post-capitalist society.[177] Apart from using this as evidence of Marx abandoning historical materialism, he further argues that capitalism does not prepare the conditions for a sustainable economy. This misinterpretation stems from the same place as his interpretation of Marx's letters to Zasulich: a lack of appreciation of the working class as the force which can reappropriate the forces of production towards useful

---

174. Tsuda 2021.
175. Kallis 2019a.
176. Hannah 2023.
177. Saito 2023a, pp.136–67.

ends.[178] Certainly the forces of production embodied in the creation of tanks and missiles would have no place; but factories can be retooled, products recycled, and so on.

For example, there is a factory in Melbourne which is involved in the production of F-35 fighter jets; but while these end products would never exist in a rational society, the heat-treatment that goes into their production could potentially find new and expanded civilian use. Capitalism makes it appear that the productive forces only develop for the benefit of capital, but this is a mystification of what is in actuality the embodiment of human powers,[179] which can be reappropriated by rational and cooperative labour. In short, Saito saps the contradictory nature of the development of the forces of production under capitalism and their potential to be used under socialism.[180] The final step to elucidating this possibility is a discussion of science, and how it can be radically transformed only after moving beyond class society.

Science: under capitalism and beyond

The possibility of growth and the expansion of the forces of production without ecological destruction depends upon understanding the nature of science and how it can be radically transformed in a future society. Our ability to interact with nature must be understood at a qualitatively different level such that productivity or population can expand without either an increase in resource use or while expanding the resource pool. So, while it is clear that under capitalism resources are primarily allocated in search of expanding profits, regardless of environmental cost, it is not enough to say that by reversing this under a communist society continued growth is therefore possible. The intellectual products of a society do not happen at random or due to the unique genius of particular individuals but are themselves products of the economic relations of the society the ideas develop out of. Marx famously argued that: "The ideas of the ruling class are in every epoch the ruling ideas",[181] but the ways in which class society determines the

178. Gibson and Empson 2023.
179. Marx 1976, pp.439–54.
180. Molyneux 2022.
181. Marx 1846.

possibility of ideas goes far beyond just the ruling ideas. The British Marxist Christopher Caudwell explored the effects of bourgeois society on culture, literature and science.[182] In his incomplete work *The Crisis in Physics*, Caudwell showed the limits of a bourgeois mechanical conception of natural science and how a dialectical method is necessary to develop beyond roadblocks around problems such as those of determinacy,[183] the position of humans in nature,[184] and metaphysics broadly.[185] Under capitalism, science is studied according to the reified logic of the mode of production.[186] The disciplines are separated despite the totality of the natural world;[187] phenomena are understood as isolated and static, when in reality they are interacting and in constant motion;[188] there is a decisive division in society between scientists and workers (mental and manual labour);[189] and the scientific method rests on a positivistic assumption, not appreciating the dialectical relationship the activity of interacting with nature has on knowing.[190] These all limit the ability of science to reach a true understanding of nature under capitalism, but there are many more socially determined limits.

John Desmond Bernal, like his contemporary Caudwell, was a communist scientist keenly interested in the interaction between politics and science.[191] He believed that a materialist dialectic was the most powerful tool not just for understanding society, but also for making scientific discoveries.[192] In *The Social Function of Science*, Bernal uses his scientific expertise to develop the fundamental limitations of bourgeois science discussed above, but also to elaborate the various ways capitalism inhibits scientific inquiry. These range from obsolescence, patents, inter-industrial competition and international

182. Caudwell 2018, pp.143–56.
183. Caudwell 2017, pp.131–48.
184. Caudwell 2017, pp.55–90.
185. Caudwell 2017, pp.22–54; see Sheehan 2017, pp.350–83 for a more complete discussion.
186. Lukács 2017, pp.88–123.
187. Sheehan 2023.
188. This includes a failure to appreciate the history necessary to understand anything.
189. Untermann 1905, pp.107–26.
190. Novack 2002, pp.155–66.
191. Sheehan 2007.
192. Sheehan 2017, pp.309–16.

secrecy,[193] to problems of the efficiency of scientific research surrounding poor pay, conditions, and management,[194] and finally the role science has in war.[195] There are near limitless ways to describe how a capitalist organisation of science and society results in innovation being limited, and many practically stem from capitalist class relations generally. As much as an individual scientist can be seen to have more freedom in their labour than a typical worker, they are still subject to the same forces of capital such as competition and exploitation that stand in the way of creative work for the rest of the labouring population. Science can therefore be transformed in the same way as all other forms of labour, through a revolution in the mode of production.

> Science puts into our hands the means of satisfying our material needs. It gives us also the ideas which will enable us to understand, to co-ordinate, and to satisfy our needs in the social sphere. Beyond this science has something as important though less definite to offer: a reasonable hope in the unexplored possibilities of the future.[196]

Following this quotation from the final chapter of *The Social Function of Science*, Bernal outlines the historic role of capitalism in the early development of science, and argues that capitalism must now be overcome if science is to fully develop its social function.[197] The new form it takes for Bernal is essentially one which is united with labour; where science is the embodiment of human collective activity and the essence of the development of our species. This comes with embracing dialectical materialism, the unity of manual and mental work,[198] and the realisation of unalienated labour. Under communism science becomes the realm in which human development occurs.

The kind of society where this new science can take hold is one in

---

193. Bernal 2010 (1939), pp.138–55.
194. Bernal 2010 (1939), pp.98–125.
195. Bernal 2010 (1939), pp.163–90.
196. Bernal 2010 (1939), p.408.
197. Bernal 2010 (1939), pp.408–16.
198. Meaning that there is no distinction between the practical labour of interacting with nature, and the theoretical act of planning and interpreting this interaction.

which the models showing the need to decrease material throughput do not apply. The kind of technological innovations that would come from a society of associated producers, working collectively towards meeting human needs, faces none of the social challenges posed by capitalism. Natural limits still exist, but their relatively would be realised directly through the development of human abilities to effectively infinitely increase efficiency and the pool of resources that could be drawn from.[199] This is not to say that growth will be constant; there may be long periods of effective stagnation as some limit constrains growth until some new development comes along. Additionally, under a society of associated producers that there would be great care for how humans impacted upon nature.[200] A communist society would not dominate nature in the way capitalism attempts to,[201] but in some form of managed harmony.[202] Engels wrote in *The Part played by Labour in the Transition from Ape to Man*:

> [A]t every step we are reminded that we by no means rule over nature like a conqueror over a foreign people, like someone standing outside nature – but that we, with flesh, blood and brain, belong to nature, and exist in its midst, and that all our mastery of it consists in the fact that we have the advantage over all other creatures of being able to know and correctly apply its laws.
>
> And, in fact, with every day that passes we are learning to understand its laws more correctly… But the more this happens the more will men not only feel but also realise their oneness with nature.[203]

Rather than the passive harmony imagined in Saito's degrowth communism, humans' unalienated creative powers could be directed towards expanding the realm of freedom while rationally managing natural metabolism. Some glimpses of this future were seen in the early

---

199. Işıkara and Narin 2023.
200. Burkett 2014, pp.239–56.
201. Kandelaars 2016.
202. Burkett 2014, pp.225–30.
203. Marx and Engels 1949, pp.82–3.

years of post-revolutionary Russia,[204] but it can only truly be realised within an advanced communist society.[205] Contrary to the proponents of degrowth,[206] it is not a simple faith in future technologies that allows for a belief in growth communism, but in the abilities of a cooperative and unalienated humanity to master nature through collective labour and science. This mastery is evidently not in the sense of a master over a slave, as humans wouldn't lord over nature but remain a part of it, but mastery in the way a tradesperson masters their craft. Communist society would have an intimate knowledge of and interrelation through labour with the natural world, shaping it to fit their needs, but while managing nature and maintaining sustainability for future generations.

To summarise: the possibility of a communism with growth rests on the revolutionary transformation of science that would occur in a society of associated producers. Just as past human societies have had their capacities expanded through innovative technologies and social organisations, the rational and collective control of our environment under communism would allow the continual transcendence of each relative limit that may be imposed.

Conclusion

To conclude I want to imagine a deep future communist society: one in which the laws of nature are so well understood that human society has completely conquered the challenges of the present – hunger, cold, climate change and so on. Motivated only by the human ethic of increasing freedom, this society could harvest the resources of entire planets, the energy of stars, without there being some dramatic revenge of nature, thanks to our collective scientific mastery. People will spend their free time labouring, but the necessary labour of ensuring everyone is housed, fed, clothed and so on is driven down to the absolute minimum. This would free up people to work creatively and scientifically, advancing upon old techniques of production to further decrease the necessary labour or spending their time dedicated to

---

204. Sheehan 2017, pp.162–5; Kandelaars 2016.
205. See Sheehan 2017, pp.213–40 for the rise and fall of the early Soviet philosophy of science.
206. Boscov-Ellen 2023.

the arts. This is not a utopian future, but one based on the material interests of the working class. It is incompatible with the actual utopian and anti-human degrowth vision of the future, in which people are somehow motivated by maintaining limits on their own freedom and incapable of growing without destroying the environment.

To be clear, this scenario does not discount the reality of relative physical limits and boundaries that would have to be worked within. And this is especially the case for a post-revolutionary society in the short and medium term, where net degrowth may very well be a necessary feature of the transition from capitalism, in a not dissimilar way to how a workers' state would temporarily require a military force. However, this is not something that can be prescribed, it must be left up to the collective decision of the international working class who make the revolution, no matter how compelling modern research is on the need to degrow our capitalist economy. It is on this limited basis that Marxist theory has anything to gain from degrowth; the synthesis attempted by Saito amounts to making a principle out of potential necessity and distorts Marx and Marxism to do so.

Despite there being nothing to add to Marxism from degrowth, I hope that this article shows the utility of a deep engagement with contrary perspectives on the climate crisis, and even of speculating about the nature of a communist society based on a Marxist understanding of nature and humans' relation to it. And through analysing the ongoing debate between degrowth and green growth a number of key points emerge, including a development of the distinction between universal and historically contingent relations, a discussion of production and science, and the centrality of freedom to the Marxist theory of international working-class revolution. It is this last point, the humanist essence of Marxism, that makes any form of degrowth incompatible with the socialist and workers' movements.

References

Ahern, Andrew 2022, "Environmentalists Need Unions, Unions Need Environmentalists: A Review of 'Climate Change as Class War'", *The Trouble*, 7 June. https://www.the-trouble.com/content/2022/6/7/environmentalists-need-unions-unions-need-environmentalists-a-review-of-climate-change-as-class-war

Andreucci, Diego 2019, "Capitalism, Socialism and the Challenge of Degrowth: Introduction to the Symposium", *Capitalism Nature Socialism*, 30(2), pp.176–88. https://doi.org/10.1080/10455752.2018.1546332

Arnove, Anthony, Peter Binns, Tony Cliff, Chris Harman and Ahmed Shawki 2017, *Russia: From Workers' State to State Capitalism*, Haymarket Books.

Bellamy Foster, John 1999, "Marx's Theory of Metabolic Rift: Classical Foundations for Environmental Sociology", *American Journal of Sociology*, 105(2), pp.366–405. https://doi.org/10.1086/210315

Bellamy Foster, John 2000, *Marx's Ecology*, Monthly Review Press.

Bellamy Foster, John 2011a, "Capitalism and Degrowth: an Impossibility Theorem", *Monthly Review*, 62(8), pp.26–33. https://doi.org/10.14452/MR-062-08-2011-01_2

Bellamy Foster, John 2011b, "On the Laws of Capitalism", *Monthly Review*, 63(1), pp.1–16.

Bellamy Foster, John 2020, *The Robbery of Nature*, Monthly Review Press.

Bellamy Foster, John 2022a, *Capitalism in the Anthropocene*, Monthly Review Press.

Bellamy Foster, John 2022b, "The Return of the Dialectics of Nature: The Struggle for Freedom as Necessity", *Monthly Review*, 74(7), pp.1–20. https://doi.org/10.14452/MR-074-07-2022-11_1

Bellamy Foster, John 2022c, "Why is the great project of Ecological Civilization specific to China?", *Monthly Review Online*, 24 June. https://mronline.org/2022/10/01/why-is-the-great-project-of-ecological-civilization-specific-to-china/

Bellamy Foster, John 2023a, "Engels and the Second Foundation of Marxism", *Monthly Review*, 75(1), pp.1–18. https://doi.org/10.14452/MR-075-02-2023-06_1

Bellamy Foster, John 2023b, "Planned Degrowth: Ecosocialism and Sustainable Human Development", *Monthly Review*, 75(3), pp.1–29. https://doi.org/10.14452/MR-072-03-2023-07_1

Bellamy Foster, John 2023c, "Marx's Critique of Enlightenment Humanism: A Revolutionary Ecological Perspective", *Monthly Review*, 74(8), pp.1–15. https://doi.org/10.14452/MR-074-08-2023-01_1

Benjamin, Walter 2002, *Selected Writings: 1938–1940*. The Belknap Press of Harvard University Press.

Bernal, JD 2010 (1939), *The Social Function of Science*, Faber and Faber.

Blackledge, Paul 2020, "Engels vs. Marx?: Two Hundred Years of Frederick Engels", *Monthly Review*, 72(1), pp.21–39. https://doi.org/10.14452/MR-072-01-2020-05_3

Boscov-Ellen, Dan 2023, "Marx(ism) in the Anthropocene", *Spectre*, 15 November. https://spectrejournal.com/marxism-in-the-anthropocene/?fbclid=IwAR2kKdKHlqWON8tAi1CwNRPjGkCw0qc5_UIhzuAJhBfE08uswq7CmHV4mio

Burkett, Paul 2014 (1999), *Marx and Nature*, Haymarket Books.

Caudwell, Christpher 2017 (1939), *The Crisis in Physics*, Verso Books.

Caudwell, Christopher 2018, *Culture as Politics*, Pluto Press.

Cliff, Tony 1964, "Russia: A Marxist Analysis", *Marxists' Internet Archive*. https://www.marxists.org/archive/cliff/works/1964/russia/index.htm

Cooney, Brendan 2022, "A Metabolic Mess: A Critique of Foster & Clark's *The Robbery of Nature*", *Marxist Humanist Initiative*, 28 April. https://www.marxisthumanistinitiative.org/economics/a-metabolic-mess-a-critique-of-foster-clarks-the-robbery-of-nature.html

Cziczo, Daniel J, Martin J Wolf, Blaž Gasparini, Steffen Münch and Ulrike Lohmann 2019, "Unanticipated Side Effects of Stratospheric Albedo Modification Proposals Due to Aerosol Composition and Phase", *Scientific Reports*, 9, December. https://doi.org/10.1038/s41598-019-53595-3

Dale, Gareth 2015, "Origins and Delusions of Green Growth", *International Socialist Review*, 97, Summer. https://isreview.org/issue/97/origins-and-delusions-green-growth

Dale, Gareth 2023, "Marxism for the Age of Climate Emergency", *Spectre*, 22 March, https://spectrejournal.com/marxism-for-the-age-of-climate-emergency/?fbclid=IwAR0aVSX2ThL0u6P9FBGXHxz2c22_lLKMh9EKnClF6N6heJokv1hJg8Q7il4

D'Amato, Paul 2014, *The Meaning of Marxism* (revised edition), Haymarket Books.

Delves, Rob 2021, "Is Green Growth Possible?" *Green Issue*, 30(3), 26 June. https://greens.org.au/wa/magazine/green-growth-possible

Dunayevskaya, Raya 2018, *Marx's Philosophy of Revolution in Permanence For Our Day: Selected Writings*, Haymarket Books.

Dunayevskaya, Raya 1975, *Marxism and Freedom*, Pluto Press.

Engels, Friedrich 1876, "The Part played by Labour in the Transition from Ape to Man", *Marxists' Internet Archive*. https://www.marxists.org/archive/marx/works/1876/part-played-labour/index.htm

Fajardy, Mathilde, Jennifer Morris, Angelo Gurgel, Howard Herzog, Niall Mac Dowell and Sergey Paltsev 2021, "The economics of bioenergy with carbon capture and storage (BECCS) deployment in a 1.5°C or 2°C world", *Global Environmental Change*, 68, May. https://doi.org/10.1016/j.gloenvcha.2021.102262

Flipo, Fabrice 2008, "Conceptual roots of degrowth", *First International Conference on Economic Degrowth for Ecological Sustainability and Social Equity*, Paris, France, pp.24–28. https://hal.science/hal-02510344/document

Fromm, Erich 1966, *Socialist Humanism*, Anchor Books.

Garnham, Sarah 2020, "New movement, new debates: The contested politics of climate change", *Marxist Left Review*, 19, Summer. https://marxistleftreview.org/articles/new-movement-new-debates-the-contested-politics-of-climate-change/

Gibson, Padraic and Martin Empson 2023, "Karl Marx's "degrowth communism"?", *International Socialism*, 180, October. https://isj.org.uk/degrowth-communism/

Hägglund, Martin 2020, *This Life*, Profile Books.

Hampton, Paul 2023, "Saito: making a mess of Marxist ecology", *Workers' Liberty*, 11 April. https://www.workersliberty.org/story/2023-04-11/saito-making-mess-marxist-ecology

Hannah, Simon 2023, "Kohei Saito's New Book Asks: Was Marx a Degrowth Communist? (Review)", *Anti-Capitalist Resistance*, 2 February. https://anticapitalistresistance.org/kohei-saitos-new-book-asks-was-marx-a-degrowth-communist-review/

Hasselbalch, Jacob A, Matthias Kranke and Ekaterina Chertkovskaya 2023, "Organizing for transformation: post-growth in International Political Economy", *Review of International Political Economy*, 30(5), pp.1621–38. https://doi.org/10.1080/09692290.2023.2208871

Henderson, George 2013, *Value in Marx*, University of Minnesota Press.

Hendrickx, Sébastien 2023, "How Degrowth Can Win Political Favour and the Masses", *Green European Journal*, 26 April. https://www.greeneuropeanjournal.eu/how-degrowth-can-win-political-favour-and-the-masses/

Hickel, Jason 2019, "Degrowth: a theory of radical abundance", *Real-World Economics Review*, 87. https://static1.squarespace.com/static/59bc0e610abd04bd1e067ccc/t/5cb6db356e9a7f14e5322a62/1555487546989/Hickel+-+Degrowth%2C+A+Theory+of+Radical+Abundance.pdf

Hickel, Jason 2021a, "How To Achieve Full Decolonisation", *New Internationalist*, 15 October. https://newint.org/features/2021/08/09/money-ultimate-decolonizer-fjf

Hickel, Jason 2021b, "The anti-colonial politics of degrowth", *Political Geography*, 88, June. https://doi.org/10.1016/j.polgeo.2021.102404

Hickel, Jason 2021c, "What does degrowth mean? A few points of clarification" *Globalizations*, 18(7), pp.1105–11. https://doi.org/10.1080/14747731.2020.1812222

Hickel, Jason 2022a, *Less is More*, Penguin Books.

Hickel, Jason 2022b, "The Global South has the power to force radical climate action", *Al Jazeera*, 29 June. https://www.aljazeera.com/opinions/2022/6/29/the-global-south-has-the-power-to-force-radical-climate-action

Hickel, Jason 2023a, "On Technology and Degrowth", *Monthly Review*, 75(3), July–August, pp.45–50. https://monthlyreview.org/2023/07/01/on-technology-and-degrowth/

Hickel, Jason 2023b, "The Double Objective of Democratic Ecosocialism", *Monthly Review*, 75(4), September, pp.14–20. https://doi.org/10.14452/MR-075-04-2023-08_2

Hickel, Jason and Giorgos Kallis 2020, "Is Green Growth Possible?", *New Political Economy*, 25(4), pp.469–86. https://doi.org/10.1080/13563467.2019.1598964

Hickel, Jason and Stéphane Hallegatte 2021, "Can we live within environmental limits and still reduce poverty? Degrowth or decoupling?", *Development Policy Review*, 40(1), January. https://doi.org/10.1111/dpr.12584

Hickel, Jason, Christian Dorninger, Hanspeter Wieland and Intan Suwandi 2022a, "Imperialist appropriation in the world economy: Drain from the global South through unequal exchange, 1990–2015", *Global Environmental Change*, 73, March. https://doi.org/10.1016/j.gloenvcha.2022.102467

Hickel, Jason, Giorgos Kallis, Tim Jackson, Daniel W O'Neill, Juliet B Schor, Julia K Steinberger, Peter A Victor and Diana Ürge-Vorsatz 2022b, "Degrowth can work — here's how science can help", *Nature*, December. https://www.nature.com/articles/d41586-022-04412-x

Holgersen, Ståle 2023, "Neither Productivism nor Degrowth", *Spectre*, 4 September. https://spectrejournal.com/neither-productivism-nor-degrowth/?fbclid=IwAR27sLCaQkkqcKKjtrpDe5R9hvJs_2IQe3UJATUgg9VDHdcVbKi3Jx uXlAw

Huber, Matt 2019a, "Ecological Politics for the Working Class", *Catalyst*, 3(1), Spring. https://catalyst-journal.com/2019/07/ecological-politics-for-the-working-class

Huber, Matt 2019b, "Ecosocialism: Dystopian and Scientific", *Socialist Forum*, Winter. https://socialistforum.dsausa.org/issues/winter-2019/ecosocialism-dystopian-and-scientific/

Huber, Matt 2019c, "Ecosocialism: Dystopian and Scientific (Winter 2019) Responses", *Socialist Forum*, May. https://socialistforum.dsausa.org/responses/ecosocialism-dystopian-and-scientific-winter-2019-responses/

Huber, Matt 2022a, *Climate Change as Class War*, Verso Books.

Huber, Matt 2022b, "Mish-Mash Ecologism", *New Left Review*, August. https://newleftreview.org/sidecar/posts/mish-mash-ecologism

Huber, Matt 2023a, "Reflections on Climate, Class, and Strategy", *Critical Sociology*, 49(7–8), July. https://doi.org/10.1177/08969205231189452

Huber, Matt 2023b, "The Problem With Degrowth", *Jacobin*, 16 July. https://jacobin.com/2023/07/degrowth-climate-change-economic-planning-production-austerity

Huber, Matt and Leigh Phillips 2024, "Kohei Saito's 'Start From Scratch' Degrowth Communism", *Jacobin*, 9 March. https://jacobin.com/2024/03/kohei-saito-degrowth-communism-environment-marxism?fbclid=IwAR37vJ UgRGC2vLAvGTOrn8i4f_ZNyCRtuMhgKVjACGZSRwqaTF2aaOR4iNc

Hughes, Jonathan 1995, "Development of the productive forces: an ecological analysis", *Studies in Marxism*, 2, pp.179–98. https://philarchive.org/archive/HUGDOT#:~:text=Jonathan%20Hughes&text=My%20aim%20is%20to%20dispute,concept%20to%20investigate%20ecological%20problems

Işıkara, Güney and Özgür Narin 2023, "Degrowth and Socialism: Notes on Some Critical Junctures", *Monthly Review*, 75(3), pp.30–43. https://doi.org/10.14452/MR-075-03-2023-07 2

James, CLR 1943, "Production for the Sake of Production", *Workers Party Bulletin*, April, pp.198–209. https://www.marxists.org/archive/james-clr/works/1943/04/production.htm

James, CLR 2013 [1950], *State Capitalism and World Revolution*, PM Press.

Kallis, Giorgos and Hug March 2015, "Imaginaries of Hope: The Utopianism of Degrowth", *Annals of the Association of American Geographers*, 105(2), December, pp.360–8. https://doi.org/10.1080/00045608.2014.973803

Kallis, Giorgos 2019a, "Socialism Without Growth", *Capitalism Nature Socialism*, 30(2), October, pp.189–206. https://doi.org/10.1080/10455752.2017.1386695

Kallis, Giorgos 2019b, "Capitalism, Socialism, Degrowth: A Rejoinder", *Capitalism Nature Socialism*, 30(2), January, pp.267–73. https://doi.org/10.1080/10455752.2018.1563624

Kandelaars, Michael 2016, "Marxism and the natural world", *Marxist Left Review*, 11, Summer. https://marxistleftreview.org/articles/marxism-and-the-natural-world/

Katz-Rosene, Ryan 2023a, "Critical engagements with *Climate Change as Class War* – towards a politics of better", *Studies in Political Economy*, 104(3), pp.181–8, December. https://doi.org/10.1080/07078552.2023.2278007

Katz-Rosene, Ryan 2023b, "Towards a socialist ecomodernism? An interview with Matthew Huber", *Studies in Political Economy*, 104(3), September, pp.113–26. https://doi.org/10.1080/07078552.2023.2234754

Kelton, Stephanie 2020, *The Deficit Myth*, John Murray.

Klitgaard, Kent A 2023, "Planning Degrowth: The Necessity, History, and Challenges", *Monthly Review*, 75(3), July–August, pp.85–98, https://doi.org/10.14452/MR-075-03-2023-07_6

Li, Jiaman, Xiucheng Dong and Kangyin Dong 2022, "Is China's green growth possible? The roles of green trade and green energy", *Economic Research-Ekonomska Istraživanja*, 35(1), April, pp.7084–108. https://doi.org/10.1080/1331677X.2022.2058978

Löwy, Michael 2020, "Ecosocialism and/or Degrowth", *Climate & Capitalism*, 8 October. https://climateandcapitalism.com/2020/10/08/ecosocialism-and-or-degrowth/

Löwy, Michael, Bengi Akbulut, Sabrina Fernandes and Giorgos Kallis 2022, "For an Ecosocialist Degrowth", *Monthly Review*, 73(11), April, pp.56–58. https://doi.org/10.14452/MR-073-11-2022-04_4

Lukács, Georg 2017 (1923), *History and Class Consciousness*, Bibliotech Press.

Maher, Stephan and Joshua K McEvoy 2023, "Between De-Growth and Eco-Modernism: Theorizing a Green Transition", *Critical Sociology*, 49(7–8), June. https://doi.org/10.1177/08969205231177370

Marx, Karl 1846, "The Illusion of the Epoch", in *The German Ideology*, Part I, *Marxists' Internet Archive*. https://www.marxists.org/archive/marx/works/1845/german-ideology/ch01b.htm

Marx, Karl 1881, "The 'First' Draft", *Marx-Zasulich Correspondence, Marxists' Internet Archive*. https://www.marxists.org/archive/marx/works/1881/zasulich/draft-1.htm

Marx, Karl 1976 [1867], *Capital*, Volume I, Penguin Books.

Marx, Karl 1978 [1885], *Capital*, Volume II, Penguin Books.

Marx, Karl 1981 [1894], *Capital*, Volume III, Penguin Books.

Marx, Karl and Friedrich Engels 1949, *Marx Engels Selected Works in Two Volumes*, Volume II, Foreign Languages Publishing House: Moscow.

Marx, Karl and Friedrich Engels 1962, *Marx Engels Selected Works in Two Volumes*, Volume I, Foreign Languages Publishing House: Moscow

Masson-Delmotte, Valérie (ed.) 2018, "Global Warming of 1.5°C", Intergovernmental Panel on Climate Change.

McCurry, Justin 2022, "'A new way of life': the Marxist, post-capitalist, green manifesto captivating Japan", *The Guardian*, 9 September. https://www.theguardian.com/world/2022/sep/09/a-new-way-of-life-the-marxist-post-capitalist-green-manifesto-captivating-japan

McNeill, Dougal 2023, "Thinking About Ecology with Marx – A review of Kohei Saito's *Marx in the Anthropocene*", *ISO Aotearoa*, 8 February. https://iso.org.nz/2023/02/08/thinking-about-ecology-with-marx-a-review-of-kohei-saitos-marx-in-the-anthropocene/

Miller-McDonald, Samuel 2021, "Ecosocialism is the Horizon, Degrowth is the way", *The Trouble*, 11 February. https://www.the-trouble.com/content/2021/2/11/ecosocialism-is-the-horizon-degrowth-is-the-way

Millward-Hopkins, Joel, Julia K Steinberger, Narasimha D Roa and Yannick Oswald 2020, "Providing decent living with minimum energy: A global scenario", *Global Environmental Change*, 65, November. https://doi.org/10.1016/j.gloenvcha.2020.102168

Molyneux, John 1983, "What is the real Marxist tradition?", *Marxists' Internet Archive*, https://www.marxists.org/history/etol/writers/molyneux/1983/07/tradition.htm

Molyneux, John 2022, "Degrowth: A Response", *Rupture*, 8, 4 December. https://rupture.ie/articles/degrowth-a-response

Murphy, Paul and Jess Spear 2022, "The necessity of ecosocialist degrowth", *Rupture*, 7, 10 May. https://rupture.ie/articles/necessity-degrowth

Nebel, Arjuna, Alexander Kling, Ruben Willamowski, Tim Schell 2023, "Recalibration of limits to growth: An update of the World3 model", *Journal of Industrial Ecology*, 28(1), February, pp.87–99. https://doi.org/10.1111/jiec.13442

Novack, George 1973, *Humanism and Socialism*, Pathfinder Press.

Novack, George 2002, *Understanding History*, Resistance Books.

Olk, Christopher, Colleen Schneider and Jason Hickel 2023, "How to pay for saving the world: Modern Monetary Theory for a degrowth transition", *Ecological Economics*, 214, December. https://doi.org/10.1016/j.ecolecon.2023.107968

Parrique, Timothée 2020, "The political economy of degrowth. Economics and Finance" (English version Stockholms universitet). https://theses.hal.science/tel-02499463

Parrique Timothée 2021, "A response to Matt Huber: Facts and logic in support of degrowth", *Timothée Parrique Blog*, April. https://timotheeparrique.com/a-response-to-matt-huber-facts-and-logic-in-support-of-degrowth/

Parrique T, J Barth, F Briens, C Kerschner, A Kraus-Polk, A Kuokkanen and JH Spangenberg 2019, "Decoupling debunked: Evidence and arguments against green growth as a sole strategy for sustainability", *European Environmental Bureau*, July. https://eeb.org/wp-content/uploads/2019/07/Decoupling-Debunked.pdf

Persson, Linn, Bethanie M Carney Almroth, Christopher D Collins, Sarah Cornell, Cynthia A de Wit, Miriam L Diamond, Peter Fantke, Martin Hessellöv, Matthew MacLeod, Morten W Ryberg Peter Søgaard Jørgensen, Patricia Villarrubia-Gómez, Zhanyun Wang and Michael Zwicky Hauschild 2022, "Outside the Safe Operating Space of the Planetary Boundary for Novel Entities", *Environmental Science & Technology*, 56(3), January, pp.1510–21. https://doi.org/10.1021/acs.est.1c04158

Phillips, Andy and Raya Dunayevskaya 1984, *The Coal Miners' General Strike of 1949–1950 and the Birth of Marxist-Humanism in the U.S.*, News and Letters, 17 June. https://files.libcom.org/files/The-Coal-Miners-General-Strike.pdf

Pineault, Eric 2019, "From Provocation to Challenge: Degrowth, Capitalism and the Prospect of 'Socialism without Growth': A Commentary on Giorgios Kallis", *Capitalism Nature Socialism*, 30(2), pp.251–66. https://doi.org/10.1080/10455752.2018.1457064

Ripple, William J, Christopher Wolf, Jullian W Gregg, Johan Rockström, Thomas M Newsome, Beverly E Law, Luiz Marques, Timothy M Lenton, Chi Xu, Saleemul Huq, Leon Simons and Sir David Anthony King 2023, "The 2023 state of the climate report: Entering uncharted territory", *BioScience*, 73(12), Special report, December, pp.841–50. https://doi.org/10.1093/biosci/biad080

Roberts, Michael 2020, "The value in GDP", *Michael Roberts Blog*, 27 January. https://thenextrecession.wordpress.com/2020/01/27/the-value-in-gdp/#:~:text=GDP%20is%20biased%20as%20a,the%20depreciation%20of%20machinery%20etc)

Rockström, Johan, Will Steffen, Kevin Noone, Åsa Persson, F Stuart III Chapin, Eric Lambin, Timothy M Lenton, Marten Scheffer, Carl Folke, Hans Joachim Schellnhuber, B Nykvist, CA De Wit, T Hughes, S van der Leeuw, H Rodhe, S Sörlin, PK Snyder, R Costanza, U Svedin, M Falkenmark, L Karlberg, RW Corell, VJ Fabry, J Hansen, B Walker, D Liverman, K Richardson, P Crutzen and J Foley 2009, "Planetary Boundaries: Exploring the Safe Operating Space for Humanity", *Ecology & Society*, 14(2). https://www.ecologyandsociety.org/vol14/iss2/art32/

Roso, Darren 2023, "Engels after Marx: A (critical) defence", *Marxist Left Review*, 26, Spring. https://marxistleftreview.org/articles/engels-after-marx-a-critical-defence/

Saito, Kohei 2017, *Karl Marx's Ecosocialism*, Monthly Review Press.

Saito, Kohei 2023a, *Marx in the Anthropocene: Towards the Idea of Degrowth Communism*, Cambridge University Press.

Saito, Kohei 2023b, *Towards the Idea of Degrowth Communism* [conference presentation], Ecosocialism 2023, Melbourne, Australia.

Saito, Kohei 2024a, *Slow Down: How Degrowth Communism Can Save the Earth*, Weidenfeld & Nicolson.

Saito, Kohei 2024b, "Greening Marx in Japan", *New Left Review*, 145, January–February. https://newleftreview.org/issues/ii145/articles/kohei-saito-greening-marx-in-japan

Sheehan, Helena 2007, "J D Bernal: philosophy, politics and the science of science", *Journal of Physics. Conference Series*, 57(1), June, pp.29–39. https://doi.org/10.1088/1742-6596/57/1/003

Sheehan, Helena 2017, *Marxism and the Philosophy of Science*, Verso Books.

Sheehan, Helena 2023, "Totality: Decades of Debate and the Return of Nature", *Monthly Review*, 75(4), September, pp.21–34. https://doi.org/10.14452/MR-075-04-2023-08_3

Suzelis, Natalie 2022, "Class Struggle Against Growth", *Spectre*, 25 August. https://spectrejournal.com/class-struggle-against-growth/

Trotsky, Leon 1906, *Results and Prospects*, https://www.marxists.org/archive/trotsky/1931/tpr/rp-index.htm

Trotsky, Leon 1931, *The Permanent Revolution*, https://www.marxists.org/archive/trotsky/1931/tpr/pr-index.htm

Tsuda, Kenta 2021, "Naive Questions on Degrowth", *New Left Review*, 128, March–April. https://newleftreview.org/issues/ii128/articles/kenta-tsuda-naive-questions-On-degrowth

UN DESA 2023, Independent Group of Scientists appointed by the Secretary-General, Global Sustainable Development Report 2023: *Times of crisis, times of change: Science for accelerating transformations to sustainable development* (United Nations, New York).

Untermann, Ernest 1905, *Science and revolution*, John F. Higgins: Chicago.

Vettese, Troy and Drew Pendergrass 2022, *Half-Earth Socialism*, Verso Books.

Vogel, Jefim and Jason Hickel 2023, "Is green growth happening? An empirical analysis of achieved versus Paris-compliant CO2–GDP decoupling in high-income countries", *The Lancet Planetary Health*, 7(9), September. https://doi.org/10.1016/S2542-5196(23)00174-2

Williams, Chris 2016, "The case against nuclear power", *International Socialist Review*, 103, Winter. https://isreview.org/issue/77/case-against-nuclear-power/index.html

ROWAN CAHILL

Review: The 1848 revolutions

Rowan Cahill has variously worked as a farmhand, teacher, and for the trade union movement as a publicist, historian, and rank-and-file activist. Currently an Honorary Fellow at the University of Wollongong. Most recently co-author with Terry Irving of *The Barber Who Read History* (2021). His website is rowancahill.net.

Christopher Clark, *Revolutionary Spring: Fighting for a New World 1848–1849*, Allen Lane, 2023.

R*EVOLUTIONARY SPRING* CHALLENGES the persistent and powerful historical view of the revolutions of 1848–49 as failures. Yes, they began tumultuously, dramatically, full of enthusiasm and dreams of new and better worlds; yes, they were relatively quickly undone, variously destroyed by internal divisions, and by increasingly violent and sophisticated policing.

Yet the notion of "failure" persists, argues Clark, because in retrospect these revolutions have been appropriated into national narratives. This enables singular treatments, depriving them of the historically transformative and Europe-wide upheavals they were.

Clark begins by creating a detailed and layered backdrop of "economic precarity", filth, disease, unrestrained labour exploitation, huge wealth, mass poverty, inequalities, social tensions and conflicts, rural and urban divides, a Europe alive with critics and dissidents "not locked into finished worldviews", a Europe where social orders were straining and waiting to break.

Against this he explores the revolutions with respect to their local roots, individualities and non-linear courses. Individual as they were, they took place simultaneously across a vast continental geography. Clark explores this and the ways they were linked. It is a huge task, and Clark's book is not a hurriedly cobbled together work. The result of years of research and writing, its origins are in his earlier studies of European history.

Characterising the revolutions as the mid-nineteenth century's "particle collision chamber", Clark argues they became an "unfinished revolution", a watershed from which Europe did not recover. This latter term should be read poetically in a political way, the sense being that the revolutions opened up the future. Not only to nationalism, the general historiographical preference, but robustly to liberative possibilities: ideas and notions about liberalism, radicalism, democracy, republicanism, socialism, social rights; the emancipations of women, slaves, Jews; the nature of government; the tactics of resistance and revolt; how to bring about social change. And some of these will always be works in progress.

The revolutions ended with counter-revolutionary policing, the counter-revolutionary forces able to build alliances which the revolutionaries failed to do. Vicious "cleansing" reprisals followed. Traditionally, Britain is portrayed as having escaped the turmoil of the period, the main dissident contender being Chartism. The line is that Chartism was too fractured with internal divisions to hold together, that the savvy British ruling class let air out of the balloon with gradual reform concessions, that the Chartists were good-natured folk after all. Well no, says Clark. Robust and mass policing involving regular police, huge troop deployments, and specially recruited constables with licence to use violence smashed the movement. Ireland was contained similarly. As Clark shows, the British model of policing became one informing continental counter-revolutionaries. Besides, Clark observes, Britain also had the offshore safety valve of its Empire and deportation to help thwart dissidence.

As Clark winds up his narrative, traces of those revolutionaries who survived the reprisals leave tracks. Some variously went quiet, changed politics, pulled their heads in and worked through the system, went underground, while a diaspora of radicals with ideas in their heads and luggage, spread globally and helped make histories elsewhere.

Running to 873 pages, *Revolutionary Spring* is a weighty tome. The canvas is vast. Clark is imaginatively at home in the Europe of the time, a rich tapestry of empires, kingdoms, states, principalities, ethnicities, demographies, all geopolitically unique with their own cultures, traditions and histories.

Maps at the front of the book assist the reader navigate this Europe before empires were variously dismantled and geographies reshaped by nationalism. Clark shows how the revolutionary zeal and political energies of the period went beyond continental Europe, ripples and convolutions variously experienced in Britain, the French Caribbean, Latin America, the United States, even colonial Australia. Readers may be surprised to find the colonies of New South Wales and Victoria part of Clark's canvas. Discussing the impact of the 1848–49 Revolutions, he deftly includes the Eureka Stockade and Australian constitutional reform as parts of the fallout.

While Clark is a European historian, with one of the history world's top gigs as Regius Professor of History at Cambridge University, he is also an Australian. Schooled in Australia, he took his first degree at Sydney University in the 1980s. The Free University of Berlin and Cambridge followed.

In part at least, it seems to me, in the art of the book's creation and writing there is the spirit of EP Thompson, in the way Clark handles the galaxy of players with agency across class divides, many unfamiliar and needing concise biographical detail to make them part of the account; and in his understandings of dissident culture in poetry, song, broadsheets, pamphlets, newspapers, meetings, conversations, in formal and in informal sites like pubs, cafés, streets. Clark is on record elsewhere respectfully referring to Thompson as a "great British historian".

Revolutionary Spring ends with 113 pages of References and Index. The References reveal the huge and diverse amount of material Clark has drawn on, multilingual material that crosses all manner of divides.

Before these there are three pages of Acknowledgements. Clark has drawn on many fellow scholars and friends for expertise, advice and comment. Some have granted access to works in progress, and works in pre-publication stages. This points to collegial trust and sharing often absent in modern academia. Clark notes that conversations are indispensable in knowledge production, and he acknowledges these individually. It is a pleasure to see this, since this tends not to be valued by the modern systems and metrics that manage scholarship.

Revolutionary Spring is an impressive work. Reader-friendly, scholarly, it is an invitation to, and demonstration of, a long view of history. It eloquently counters a historical tradition that gives *failure* hegemonic import, and which paves ways for shadows of futility and despair to hover over radical dreaming and activism. For people on the right side of history, in a time when a great deal of energy, power and politics is destructively and mischievously fed into generating messages of despair and end times, *Revolutionary Spring* is worth consideration; a book for our times.

LUCA TAVAN

Review: How I learned to stop worrying and love the Squad

Luca Tavan is a member of Socialist Alternative and contributor to *Red Flag* and *Marxist Left Review*.

Ryan Grim, *The Squad: AOC and the Hope of a Political Revolution*, Henry Holt and Co, 2023.

66 "IT'S TOUGH BEING a member of the Squad these days", wrote Branko Marcetic last year in the pages of *Jacobin Magazine*, lamenting the fact that "even committed socialists question what the point of the Squad has been".[1]

Alexandria Ocasio-Cortez's successful bid to unseat long-term Democratic powerbroker Joe Crowley from his New York congressional seat in June 2018 had unleashed an avalanche of expectations on the American reformist left. Ocasio-Cortez, known as AOC, was joined by three other successful progressive challengers. Ilhan Omar, Rashida Tlaib and Ayanna Pressley, were, together with AOC, dubbed "the Squad" by the media. *Jacobin Magazine* – a publication aligned with the Democratic Socialists of America (DSA) – presented the victory of AOC and her colleagues as vindication of their longstanding claim that the Democratic Party could be the unlikely site of a new socialist movement.

Miles Kampf-Lassin wrote: "it's no shock that Ocasio-Cortez and her

---

1. Marcetic 2023.

cohort are being treated as a threat to a party establishment that has cozied up to corporate power and helped maintain the deeply unequal economic and political order in this country. It's because they are one".[2] In another article, AOC was called "a righteous disturber of the peace, an adept orator for the working class, a creative user of new platforms. Though still on the periphery of power, she is showing us a different kind of politics. Instead of accommodating herself to the powers that be, she's expanding people's sense of the possible".[3] Her role was even compared to the heroic period of the German Social Democratic Party, a socialist workers' party which claimed a million members in the early twentieth century.

Five years later, the Squad has lost its sheen. Rather than taking the hammer to the Democratic establishment, the Squad has become its enthusiastic left flank. AOC has endorsed Biden for re-election, stating in a recent interview with CNN: "I know who I'm going to choose. It's going to be one of the most successful presidents in modern American history".[4] Commitment to party unity has meant accepting the Biden administration's right-wing domestic and international agenda, from voting to unilaterally impose a contract on railway workers and quash their right to strike, to voting to fund Israel's Iron Dome.

What the hell happened to the group that was supposed to "burn it down", in the words of one of AOC's staffers?

The new American reformist clique around *Jacobin* has portrayed the Squad as insurgent leftists trying to confront the Democratic Party machine. Ryan Grim's new book *The Squad: AOC and the Hope of a Political Revolution* is different. Grim is an effusive supporter of AOC's attempts to rehabilitate the Democrats. But unlike the *Jacobin* crowd, he makes no attempt to disguise the Squad as a genuine challenge to the Party machine. His work is useful for revolutionaries, not because it condemns the Squad, but because it provides candid evidence that can furnish a radical critique. The book proves, intentionally or not, that the Squad are nothing more than moderate and aspirational liberal Democrats.

---

2.   Kampf-Lassin 2019.
3.   Sacks 2019.
4.   Quoted in Elliot 2024.

Grim's account describes how each member of the Squad established their careers within the Democratic Party machine. Ayanna Pressley worked her way up as an intern for a member of the Kennedy dynasty, before becoming political director for John Kerry, one-time Presidential hopeful and current US climate envoy. Rashida Tlaib worked as a Democratic staffer from 2004, eventually serving in Congress in Michigan, while Ilhan Omar did the same in Minnesota from 2013. Alexandria Ocasio-Cortez interned for Ted Kennedy, before establishing a Bronx-based company publishing children's books. In 2012 AOC appeared alongside Democratic Senator Kirsten Gillibrand at a press conference unveiling a tax break for new businesses; as Gillibrand intoned: "We know that government doesn't create jobs, businesses do". In a weak defence of AOC's working-class credentials, Grim dismisses this awkward history by emphasising her one-time stint in the hospitality industry, adding: "Despite her earlier ambitions, by this point in her life, the proper way to understand Ocasio-Cortez was as a bartender" (ch. 1).

The Squad's breakthrough came two years after the insurgent campaign by Bernie Sanders for the Democratic presidential nomination. Sanders began his campaign with a series of scathing attacks on the Democratic establishment, but by July 2016 had endorsed Hillary Clinton, championing the neoliberal warmonger's policy platform as "the most progressive in history".[5]

AOC serves as the major focus of Grim's book, reflecting her role as the leading and most influential member of the grouping. One of AOC's first acts was her early occupation of House Speaker Nancy Pelosi's office alongside climate activists from the Sunrise Movement. Grim shows that even this disruptive action was couched within an approach which sought to gently nudge the party in the right direction. When asked whether her occupation was a direct challenge to Pelosi (and by extension the Democratic establishment), AOC replied: "One of the things I admire so much about Leader Pelosi is that she comes from a space of activism and organising, and so I think that she really appreciates civic engagement. And really what I'm here to do is just to

---

5.   Quoted in Roberts 2016.

support the folks who are here"; adding "Should Leader Pelosi become the next Speaker of the House, we need to tell her that we've got her back" (ch. 3).

The Squad did indeed have Pelosi's back. They supported the venture capitalist – who has an estimated net worth upwards of $100m – for re-election as party leader at the end of 2018. Soon AOC had christened her the "mama bear" of the Democratic Party. This established a pattern: members of the Squad would trade loyalty to the Democratic leadership for a shot at sitting in on influential Congressional Committees. AOC soon began withholding endorsements for other progressive primary challengers, and funnelling money from her "Courage to Change" fundraising committee to centrists. In 2023 the Squad unanimously backed Pelosi's successor, Hakeem Jeffries, whose extreme hostility to the left was infamous in progressive circles.

At the time, the steadfast loyalty of the Democratic Party's left wing contrasted awkwardly with dynamics playing out on the other side of the aisle. The far-right Freedom Caucus was giving a masterclass in obstructionism, blocking the election of establishment Republican Kevin McCarthy to the House Speaker position for days on end. AOC was forced to respond to an obvious question: Why doesn't the Democratic left fight their leaders as hard as the Republican right fight theirs? Her response was revealing:

> When people say, you know, why don't we do this? First of all, there's a lot of cost and dysfunction... Second of all, those people who are holding out right now, they may have made certain structural gains, but they have also made incredible reputational and relational harm within their caucus. And so, if you are trying to get something done within your caucus moving forward, you still need members of your caucus. And that, at the core, is an element of electoral politics that is simply inescapable (ch. 20).

While some issues created tension between the Squad and the Democratic leadership, this was never translated into an open political battle. AOC ruffled feathers by referring to the Israeli "occupation of Palestine" in a 2018 interview. But since then, she has waffled and evaded on the issue, culminating in her 2021 decision to vote "present" rather than "no" on a vote to fund Israel's Iron Dome. This shocked many in left-Democratic circles, sparking debate about whether this represented a capitulation, or some subtle tactical masterstroke. The rationale that Ocasio-Cortez herself provided is far more banal: "I felt voting P[resent] was the only way I could maintain some degree of peace at home – enough to bring folks together to the table[,] because all this whipped things up to an all out war" (ch. 18). Maintaining friendly relations with right-wing Democrats and upholding party unity trumped principle and the possibility of mobilising sentiment against the craven pro-Israel politics of the Democratic establishment.

The relationship between the Democratic left and centre was consummated under Biden. After swiftly dispensing with the half-hearted challenge from Bernie Sanders in the 2020 primaries, he moved to co-opt the left and adopt some elements of their rhetoric as part of his policy agenda. AOC joined Biden's "climate unity" task force with John Kerry, while Sanders was handed a plum spot on the Senate Budget Committee. Grim writes: "while Ocasio-Cortez and the Squad spent much of 2019 in conflict with party leadership, and spent the first half of 2020 trying to nominate Sanders for president, AOC had been a team player in the general election, and through Biden's term, she had consistently framed her advocacy as in support of his administration and his agenda" (ch. 20).

Grim presents Biden's suite of economic and social policies, dubbed "Bidenomics" by the press, as a victory for the left, something at least approximating the reformist vision of a Green New Deal. US socialist Ashley Smith argues that Bidenomics should better be understood as a project of "imperialist Keynesianism" – a capitalist project which includes three connected goals: "1) rebuilding the foundations of U.S. capitalism, 2) stabilizing domestic politics under the hegemony of the Democratic Party, and 3) restoring and protecting Washington's imperial supremacy over China and Russia."[6]

Rather than pulling Biden to the left, Sanders and the Squad were pulled to the right, abandoning their reformist program to cheerlead

---

6.   Smith 2023.

an administration overseeing attacks on workers at home and militarisation abroad.

Grim's insider account reveals that this approach clashed with some of the expectations of AOC's staffers who wanted a combative politics: "Her staff and many of the backers of Justice Democrats wanted to go to war against the people they saw as in the way of progress, AOC's one-time policy adviser Dan Riffle said. They wanted a real political revolution" (ch. 10). In the end, AOC resolved this contradiction by replacing her two closest political advisers with Washington insiders.

Grim's book makes it clear that the "activist" sphere with which the Squad interacts is the well-heeled NGO-industrial complex. If anything, this exerts a further conservatising pressure on elected officials. Grim recounts one tragicomic example on the issue of abortion. AOC's staffers considered bringing a vote to Congress to repeal the Hyde amendment, prohibiting federal funding for abortion services. This longstanding piece of legislation is defended by Biden. They were discouraged from pushing for the legislation's repeal by Planned Parenthood lobbyists, who explained that if they brought forward a vote to repeal the law, the NGO would be forced to publicly criticise Democrats who voted to maintain it. This was something they were not keen on, and the vote was abandoned (ch. 10).

Could things have gone differently? Could more organised left-wing pressure on the Squad have pushed them towards a more principled path? Adam Sacks' *Jacobin* article comparing AOC to the German Social Democrats suggested so, stressing that "Going forward, we'll need nationwide networks of left politicians, real structures outside the Democratic Party, and a vibrant working-class movement that can groom the next generation of socialists".[7]

This statement has no relationship to the actual project of the Squad. As a grouping of elected officials, they have expressed no desire to foster independent organisations that can hold them to a baseline set of political principles. The organisations that helped propel the Squad into office, like the DSA and Justice Democrats, are ginger groups that operate within the framework of Democratic party politics, not

---

7.   Sacks 2019.

independent working-class organisations. As the strategy of electing left Democrats has been exposed as a dead end, organisations built around this project have gone into decline. The DSA is mired in crisis, with falling membership, while Justice Democrats were forced in 2023 to lay off nearly half of their staff. Years of organisational investment into the Squad has only put left-wing organisations in the US in the discrediting position of feeling compelled to apologise for their unchecked backsliding and political capitulation.

More than five years on from the shock election of the Squad, there is a need for a serious critique of their project. Much of the criticism of AOC in leftist circles focuses on individual outrages – from her rebranding of Trump's migrant "concentration camps" as "overflow facilities" under Biden, to her rebuttals of left-wing criticisms of his administration as "privileged" and "bad faith". While these statements are pretty repugnant, the left needs a deeper critique of the arguments mobilised to justify the Squad's project.

The strategy promoted by the American reformists operating around the DSA is that the Democratic Party can be taken over, split or disrupted by socialists running in elections as Democrats. This is an utterly unrealistic, distorting and disorganising perspective for any serious left.

The Democratic Party is the oldest and most established capitalist party in the world. Its list of crimes is the longest of any, given the party's central role in administering one of the most brutal capitalist states on the planet – a state which has spent 80 years as the largest and most aggressive empire the world has ever known. The Democrats are the party of slavery and segregation, of Hiroshima and the wars on Vietnam and Gaza, of union-busting and austerity.

The very name "Democratic Party" is an oxymoron. Its structures are profoundly undemocratic and it's not really a party. Rather, it's a series of fundraising cabals controlled by a powerful wing of the US capitalist class. The speed with which the Democratic Party apparatus mobilised to defeat Sanders after his surprise breakthrough in the 2020 Las Vegas primaries is evidence of the imperviousness of these structures to democratic will. No genuine socialist could politically operate within its institutions.

This raises a broader question unexplored in Ryan Grim's book and seldom touched in the pages of publications like *Jacobin*: what is a socialist? The label has been everywhere in the last decade. As an adjective, "socialist" appears 28 times in the book, reflecting its widespread adoption, even by very moderate politicians and organisations. The noun "socialism", however, doesn't appear once. It's peculiar that a book covering five years of what has often been portrayed as an insurgent socialist movement doesn't contain a single paragraph of discussion of socialism as a political objective, what it means and how to get it.

Socialism is about uprooting the capitalist system; it is about eliminating exploitation and doing away with the existing state. Socialism is a radical end that can only be achieved through radical means. To be a "socialist" requires a relentless hatred of the capitalist class and their institutions.

The best representatives of the socialist movement have always understood this. The American revolutionary Eugene Debs once said: "There was a time in my life, before I became a Socialist, when I permitted myself as a member of the Democratic party to be elected to a state legislature. I have been trying to live it down. I am as much ashamed of that as I am proud of having gone to jail."[8]

The balance sheet of the Squad's first five years shows that a grouping of aspirational, progressive political careerists can exist comfortably in the swamp of the Democratic Party, despite occasional ideological tensions and policy clashes. A socialist movement is something different – it will have to be built based on an implacable hostility to the oldest, most powerful capitalist party on the planet.

References

Elliot, Phillip 2024, "How Alexandria Ocasio-Cortez Became One of Joe Biden's Most Valuable Boosters", *Time*, 16 February. https://time.com/6695367/alexandria-ocasio-cortez-joe-biden/

Kampf-Lassin, Miles 2019, "They're Not Just Mad at AOC – They're Scared of Her", *Jacobin Magazine*, 15 July. https://jacobin.com/2019/07/alexandria-ocasio-cortez-aoc-nancy-pelosi-democratic-party

---

8.   Quoted in Lepore 2019.

Lepore, Jill 2019, "Eugene V. Debs and the Endurance of Socialism", *New Yorker*, 11 February. https://www.newyorker.com/magazine/2019/02/18/eugene-v-debs-and-the-endurance-of-socialism

Marcetic, Branko 2023, "AOC and the Squad's List of Left-Wing Accomplishments Is Quite Long", *Jacobin Magazine*, 16 August. https://jacobin.com/2023/08/alexandria-ocasio-cortez-aoc-the-squad-left-criticism-policy-accomplishments

Roberts, Dan 2016, "Bernie Sanders officially endorses Hillary Clinton for president", *The Guardian*, 13 July. https://www.theguardian.com/us-news/2016/jul/12/bernie-sanders-supports-hillary-clinton-president

Sacks, Adam J 2019, "Before AOC, There Was the SPD", *Jacobin Magazine*, 6 December. https://jacobin.com/2019/06/social-democratic-party-germany-ocasio-cortez

Smith, Ashley 2023, "Trapped in the Democratic Party", *Tempest*, 21 August. https://www.tempestmag.org/2023/08/trapped-in-the-democratic-party/?fbclid=IwAR1aONtYk_esVijhDO5WVChOJ_jCE8_5IujllM2ZP1KdZ6JbdRTYU6_rX2w

www.ingramcontent.com/pod-product-compliance
Lightning Source LLC
Chambersburg PA
CBHW011833020426
42335CB00024B/2850